SALUTE TO

THE JOLLY ☠ ROGERS

"Blackburn was an exceptionally talented, resourceful, inspiring leader who imparted to his men a fierce warrior ethic . . . especially noteworthy is the author's straightforward description of the methods he used organizing, training, leading his pilots in combat, and developing air tactics."

—*Publishers Weekly*

"Tom Blackburn has more than a few stories to tell, some funny, some sad, but all exciting. . . . The men of the VF-17 live on in Blackburn's book."

—*Orlando Sentinel*

"A macho, like-it-was memoir . . . a gritty, action-packed slice of WW II life."

—*Kirkus Reviews*

"Tom Blackburn is one of the most successful fighter squadron commanders the U.S. Navy has ever produced . . . not only a crackling good story, but a valuable primer on dealing with the rugged individualists who populate naval aviaton. Highly recommended."

—*The Hook*

"Excellent . . . a well-rounded, coherent story . . . As a professional's account of his squadron's . . . war, Blackburn's has no peer."

—Naval Institute's *Proceedings*

A Military Book Club Dual Main Selection

TOM BLACKBURN commanded the aircraft carrier *Midway* after World War II. He retired as a captain and lives in Jacksonville, Florida.

THE JOLLY ROGERS

The Story of Tom Blackburn and Navy Fighting Squadron VF-17

TOM BLACKBURN

POCKET BOOKS

New York London Toronto Sydney Tokyo Singapore

POCKET BOOKS, a division of Simon & Schuster Inc.
1230 Avenue of the Americas, New York, NY 10020

ISBN: 0-671-69493-6

First Pocket Books printing August 1990

10 9 8 7 6 5 4 3

POCKET and colophon are registered trademarks of
Simon & Schuster Inc.

Printed in the U.S.A.

For the Fallen . . .

JOHN KEITH

Missing in Action
November 1, 1943

BRADFORD BAKER

Missing in Action
November 16, 1943

CHARLES PILLSBURY

Missing in Action
November 21, 1943

ROBERT HOGAN

Missing in Action
January 26, 1944

JAMES FARLEY

Missing in Action
January 26, 1944

THADDEUS BELL

Missing in Action
January 27, 1944

THOMAS KROPF

Missing in Action
January 30, 1944

DOUGLAS GUTENKUNST

Killed in Accident
January 30, 1944

HOWARD BURRISS

Missing in Action
January 31, 1944

DONALD MALONE

Missing in Action
February 4, 1944

PERCY DIVENNY

Missing in Action
February 4, 1944

CLYDE DUNN

Missing in Action
February 17, 1944

JAMES MILLER

Missing in Action
February 17, 1944

Contents

· · · · · · · · · · ·

Introduction

• • • • • • • • • • •

This is the story of the fighting days of a naval officer who shaped my life. John Thomas Blackburn was forty-five or forty-six years old during the time I spent with him on the aircraft carrier *Midway* in the late fifties. He was, to be sure, that great ship's commanding officer, but to her four thousand officers and sailors, and particularly to her pilots, he was The Immediate Presence, the mentor, the guide— the man we all knew could do anything better than anybody aboard without half trying. He could turn the ship around on a dime in a narrow channel, take over from a boat coxswain in high winds and choppy seas, and make a flaw- less approach and landing at the accommodation ladder, or outfly the hottest fighter pilots with aplomb. He "had it" upstairs, at the tips of his fingers, in the seat of his pants. If ever a man was tailor-made to be an across-the-board role model and leader of men flying and fighting from ships at sea, it was Tommy Blackburn.

This book tells how he got that way. You get the feel of tension and drive as the young fighter pilot, son and younger brother of naval officers more comfortable with the peacetime Navy than he, taxes himself, subconsciously prepares himself for the crucial tests of World War II. He becomes a perfectionist in the techniques of getting masses of airplanes on and off aircraft carriers at sea, smartly. I was a lead fighter pilot on that carrier, *Midway,* in 1958 and 1959, and we all felt the teeth and sting of his perfectionism, but it wasn't until I read this story that I got the feel for how it was developed, or an appreciation of how it had paid off in his fighting days.

In November 1943, at the age of thirty-one, Tom Blackburn was commanding his second fighter squadron in combat. On New Year's Day of that year he had commissioned VF-17, the Navy's second squadron, to fly the F4U Corsair. By October the squadron had become the first to fight in the airplane, and on this November 11, in the predawn darkness, he was leading twenty-four of his Corsairs from the island of New Georgia toward Japan's primary fortress in the South Pacific, Rabaul. En route, they were to fly cover over a force of three carriers and nine destroyers from darkness into light, and then land aboard and refuel and rearm while the carriers' planes attacked Rabaul. Time was of the essence because VF-17 had to relaunch to face the horde of Japanese fighters that could be expected to follow the carrier planes back to their ships. In the early light, after shooting down a Japanese prowler over the ships in the dark, Tom picked up the "Prep Charlie" visual signal flashed from the carriers, and watching aircraft launching on the decks below, maneuvered his planes in radio silence to be at the ramp, landing gear and hooks down, ready to start landing the instant "Clear Deck" was signaled.

To know the man and his element is to appreciate the joy in Tom's heart as the ships, heading into the wind, sailing ever closer to enemy territory, received VF-17's planes, at tight interval, no wave-offs, quickly and silently. And these were the first carrier landings any of VF-17's pilots had made in over two months. (They had been based ashore for logistic, not operational, reasons.)

And yes, the squadron did launch in time to face one hundred or more inbound Japanese planes and, in the next hour that morning, they were credited with 18.5 kills (including another for the skipper). When I was serving in Blackburn's ship fifteen years later, I was making a pioneer deployment in the F4U Corsair's grandson, the F8U Crusader. In no small measure trading on Tom Blackburn's inspiration, I took the F8U Crusader through a squadron and wing command and introduced it into the war in Vietnam, in which it achieved the highest kill-to-loss ratio of any Navy, Marine, or Air Force fighter type in the conflict. But in the course of the whole war it shot down only as many planes as Blackburn's squadron shot down that morning of November 11, 1943.

Of course, we all know that World War II was the place to set kill records. The targets were plentiful, the closing rates were somewhat less, and the enemy planes were very vulnerable. But as the following pages will make clear, VF-17's combat record in the Solomons was unbeatable. That one squadron, in seventy-six combat days, had a confirmed kill score of 154.5 Japanese airplanes with a kill to loss ratio of over eleven. Thirteen pilots of VF-17 made ace in this period. This, by a factor of more than a third, exceeds the scores of the Black Sheep Squadron made famous in the modern television serial. True, Tom Blackburn was generally operating with a third more planes than his Marine counterpart, but even after applying this factor, his numbers still come out higher.

But inspiration is what I'm writing these few pages about, and that was the legacy that Tom left all fighter pilots. He saw his war in a heroic, go-for-the-jugular, romantic context. I think he's right when he suggests that destroying their fighter planes and pilots in air-to-air combat may have done Japan's self-confidence more violence than bombs. But it was his manner, his conviction, and his courage (including the physical kind, in a supersonic Crusader cockpit) that stuck with me from those days on the *Midway*. Perhaps it's no coincidence that I realized my greatest aspirations for service—mine in a North Vietnamese prison—when I was the same age as he was when his tremendous influence on me counted most: forty-five or forty-six.

James Stockdale
Vice Admiral
U.S. Navy (Ret)

Glossary

· · · · · · · · · · · ·

A/C aircraft
Acknowledge voice-radio directive: "If you understand and will comply with the order given, reply 'Wilco' "
Airflow spoiler a fitting or device to destroy lift when desired
AirLant Air Force Atlantic Fleet
Ammo ammunition (bullets)
Angels fighter direction code for altitude in thousands of feet
Anti-G suit rig to minimize blackout from gee (*see* G)
Anzac military man from Australia/New Zealand
ASAP as soon as possible
Augered in crashed, originally used with tailspin accidents
AvCad Navy rank, Aviation Cadet

B-24 Consolidated's Liberator; four-engine heavy bomber
B-25 North American's Mitchell; two-engine medium bomber
Back to battery return to normal
Bail out to jump out of an a/c
Bastille prison, jail, slammer, calaboose, hoosegow
Beach land area; opposite of "at sea"
Betty IJNAF land-based twin-engine bomber, appearance like Martin B-26
Black Shoes nonaviation Naval officers (aviators: brown shoes)
Bogey fighter direction code: unknown aircraft
Bomber One the main landing strip at Espiritu Santo
Boresight to align guns and sighting devices

Boresighted, he had me enemy in perfect firing position

Bought the farm fatal crash, usually associated with home base

Brain bucket crash helmet or hard hat

Bridge the topside control station of a ship

BT-1 Northrop monoplane dive bomber, prototype of SBD

Bulkhead nautical term for wall; also vertical panel in a/c

Bunker Hill CV-17, *Essex*-class carrier (36 F6F 36 SB2C 19 TBF)

CAG Carrier Air Group Commander

'Canal short for Guadalcanal

CarQual qualify for carrier flight operations (landings and takeoffs made under controlled conditions)

Cat catapult; also short for Wildcat; part of the capstan used in handling anchor chain

Cat, walk back the reverse a policy or dictum

Catwalk walkway just below flight deck level, providing shelter and fore and aft access

CAVU Ceiling and Visibility Unlimited; weather

Chandelle a steep climbing turn, usually started at high speed (*see* Zoom)

Charger USS *Charger* CVE 29, small merchantman converted to flattop

Chennault's Flying Tigers the American Volunteer Group in China pre–WW II

Chocked wheel held in place by wooden blocks

Church key beer can opener

CInCPac Commander in Chief Pacific Fleet

Clocks aircraft instruments, especially flight aids

Cockpit coaming the rim

ComInCh Commander in Chief (of the U.S. Navy)

ComAirLant Commander Air Force Atlantic Fleet

ComAirPac Commander Air Force Pacific Fleet

ComAirSols Commander Air Forces Solomon Islands

ComAirSoPac Commander Air Forces Southern Pacific

ComSoPac Commander Southern Pacific Area (VAdm W. F. Halsey, USN)

ConForSols Confederate Forces, Solomon Islands

CV large aircraft carrier
CVE small "escort" carrier, usually converted merchantman
CVL "light" carrier, U.S., normally converted cruiser

Dauntless *see* SBD
DD destroyer

Echelon aircraft formation with planes following on a single line of bearing from leader; level of command; ancillary unit
Essex CV-9, *see Bunker Hill,* except VB: 36 SBD
ETA estimated time of arrival
ETD estimated time of departure

F2A Brewster Buffalo, early monoplane fighter
F2F, F3F Grumman biplane fighters
F4B Boeing biplane fighter (AAF P-12)
F4F Grumman Wildcat, small midwing monoplane, Vmax 325, standard equipment for all VF squadrons till early 1943
F4U Vought Corsair, the Hog; also U-Bird; gull-winged, Vmax 400, Navy and Marine Corps Fighter and Fighter-Bomber squadrons
F6F Grumman Hellcat, low square-tipped wing, Vmax 375; principal fighter in Navy squadrons, after F4F, until VJ Day
FW 200 German four-engine long-range recco
Fairey Fulmar British two-seater carrier-based "fighter"
Fam, fammed familiarize(d)
Fan propeller
Feathered propeller blades aligned with flight path to reduce drag and stop rotation (*see* Windmill)
FFT for further transfer (transportation)
Fifties U.S. machine guns, bullet diameter 0.50 inch
Filled to the gunwales (gunnels) loaded to capacity
Fire-wall, fire-walled partition immediately aft of engine, hence throttle to max forward (open) position
Fish a torpedo
Five squared (5 by 5) voice radio: strength five (max); readability five; also "loud and clear"
Flak antiaircraft fire; also adverse criticism

Flat-hatting flying at very low levels, usually exhibitionistic
Flipper aircraft horizontal control surface; elevator
Fokker Dreidecker German triplane fighter of WW I (Richtofen)
Freeboard vertical distance from surface of water to gunwale (edge of boat)
Full bore maximum engine power

G, Gee force of gravity used as a measure of (usually) vertical acceleration or deceleration
Gauges *see* Clocks
GP bombs general purpose explosive (contrasts with incendiary, for example)

Hack, in officer's punishment: relieved of duty and restricted to quarters
Hamp Japanese fighter, square-wingtip version of Zero
Hand on the helm in command of
Heave around work hard; get busy at assigned task
Helen Japanese medium two-engine bomber, similar in appearance to B-25
Hellcat *see* F6F
High blower an engine supercharger setting used at high altitudes
High-side run a fighter attack pattern using steep dive from the side (*see* Overhead)
Hit the silk to parachute, or bail out
Hog *see* F4U

IJAAF Imperial Japanese Army Air Force
IJNAF Imperial Japanese Naval Air Force
Independence CVL-22, (24 F6F 9 TBF)
Island the superstructure above the flight deck of a carrier, incorporates bridge(s), mast(s), smokestack, etc.

Jeep carrier a CVE
JU-88 German two-engine medium bomber

Kate IJNAF torpedo bomber
Kiwi a New Zealander
Knucklehead U.S. strip in Russell Islands; someone not bright

LCI landing craft infantry; a small seagoing vessel for landing troops on beaches

LCT landing craft tank; a boat carried by ships of amphibious forces to land tanks, light artillery, and small numbers of troops

LSO landing signal officer; the controller of aircraft on final approach to carrier landing

LST landing ship tank; a 280-foot seagoing vessel to carry men and equipment to beachheads (also known as large slow target)

Lufbery (circle) a horizontal ring of fighters for mutual defense (WW I)

Main mount large wheel and tire of a/c

Maru Japanese "ship"

ME-109 German fighter, principal equipage of *Luftwaffe*, Vmax 350

Meat wagon ambulance portion of airfield crash crew

Mil(s) gunnery term of angular measurement, 1 mil equals 1 foot of arc at 1000 feet

Milk up raise gradually

Mosquito British two-engine light bomber, designed for low level ops

NAAS Naval Auxiliary Air Station; usually a small satellite field to an NAS

NAS Naval Air Station

NJ North American, fixed landing gear, the first U.S. monoplane trainer, prototype of SNJ

Nugget a fledgling pilot

O'clock relative bearing code using straight ahead as twelve, dead astern as six, etc.

Oleo, oleo struts shock absorber(s)

One-eighty (180) a turn of 180 degrees, course reversal

Oscar obsolescent IJAAF fighter, fixed landing gear, Vmax 300

Out radio code: end of transmission, reply is neither requested nor desired, never used with "Over"

Over   radio code: end of transmission, but reply is requested
Overhead   aboard ship; the ceiling; aerial gunnery; a steep diving run from directly above target

P-38   Lockheed Lightning two-engine fighter, Vmax 350
P-39   Bell Aircobra fighter, Vmax 325
P-40   Curtiss Tomahawk; no further comment
P-51   North American Mustang, Vmax 400
P&W   Pratt and Whitney (Aircraft Engine Company), makers of high HP radial engines
Part brass rags   to sever connections with a close associate
PBY   Consolidated two-engine seaplane (and amphibian)
Photo recco   photographic reconnaissance
Plank owner   member of ship or squadron complement from date of unit's commissioning
Plebe   U.S. Naval Academy freshman
Plowback   school graduate retained as an instructor
Poilu   French common soldier
Pollywog   one who hasn't crossed the equator
Porpoised   as with torpedo broaching after initial plunge
Prep Charlie (PC)   prepare to land aboard (carrier)
Pri fly   aircraft carrier's flight operations nerve center (usually on aft end of island structure)
Princeton   CVL-23 (24 F6F 9 TBF)
PT   motor torpedo boat

Refam, refammed   refamiliarize(d)
Retread   officer with WW I service brought back to active duty from civilian life
Revetment   horseshoe-shaped embankment for protection from horizontal blast

SBD   Douglas Dauntless, divebomber; standard equipment for Navy and Marine VB squadrons 1941–43; wings did not fold
SB2C   Curtiss Helldiver (the Beast), divebomber, replaced SBD starting in late 1943
SB2U   Vought Vindicator, Navy's first monoplane divebomber, replaced by SBD prior to December 1941

SNJ North American advanced trainer (USAF AT-6); the mainstay of U.S. military fighting training

Saddle position astern of another aircraft in position for attack

Saratoga CV-3, built on battle cruiser hull (36 F6F 24 SBD 18 TBF)

Scramble launch a/c as fast as possible

Scuttlebutt rumor, gossip

Seven-point-seven (7.7) mm bullet diameter of Japanese machine guns (about 0.27 inch)

Shellback a seafaring man who has crossed the equator

Sick bay medical area aboard ship or Navy Base

Skip bombing very low level bombing wherein bomb skips into target from water (or land) like a flat rock

Slipstream the turbulent blast of air created by an a/c prop

Slot, the New Georgia Sound, the passage between the Solomons from Bougainville to Guadalcanal

Snoop, snooper to hang around a ship or force observing from a distance; surveillance

Sonar device for submarine detection from sound reflection

SoPac South Pacific; the command area embracing the islands from New Ireland to New Caledonia, including the Solomons

Spad Allied WW I biplane fighter

Spin in to crash, especially from a tailspin

Spitkit (Nautical: spittoon) a small ship

Spliced get married

Split-S, split-essed a violent half roll to an inverted position; go as quickly as possible from level flight into a vertical dive

Spook startle; scare off

Stall, stalling out breakdown of smooth airflow resulting in loss of lift

Standard rate turn a gentle turn of approximately 3 degrees per second

Tail-end-Charlie the rearmost plane of a formation

TBD Douglas Devastator; torpedo plane, the Navy's first service monoplane; replaced by TBF starting mid-1942

TBF Grumman Avenger; torpedo plane, used also as glide bomber. Standard equipment for Navy and Marine squadrons after mid-1942

TBM Avenger, built by General Motors

Tojo IJAAF radial engined fighter; follow on to Zero, Vmax 400(?); never appeared in significant numbers

Tokyo express high speed Japanese resupply and reinforcement by ship, especially through the Slot to Guadalcanal at night

Tokyo Rose The English-speaking DJ on Radio Tokyo who broadcast propaganda and "seductive" messages in a honeyed female voice

Tony IJAAF in-line engine fighter; no relative of, but looked like, Me 109; Vmax 350

Torpecker torpedo plane or pilot

Turkey an *affectionate* name for the Grumman TBF

Turkey shoot a one-sided bloody aerial battle

Uncle Sugar the U.S.A.; the U.S. government

V true airspeed; Navy letter denoting heavier than air (VP = patrol plane, ZP = blimp, CA = cruiser, CV = aircraft carrier)

Vmax sustained top speed in level flight

VAL Japanese dive bomber; fixed landing gear

VB, VF, VF (N), VP, VT aircraft type and squadron designators; bomber, fighter, night fighter, patrol, torpedo; when followed by number denotes unit

Washing Machine Charlie Japanese high-altitude night heckler over Solomons beachheads

WestPac almost all of Pacific area west of Hawaii except SoPac

Windmill propeller rotating on dead engine

Zero, Zeke Japanese fighter, principal VF equipment of IJNAF from 1940 on; Vmax 350

Zoom a steep climb started at high speed for maximum altitude gain

Zoomie Black Shoe equalizer term for aviators

Danny Boy
· · · · · · · · · · ·

Bougainville
February 19, 1944
  "Honest, Duke, this second Zeke did the same dumb thing. After Oc came in too fast, missed, and chandelled out, the Zeke pulled up in a forty-five-degree climb, straight ahead. He was just hanging there. I opened up inside two hundred yards, dead astern, led him about fifty mils. Just like the skipper keeps telling us: 'Get close before your shoot; you're never as close as you think!' I waited until he filled my whole windshield. I was right on. I squeezed the trigger and BLOOIE!—the biggest ball of fire I'll ever see. I went right through it; got a load of oil on my windshield. I think my first bullet flamed him. Couldn't have been more than a half-second burst. Jesus, those two poor bastards never knew what hit 'em. One minute they're fat, dumb, and happy; the next, they're exploded in the goddamnedest blossom of orange you ever saw.
  "I lost Oc on this run . . ."

The official action report written that evening by the VF-17 air combat intelligence officer, Lt(jg) Duke Henning, is more laconic. By February 1944 Duke had heard many combat reports related by successful pilots still hyperstimulated by the mind-blowing pressures of air-to-air combat. While not unbelieving, Duke was obliged to expunge the hyperbole and reduce the tales to their reportable essentials:

"Lt [Oscar] Chenoweth and Lt (jg) [Daniel] Cunningham were the only F4Us to complete the mission. They arrived at the target area at about 1005, twenty minutes ahead of the bombers. They came in at 30,000 feet and circled, letting down to 24,000 feet. They saw six to eight Jap fighters over St. George Channel at 18,000 feet. Chenoweth made a firing run with Cunningham on his wing. Then Chenoweth followed the Zeke down to 12,000 feet (Cunningham stayed at 18,000 feet) and saw him crash on Cape Gazelle. He then climbed and rejoined Cunningham. The section made a second run. Chenoweth overshot, and as this Zeke pulled up he was an easy target for Cunningham, who burned him. The section recovered and headed westward over Blanche Channel where they spotted Zekes below them on the same course. A section run was made, and Cunningham again caught a Zeke as he pulled up and set him afire. In both cases, the Zekes were slow and Cunningham used less than 75 mils lead. . . . As he made his kill, Cunningham lost Chenoweth.

"When Cunningham lost [sight of] Chenoweth he was over Simpson Harbor at 5,000 feet. He headed for Blanche Channel at full throttle. Spotting an F4U he turned north to join up, but the F4U also turned north in pursuit of another Zero. Cunningham spotted a second one coming down behind him. He turned hard into the Jap, but the latter evaded, going for the other Corsair. Cunningham closed and sent him down flaming. Recovering at 3,000 feet, he headed for Cape Gazelle, saw another single close to the covering fighters with our retiring bombers. Shooting from . . . 150 yards, he put a fourth flamer into the water. He then joined the bomber cover heading home."

Oc Chenoweth had joined VF-17 in January, another in a long line of castoffs from other squadrons. Danny Boy Cunningham was the squadron shorty; he could not properly operate the huge F4U's rudder pedals without a special rig. Had it not been for his plaintive "I *can* do it; give me a chance," he would have been banished. On February 19, 1944, Oc got 3 confirmed kills, bringing his total score to 8.5, and Danny Boy got 4, bringing his total score to 7. That day, VF-17 pilots scored 16 confirmed kills.

In all during VF-17's two combat tours under my command, we were credited with 154.5 Japanese airplanes destroyed, 27 probably destroyed, and 25 damaged. Until then, no U.S. Navy or Marine fighter squadron in World War II had done as well.

BOUGAINVILLE

○ JAPANESE AIRBASE

ELEVATIONS IN FEET

| 0 | 1000 | 3000 | 5000 AND ABOVE |

0   10   20   30   40 MILES
0   10   20   30   40 KILOMETERS

Green Is

TO TRUK 900 MILES

BUKA I

TO RABAUL 190 MILES

BUKA
Buka Passage
BONIS

BOUGAINVILLE

ISLAND

EMPEROR RANGE

Mt Bagana
Numa Numa
TENEKAU

MAWARAKA
NOROVANA BAY
KIETA
Cape Torokina
Kieta
EMPRESS AUGUSTA BAY
CROWN PRINCE RANGE

KARA
KAHILI
Buin
Erventa
Tonolei Hbr
BALLALE
Fauro I
SHORTLAND
Faisi I
Poporang I
Alu I

SOLOMON

SEA

Mono I
TREASURY IS
Stirling I

F Temple

PART I

. . . .

To War

1

· · · · · · · · · · · ·

My war began in January 1941 when I received orders to join the newly created instructional staff at Naval Air Station, Miami. NAS, Miami, or Opa-Locka, as the base was also called, was to be the Navy's finishing school for carrier-bound fighter, dive-bomber, and torpedo pilots.

To say that I was underwhelmed at being dragged out of an active carrier-based fighter squadron to play nursemaid to an endless stream of youngsters fresh out of primary flight training is putting too good a face on my feelings. I was incensed. My squadron, VF-2, the so-called Fighting Chiefs, was considered one of the best in the U.S. Navy, and being one of only several officers flying beside the finest enlisted naval aviation pilots (NAPs) was a singular honor. The blow was doubly hard to swallow because of the timing. Throughout 1939 and 1940, professional officers expected to be at war within days or weeks. Training new pilots to fill the Navy's burgeoning ranks was vital duty, I realized, but my entire ten-year Navy career had been focused on just one thing: preparing myself to fly a Navy fighter in combat. On the day the new orders reached me, and for many months thereafter, I just *knew* that I was to be cheated of an opportunity that could arise only once in a generation.

The fact was that instructing at Opa-Locka was an honor as well as an unparalleled opportunity to hone my skills and learn more about flying fighters than I could ever have learned in the Fleet during peacetime.

NAS, Miami, was still under construction when I reported aboard in March 1941. Essential structures had been completed and others were abuilding. Most of the concrete for the runways and working areas had been poured, but the runways had no shoulders, just the 8-inch drop-off to the sandy soil on which the base was being built. Going off the hard surface at any significant speed equaled a crash. There were no runway lights; necessary night operations were thus truly hairy because the torch pots provided confusing and erratic lighting of the runways and taxiways.

The station commander and director of the training program was Cdr Jerry Bogan, a tough, feisty little man who, I found, had handpicked his subordinates. The command thus bore his indelible stamp. He demanded and got high performance. From the start, our unspoken motto was: Work hard, play hard, don't alibi, produce.

My immediate superior was Lt Joe Clifton—Jumping Joe. He graduated from the Naval Academy in 1930, three years ahead of me. His nickname derived from his days as a star 165-pound fullback. Joe was a fitness nut decades before most Americans heard of fitness, a dynamo of nervous energy, a man of enormous charisma. He was a natural leader, an activist, a born delegator of tiresome details of administration. As Joe's immediate subordinate, I not only found myself flying a lot, I made up and modified schedules for instructors and students, and worked up and superintended the ground phase of the training program. Not the least of my responsibilities was making certain that the mercurial Lieutenant Clifton arrived from his myriad other activities on time for hops and lectures.

Another standout staffer was Lt(jg) Roger Hedrick, a fine

pilot and superb marksman. Cool, calm, and capable, Rog was to be my strong right arm. Much for what I have been given credit then and later in the war was Rog's doing. Unlike most of his superiors at the school and in naval aviation in general, Rog was not an Academy man. Rather, he was one of our direct links with most of the young pilots we would be training at Opa-Locka. Rog was an AvCad, a Naval Aviation Cadet who had been flying with the Fleet since completing flight school in 1936. This contrasts with my career pattern and, to a greater or lesser degree, those of all the Annapolis graduates in naval aviation; we had all been obliged to serve for two years in the Fleet before entering the flight-training program and earning our wings. Roger Hedrick's assignment to our staff was not only a personal triumph for Rog, it was proof positive that the AvCad program had arrived.

It is hard to say too much in praise of all the early AvCads on our faculty. The first AvCads to complete training had joined the Fleet in mid-1936 and most of them had elected to remain on active duty after the conclusion of their four-year contracts. This, despite the fact that they were not then officially ranked as officers and did not draw full officers' pay. All of our AvCad instructors—and all the Academy men—had extensive carrier service under their belts. The early AvCads were an exceptionally select group in that, at the inception of the program, only absolutely perfect physical specimens had been selected. As little as one dental filling led to disqualification, a consciously absurd criterion meant to limit access to the program from among a throng of Depression-age candidates. On the other hand, every one of them was a highly qualified college graduate who, in 1935, did not have the draft breathing down his neck. Thus, the early AvCads were highly motivated volunteers, willing to earn less status and less pay if only they could become naval aviators.

Our band of instructors steadily grew as our student load increased, for the flight schools at Pensacola and Jacksonville were really churning them out. Some of the new instructors, AvCads and Annapolis men, joined us from the

Fleet, but many were plowbacks—selected students retained upon completion of their training, not only because they were excellent students with much promise but because they appeared to possess the temperaments of good trainers.

At the time we opened NAS, Miami, in mid-1941, Annapolis graduates had to serve two full years in the Fleet before being accepted for flight training. This, combined with the limited number of Regulars who could be spared for flight training, the virtual closure of the enlisted pilot program, and the burgeoning needs of the Fleet, stressed the importance of the Naval Aviation Cadet program in the job of building naval aviation manyfold its size while maintaining world-class standards.

By 1941 the AvCad program, which had undergone numerous changes since its inception in 1935, was accepting candidates with as little as two years of college, though we had our share of cadets with postgraduate degrees as well. In return for a guaranteed bonus of five hundred dollars a year, to be paid at the conclusion of a four-year contract, AvCads were trained to fly and commissioned in the Navy Reserve or Marine Corps Reserve upon earning their wings at Opa-Locka or at the Navy's multiengine training base.

By 1940 the physical entrance standards for the revived AvCad program had been relaxed to reasonable levels. This, because the objective was to churn out a great number of pilots from a much vaster pool of physically and mentally qualified applicants. Most of our students had been subject to the draft and had thus volunteered for the program under some duress. That is no reflection on them; our qualified candidates could have chosen from among a lot of easier, less dangerous jobs than flying combat aircraft. The people we washed out reverted to enlisted rank and were obliged to serve out the terms of their contracts, but I suspect that most of them eventually wound up with commissions, for they were still among the best young men our nation was producing.

In addition to the Academy men and AvCads we trained was a small number of Reserve officers who had served on active duty with the Fleet and were between the ages of twenty-five and thirty. For the most part, these were men who had graduated from civilian colleges after completing the Reserve Officers' Training Course (ROTC).

Paralleling our efforts to turn out competent fighter pilots were the scout-and-dive-bomber unit and the temporarily moribund torpedo unit. The sum of our efforts at Opa-Locka was to produce pilots for the burgeoning carrier and Marine air groups. This was not accomplished without setbacks, among which was the complete unavailability of even obsolescent torpedo bombers, a factor that obviated torpedo training per se.

The airplanes we did have at Miami were castoffs from the Fleet, which was itself only beginning to receive relatively modern new fighter and bomber types. Initially, we flew and trained in a mixed bag of obsolete Boeing F4Bs, Grumman F2Fs, Grumman F3Fs, and others—biplanes all—supplemented by several two-seat North American SNJ advanced trainers, our only monoplanes, and a half-dozen biplane basic trainers with which we taught techniques for recovery from inverted spins. Mercifully, I had no connection with aircraft maintenance, but we did have a dedicated band of mechanical miracle workers to undertake that unenviable job of keeping our ungodly mixed bag of a working aircraft museum airborne. As it was, a single day's flying might find an instructor belting up in any of several of the numerous types in our possession. Thus, the instructor's expertise was paramount, for our fledglings had to have example as well as precept. Moreover, whenever required by the student load of the moment, instructors were expected to switch between fighters and dive-bombers.

Although all our students had completed primary flight training at Pensacola or Jacksonville, they were anything but finished products. About all they had proved was that they could regularly take off, perform basic aerobatics, and safely land. As a finishing school for Navy and Marine pilots bound for operational Fleet combat units, our syllabus included ground school with the pilot's handbooks for both fighters and bombers, cockpit checkout, supervised touch-and-go landings at unpaved outlying fields, elementary formation work, and field carrier training—simulated carrier landings on a paved runway. Next, all student pilots learned air-to-air gunnery over the Everglades against towed target sleeves. If successful, they went on to dive-bombing, where it took three hits for five drops on a 50-foot circle to get an "up"—a passing grade. If the fighter student made it that far, he went on to dogfighting, which we called "grab-ass," and then on to aerobatics. The final leg was night-flying familiarization, mostly landings and takeoffs rounded out with some extremely tame night formation flying. I doubt if the total flight time for any Miami student of the day came to 150 hours.

We did no high-altitude work at Miami. Almost without exception, the highest we took our students was 12,000 feet, where oxygen was not needed unless we were going to stay up for a long time. Thus, the mysteries of high-altitude flying—particularly the problems encountered in the use of oxygen equipment—simply were not addressed during our training course. As with everything, it was a matter of not having the equipment, which was in short supply even in the Fleet.

Each student who completed this course—each in his own time, within reason—was commissioned a Navy ensign or a Marine second lieutenant, given his wings, and sent on to the Fleet. If a student could not cut it as a fighter or dive-bomber pilot, we could send him to multiengine school. Most of us—instructors and cadets alike—considered that to be a fate worse than death, a purgatory of disrespect. It was not really our job to wash pilots completely out of the program—the incompetents theoretically did not make it as far as advanced training—but we had to do so on occasion, mostly as a result of ongoing disciplinary problems or because a cadet lost his nerve. The surest ticket out of the program—one that was punched with astounding rarity, given our rickety equipment and frenetic pace—was being killed or maimed in an accident.

*   *   *

The gunnery training that we gave to students at Miami was high-deflection-angle shooting. The runs we taught were the overhead, the high-side, and the flat-side.

In the overhead run, one comes over the target on an opposite course and approximately 3,000 feet above it. At the right moment, the pilot goes into a half roll to the inverted position and pulls through in a very steep dive. At the point of opening fire, approximately 500 feet from the target, the ideal is to be in a vertical dive perpendicular to the horizontal target. This requires maximum deflection—lead—because the relative motion of the target is greatest. As the dive progresses, the angle of the dive decreases and, thus, the amount of deflection needed also decreases. If properly executed, a pass close aboard the target will find the attacker in about a 45-degree dive. With recovery beneath the target, the speed obtained in the dive is used to zoom back up to get ahead and in position for the next run.

The high-side run is somewhat similar to the overhead run, except that the dive starts about 1,000 feet to one side of the target. The attacker should be in a steep dive abeam of the target so that the shooting is done at a 45-degree deflection angle both in the vertical plane and at the four o'clock position or eight o'clock position. (The target's nose is considered to be pointed at twelve o'clock.) The recovery is executed much as from an overhead run.

In the flat-side run, the optimum position for opening fire is 90 degrees to the course of the target. This narrows to a maximum deflection shot of 45 degrees as the attacker passes astern of the target and recovers.

These runs were designed to minimize the exposure of the attacking airplane to the flexible guns of bombers. They were extremely effective once they were mastered in that they made for a very tough shot for the bomber's gunners.

During aerial gunnery instruction, the instructor flew above and to the rear of the target sleeve so he could observe the students during their runs. When the radios worked—not very often—the instructor could coach the students as well as be available to issue warnings in case of hazardous situations, as when two people tried to make their runs at the same time. The instructor kept notes on each run of every student for a postflight skull session—debriefing.

The hectic training schedule and rickety equipment claimed a few student lives, but the pace did not allow for much in the way of lamenting such losses. We replaced the dead bodies with live ones and the ruined equipment with whatever they sent us, and we went on in our mad race against history.

Throughout my tour at Opa-Locka, the training staff was starkly aware that our course was quite rudimentary when taken against what we knew our "nuggets" would need to know in combat. But we also knew that we were locked on the horns of competing dilemmas. In the first instance, the Fleet was crying for new pilots to fill new billets created by ongoing programs aimed both at expanding the size of existing units and creating new units altogether. In the second case, we were just a stopover in the pipeline between the primary schools and the Fleet; we had strictly limited facilities with which to train ever-increasing numbers of cadets flowing out of the two Florida-based primary schools. Acute equipment shortages in the Fleet prevented us from training our students in the actual models of airplanes they would be flying in the Fleet.

Our training program was essential, but it was by no means comprehensive. And we by no means suffered under the illusion that we were turning out Fleet-ready pilots, but we did teach them a lot and we did inculcate them with the spirit of self-confidence as well as transmitting to them the esprit de corps of naval aviation. If anything, our most important task, aside from the physical and mental skills we imparted, was to teach our students a brand of *perfectionism*. Indeed, this was the philosophical basis of all the training those young men received at primary and advanced flight-training schools. Ours was a truly high-risk business; a really elevated level of self-awareness and devotion to doing things perfectly were needed by these naval aviators to survive the rigors of simply flying high-performance airplanes in carrier operations—not to mention triumphing over adversaries flying other high-performance airplanes.

Our first cadre of instructors at Miami literally was in on the ground floor of the U.S. Navy's incredible, unprecedented growth toward its eventual full wartime strength. However, though much of what would come later was certainly in the air, our pace at the outset was not frenetic or tinged with a do-or-die mind-set. The senior staff, including Rog Hedrick and several of the other early AvCads, had been painstakingly trained over long years, and that is how we hoped to train our first flock of cadets. We well knew the shortcomings of the physical plant and we certainly heard the calls from the Fleet, but we were determined to impart all the skill and knowledge that we could in the few months allowed to us. As pressure from both sides picked up—as the Fleet yelled louder and as the primary schools churned out ever greater numbers of nuggets—we were obliged to speed things up, to cut some corners, to shave some of the fine points off our instructional program. This placed the burden of truly completing the training cycle upon the Fleet and initially left us feeling that we had not quite done our jobs. But even these feelings fell prey to the ever-increasing pressures the coming war imposed.

One event that relieved some of the pressure, albeit imperceptibly, was the commissioning of a new primary flight school at Corpus Christi, Texas. In the fall of 1941, as the new school was being created, we at Opa-Locka were called upon to train a cadre of experienced Fleet pilots who would set up an advance school there identical to our own. If nothing else, at least we did not have to take on the flow of Corpus Christi's primary school graduates ourselves.

2

. . . .

Miami was by no means all work and no play. We had no officers' club at Opa-Locka, but we were welcomed at the Tatem Surf Club in Miami Beach. These luxurious facilities, including a huge pool adjacent to the surf, came to us at nominal cost. We flocked there on torrid summer afternoons at the conclusion of flight ops, and, until the pace picked up, practically lived there on weekends. My son, Mark, who was nearly four, was a real water rat and a great favorite of the young studs. To his mother's terror, they induced him to go off the high board and tossed him back and forth medicine ball fashion in the shallow end.

As a rule, we drank a lot, ate well, and danced up a storm. The few wives in attendance loved having slews of bachelors around, but I have no knowledge of extracurricular activities.

Two of our standout instructors were Lt(jg) Harry Harrison, a colorful if somewhat laid-back scion of the Philadelphia Main Line, and Lt(jg) Sam Silber, a former all-American lacrosse player from the University of Maryland. These two early AvCads delighted in playing practical jokes on our boss, Joe Clifton, primarily through the medium of Joe's prized new Buick. One day Harry and Sam jacked up a rear wheel so that the tire was just touching the ground, a fact that was obscured by the tall weeds growing in the parking lot. When Joe charged out to the lot a little late for a squash date in Miami, he characteristically jumped behind the wheel without looking, thrust the key into the ignition, and impatiently fire walled the gas pedal. A large audience that had unobtrusively gathered for the event witnessed Joe's frantic reaction to the engine's overrevving scream and the rubber smoke thrown up by the screeching tire. Another time, the two miscreants loaded several empty cartridge cases into one of the Buick's hubcaps. This produced a fearsome racket which disappeared at cruising speed. It took Joe some time to track down the source of the noise, but no time at all to decide who had planted the cartridge cases. Such high jinks helped relieve the tension of the job.

Instructors and students often enjoyed close personal associations that carried over into our off-duty hours. This close association was both a carryover from the days of an exceptionally small naval aviation service, when all of us formed a band of brothers, and a recognition of the rite of passage our course represented. On the other hand, however close we felt to our students, training time on the station—in the air or in classrooms on the ground—was marked by the strict adherence to military discipline and courtesy, for it was still our duty to inculcate our students into the rigors of the undemocratic, nonegalitarian military society for which they had volunteered. We did have mavericks to deal with from time to time, and we came down hard when they revealed themselves.

Lacking a war of our own, we followed the triumphs and travails of our British cousins as closely as we could, primarily in the press. No doubt, the Office of Naval Intelligence received a huge steady flow of information on tactics and equipment—Allied and Axis—but they did not deign to share it with any of us who might actually be able to use it. We were thus completely unaware of the appearance over China of the superb Japanese Zero fighter, a nimble airplane that was a full generation ahead of our most advanced

Fleet-type monoplane fighter, the lamentable Brewster F2A Buffalo. The same held true in the case of the most advanced British Royal Air Force fighters; we were thus mystified by the Germans' inability to turn the Mediterranean into their own lake. Meantime, like us, the Royal Navy's Fleet Air Arm was struggling along with antiques of every type. This resulted in a criminal waste of resources and a vital need for pilots. Yet, somehow, the Fleet Air Arm gave the Germans and Italians stiff enough opposition to help keep the supply lanes to Malta and North Africa open.

Little did we know how closely our early war experience would parallel the Fleet Air Arm's in terms of such losses—and such closely run triumphs.

Through August 1941 we flew a five-day week. Then we flew six days. After December 7, flight-training operations were conducted every day, though instructors and students alike flew a staggered schedule so that all hands got one day off in seven.

News of Pearl Harbor came over the commercial radio as several of us were beering up at my house following a relaxed Sunday morning round of golf. We had no idea of the magnitude of destruction. Indeed, our initial reaction was one of satisfaction that the issue, so long a threat, was now joined. We assumed that our patrol bombers out of Hawaii would quickly locate the enemy task force and that our counterattack would be devastating. As the facts slowly emerged, however, we became as horrified as we were incredulous at the ineptitude of our Pacific commanders.

Withal, the commander in chief of the Japanese Combined Fleet, Adm Isoroku Yamamoto, was correct in opposing the Pearl Harbor attack while it was in the planning stage. He said, "No matter how successful it may be, it will wake the sleeping dragon." Unwittingly, the Japanese did us another service in addition to uniting our nation for the war; it was a favor that ultimately saved more lives than were lost at Pearl Harbor. By pure luck, none of our six precious fleet-type aircraft carriers were lost on December

7, 1941. Indeed, by crippling our battleship forces, the Imperial Navy forced the U.S. Navy to completely change over from a strategy based on a powerful surface fleet to one based on the employment of carrier air. The U.S. Navy was forced by its losses in battleships at Pearl Harbor to use the emerging carrier-based air arm as its primary offensive weapon from the onset of the Pacific War.

Of immediate use to us in the earliest weeks of the war was the Fleet's decision to scrap the Brewster F2A monoplane fighter in favor of the far better but still somewhat outclassed Grumman F4F Wildcat. As soon as more new Wildcats reached the carrier air groups and Marine squadrons, around the first of the year, Buffalos were released to the training command. The modern Buffalos were an invaluable supplement to the obsolete biplane fighters that we heaved around in, checking out ourselves and our students. While inadequate for combat, the F2As were ideal for our purposes, especially for approximating the level of engine power and flight characteristics our graduates would experience in the new Wildcat.

The introduction of the Buffalo at Opa-Locka temporarily boosted my prestige, for I was the only instructor who had flown it or any monoplane fighter in the Fleet, it having made its Fleet debut with VF-2 during my last year there. Of course, at the outset, my work load was increased, for I had to check out instructors after teaching them the vagaries of this quirky, hard-to-handle compromise airplane. Moreover, I had been VF-2's engineering—ground maintenance—officer when the Buffalo made its debut with VF-2, so it also fell on me to help get the Opa-Locka maintenance staff up to speed on that dog's gremlins, which were legion.

After we had processed our first batch of students in the newly acquired F2As, Roger Hedrick and I were introduced to a new sort of teacher, LCdr Charles Evans, of the Royal Navy, a combat veteran fresh from the perils of flying the ghastly, inadequate Fairey Fulmar against German Messerschmitt Me-109s in Europe.

It would be an understatement to brand Lieutenant Commander Evans a mere "character." With a neatly cropped red mustache and beard—unheard of in the U.S. Navy—and a swagger stick in hand, this slight, handsome Britisher was the epitome of quiet self-confidence. He was unmistakable in his black silk scarf, octagonal-lensed goggles, and standard Royal Air Force leather flying helmet, which he wore in even the hottest weather. He was a superb, extremely skilled pilot and a warm, perceptive gentleman. With Lieutenant Commander Evans's arrival came news that Roger and I would receive as our next class a complement of Royal Navy trainees.

Once Evans had had a chance to study the pilot's handbook and receive a cockpit checkout in one of our F2As, he took off for a one-hour familiarization flight. Rog and I carefully monitored his ground-handling technique, takeoff, and final landing, and we saw that he handled the airplane expertly and smoothly. As Evans rolled up to the hardstand, Rog and I both knew what was coming next.

"Tom, I'd like to fly with you chaps. Can we take three of these aircraft out for a little formating?"

"Certainly, sir. We'll get our gear and be ready to go in fifteen minutes." As Rog and I turned to leave, we could not help grinning at one another, for we had both evaluated a lot of pilots just this way ourselves.

Rog and I followed Evans closely as we taxied out, and Evans looked briefly startled as we pulled into a tight vee for a formation takeoff. Routine climb-out, shallow dives, turns in each direction—Rog and I stayed locked in tight throughout. Next, Evans headed out over the cobalt Gulf Stream, eased down to about 30 feet above the whitecaps, and started a series of turns. The trick here is for the pilot on the inside to drop below the leader in order to keep formation; the tighter the turn, the lower he has to go. This is routine flying at most operating levels, but it gets a mite hairy when you know that your outboard wingtip, which you cannot watch, is getting ever closer to the water. You only snag once in that sort of situation.

After giving both of us a good trial by fire to see if we

would clutch or sky out, Lieutenant Commander Evans pulled up, gave each of us a smile and a thumbs-up, and headed back to base to land. After that, whatever Rog and I did with the Brits was okay with him. This was most helpfully the case when one of the British students tried showing off for his girlfriend and augered in. I was sick but furious as I called all the Brits together and read them the riot act; I brusquely informed them that any more unauthorized flying at low level would be cause for immediate grounding and that Lieutenant Commander Evans would probably recommend that the offender be sent home in disgrace. The students groused a lot behind my back, but to no avail; Evans backed me all the way. We had no further discipline problems with the Brits, but they never forgave me for saying, "Your mate killed himself by his own stupidity."

Later in the war, when we led VF-17, Rog and I invariably employed LCdr Charles Evans's low-level checkout technique with pilots who wanted to fly with us.

Our Royal Navy students were eager, dedicated young men to whom war was much more a reality than it was to their American counterparts. However, by early 1942, the Royal Navy was reaching fairly far down into the barrel for pilot candidates, and it is fair to say that these Brits were not of the same caliber as their American fellow sufferers at our hands.

Lieutenant Commander Evans wound up paying NAS, Miami, one of the finest compliments it ever received. In commenting on the quality of the Royal Navy students we were turning out, Evans said that they were better trained than those the Royal Navy was turning out for itself at home. This, from a combat veteran representing a service that had been at war for two years.

3

. . . .

The CO, Cdr Jerry Bogan, made short shrift of my official January 1942 letter to the Navy Department requesting orders for sea duty. As soon as the letter reached Bogan's desk for an endorsement, I received the word, "Report to the commanding officer at once."

"You sent for me, sir?"

"You're goddamn right I did. I need you and all the other able-bodied instructors I can get for a long time to come. I will not so much as forward your request for sea duty recommending disapproval. Take it, get out of here, and don't waste my time again. Is that clear?"

"Yes, sir."

"Okay, Blackburn, shove off."

I was zero for two in my efforts to buck the system: My original assignment to Opa-Locka had stuck before there was a war, and my official request to get out of there had been turned back now that there was a war. Shortly after leaving Commander Bogan's office, however, I dropped a note to a personal friend working at the Aviation Detail Office, in Washington, and put in an unofficial request. Later still, I happened to be in Dallas picking up a new SNJ trainer to ferry to Miami when a recruiter for Claire Chennault's American Volunteer Group—the Flying Tigers—came through Opa-Locka. I was so frustrated at being kept from the war that I probably would have resigned my commission and signed on with Chennault if I had been home to see the recruiter.

But all was not lost.

"How the hell did you do this," Commander Bogan yelled as he waved a sheaf of official papers at me from behind his desk.

It was May 1942, long after I had given in to my sorry lot of being a beached fighter pilot playing nursemaid to tyros. I had no idea what the skipper was talking about, so it was no work at all adopting the look of honest, injured innocence I would have had on my face even if I had known what was going on.

The "this" turned out to be orders detaching me in June to travel to NAS, Norfolk, to form, commission, and command Escort Fighting Squadron 29 (VGF-29). Once formed, VGF-29 would report for duty aboard the new escort carrier, *Santee*. I was breathless and, for once, speechless.

Bogan cooled down a bit as he slowly came to realize that my look of surprise and delight was unfeigned. "Come on, Tommy, I've got connections you wouldn't believe, and *I* can't get sprung from here. You son of a bitch, how did such a junior lieutenant do it? Who do *you* know?"

I held my features deadpan as I rejoined, "Sorry, skipper, but that's classified information."

The skipper tried several unsuccessful approaches to get a clue, then finally growled, "Okay, shove off. Get back to work." As soon as I could, I sent a fifth of very good scotch to my friend at the Aviation Detail Office. It was the best investment I ever made.

When I picked up my orders from the skipper's office as I was checking out of Miami in June, I was flattered as well as touched to see that Jerry Bogan had penned in "with regret" after the standard typed-in phrase, "Detached this date."

*   *   *

July 1, 1942, was a typical blistering day at Norfolk when I read my orders aloud before twelve officers, eighty-plus sailors, and a handful of well-wishers: Escort Fighting Squadron 29 was formed and commissioned. Flight ops commenced several days later, as soon as we were equipped and checked out in a dozen factory-fresh Grumman F4F-4 Wildcat fighters.

Two of my officers were combat veterans of the new war, and one had even flown and scored kills in the Wildcat in combat, albeit his fighter was the earlier F4F-3 variant. The F4F-4, which was just then making its way into the Fleet, was the first folding-wing fighter ever to be purchased by the U.S. Navy. The folding wings would prove to be a must aboard the cramped escort carrier to which VGF-29 was bound. The F4F-4 mounted a solid battery of six .50-caliber machine guns, three in each wing, and sported a good reflector gun sight. On the down side, the airplane was moderately underpowered and therefore quite slow in the climb, a compromise necessitated by the wing-folding mechanism, heavy armored seatbacks, and heavy ammunition load required for the six machine guns. About the best thing that could be said about the added weight was that it would help Wildcats get away from most Japanese and German fighters while in a dive. Already proven at the Coral Sea and Midway, the Wildcat had a reputation for standing up to heavy fire and bringing its pilot home.

The Wildcat was a far better airplane than the transitional Brewster F2A Buffalo it replaced, but it had some weird quirks and terrible ground-handling characteristics. The powerful engine torque could cause an unwary or inexperienced pilot to ground loop to the left on takeoff, sometimes with fatal results. Also, its retraction mechanism for the main landing gear was a chain attached to a handle that the pilot was obliged to turn about twenty-seven times while he was doing all the other things required of him right after takeoff. Many an unwary or inexperienced Wildcat pilot sported painfully bruised shins after the handle got away from him while he was raising or lowering the landing gear. While no thoroughbred, the Wildcat was still the best, most powerful, most reliable production fighter the Navy had thus far put into service. I, for one, was glad to have it.

The training got off to an intense start, a holdover from my recent instructional duty. Within days, it became apparent that my exec, an old hand at flying multiengine patrol planes, was not making the grade as a fighter pilot despite a valiant effort on his part. He was unable to break ingrained habits and I was thus forced to send him back to multiengine flying. That left me with the job of choosing a new exec from between two experienced combat pilots whose squadrons had been lost when fleet carrier *Lexington* had been sunk in the Coral Sea in May. One, Lt(jg) Harry "Brink" Bass, was a 1938 Annapolis graduate who had earned a Navy Cross planting one of the bombs that sank the Japanese light carrier *Shoho* at Coral Sea. The other, Lt(jg) Bill Eder, was an ex-AvCad who had earned a Distinguished Flying Cross and whose score thus far in fighters was 1.5 confirmed kills and 1 probable. Brink, who had only just transitioned from dive-bombers to fighters, was senior to Bill, and fortunately a much better leader, so he got the nod despite Bill's combat record in fighters.

All the rest of the pilots under my command were fresh-caught ensigns right out of the advanced school at Corpus Christi. Rounding out VGF-29 was a sound, devoted ground staff. From the start, it was a happy, hardworking outfit.

Shortly after I formed the squadron, I was promoted to lieutenant commander. And shortly after that, we escaped the complications and strictures of a big-time base like NAS, Norfolk, and moved to our own operating base. Naval Auxiliary Air Station (NAAS) Pungo was in the boondocks 15 miles south of Norfolk, on the eastern edge of the Dismal Swamp. Pungo wasn't much, but it was mine, for I was the senior aviator present. With only our twelve Wildcats assigned to the station, we were free to set our own schedules and traffic patterns, and come and go as we pleased.

We came through our brief training at Pungo very well, though we lost one pilot who clutched and rode his Wildcat into the ground when he got into a spin trying to stream a towed target sleeve. In good time, all hands carrier qualified aboard jeep carrier *Charger,* a small converted merchantman, and we were all set to board Cdr Bill Sample's *Santee* when she completed conversion from fleet tanker to escort carrier in September. At that time, we joined the balance of the new escort air group, nine Grumman TBF Avenger torpedo bombers and nine Douglas SBD Dauntless scout-bombers. The bomber leader, LCdr Joe Ruddy, an old friend and comrade, was several years senior to me and thus filled in as air-group commander.

The very real German U-boat threat curtailed practice operations in the Atlantic, so we did our group workups while *Santee* remained in Chesapeake Bay. It was during the early part of the carrier work that I got caught with my pants at half-mast and made a beautiful comeback.

It happened when the fighter director, LCdr Red Gill, another *Lexington* survivor, called me by voice radio during one early flight: "Fighter Leader, this is *Santee*. My call sign is Romeo. What is yours? Over."

There followed a dismal pregnant silence. I had not thought about a call sign for the squadron; it had never occurred to me that we would be needing one. I had no response ready, but I had been taught as a plebe at the "trade school" —Annapolis—never to say "I don't know"; a dumb answer is better than no answer. I was not about to lose face over this one, not with the whole squadron and possibly the whole ship listening.

"Arrgh . . . Romeo, this is . . . Shillelagh Leader. Send your message. Over."

Our unofficial squadron insignia soon appeared on the left shoulder of our flight coveralls. It depicted a stylized Irish war club within a kelly green border.

Santee sailed for Bermuda in October 1942 as part of a task force bound for Operation TORCH, the invasion of North Africa. Of course, we had no idea what lay ahead, but we sensed that it was something of importance.

Our immediate group comprised one small fleet carrier and three CVEs, *Santee* and two other escort carriers converted from fleet tankers. Our flagship was *Ranger,* a small fleet-type carrier that was to have been the first of a line of many such economical carriers. However, *Ranger* had been found wanting because of the lack of a third elevator between her flight deck and hangar deck that resulted in very slow launch and recovery operations. Though fleet carrier *Wasp* was really an updated *Ranger*-type carrier, the addition of a third elevator allowed her to participate in dangerous offensive operations. *Ranger* was not really up to taking part as a full participant in the strategically critical battles then raging in both the Pacific and Mediterranean, so she had been relegated to serving as an oversized escort and escort leader.

We conducted five days of intense warm-up exercises in Bermudan waters. It was a meager shakedown for new ships operating with new squadrons.

During the Bermudan interlude, one of my gang managed to wreck a Wildcat in a bad landing. Upon returning to the anchorage for a final resupply before heading east toward Africa, we received a message from the task force commander: "Replacement aircraft arriving aboard *Chenango* [on October 15]. All ships submit [aircraft] replacement requirements." Captain Sample called LCdr Joe Ruddy and me to his cabin and showed us the message.

"Captain, I recommend that we ask for two fighters. That'll improve the chances of getting the one we need."

The skipper nodded with a look that spelled "conniver," but he said, "Okay, Tommy, I'll do that."

The following day I was told to report to the captain's cabin "on the double." There, I found Bill Sample with a big grin on his coppery face. "Tommy, I just got word that *two* fighters will be arriving by barge this afternoon. That's thirteen planes for twelve pilots! I can't have a spare plane I can't use cluttering up my ship. You got us into this, so you go get us out!"

My mind was already at work. "Aye, aye, sir. Do I have your permission to go talk to the people aboard the flagship?"

"Yeah. Do whatever's needed. We don't have much time."

Once aboard *Ranger,* I headed straight for the cabin of the task group chief of staff, Capt John Ballentine. I told the unvarnished truth and saw the amusement in Captain Ballentine build to a great belly laugh. When I quit talking and he quit laughing, the captain asked, "Okay, Blackburn, what do you want from me?"

"Sir, I'd like to talk to your personnel people and see if somebody has a Wildcat pilot he can spare. If so, I'd like to get him temporarily transferred to us."

Unbelievably, the chief of staff bought the idea. This meeting with Captain Ballentine was to have a significant impact upon my future.

On our first day out of Bermuda, we had a mishap involving an SBD as it was being launched by catapult to take its turn on the antisubmarine patrol. As usual, the scout was armed with a 500-pound general-purpose bomb, fused so that its pilot could select the mode of detonation—upon high-speed impact with the surface or as a depth charge, 40 feet below the surface. As the Dauntless flew off, the suspension lug holding the bomb failed. We onlookers gawked with terrified fascination as the explosive device bounced and rolled down the flight deck and then fell over the bow.

The bomb went off as a depth charge—with a great roar and a mighty upheaval of water directly below the aircraft elevator. An optical rangefinder weighing 300 pounds toppled down upon the open bridge, narrowly missing the skipper and bruising several men before it came to rest. Word was instantaneously passed over the ship's public-address system that the explosion was from one of our own depth charges, and not a torpedo hit. This news came as an immense relief to all hands who had not seen what had happened.

It was immediately discovered that the aircraft elevator had been jammed in midposition, and that resulted in the damage-control party being called out. The damage-control people also learned in short order that the tough double tanker hull had apparently oilcanned, a remarkably fitting technical term meaning that it had first dished in and then had snapped back out. No leakage or apparent other damage was found. However, of direct interest to me and four other members of VGF-29, the detonation had fouled up our aircraft homing device, a malfunction that would not be discovered until it was too late.

4

· · · · · · · · · · ·

The four small carriers and their meager screen of destroyers sortied from Bermuda on schedule on October 25 and
joined with the rest of the North Africa invasion armada on
October 27. TORCH, the first major American amphibious
assault of the war in the European Theater of Operations,
brought together in its U.S. component 102 ships of every
type and size, from battleships to fleet tugs. The Navy's job
was to get the Army ashore in French Morocco before the
winter storms and soggy fields made the landing and break-
out unacceptably risky.

On Halloween, at 0200, *Santee* came frantically alive
with the clanging of the General Quarters alarm—a bugle
blast and PA blatting, "General Quarters. General Quarters. All hands man your battle stations." As we ran through
the hangar deck on our way to the squadron ready rooms,
we felt the shock waves of depth charges transmitted through
the steel deck and, seconds later, heard the loud *boom,
boom, boom* of the detonations. Every one of us had seen
tankers burning off the Atlantic coast, so we were all scared.

After a long hour in the ready room, we got the word
that we had been the victims of a false alarm, that no
submarine had been found and that a destroyer's sonar

contact had apparently been erroneous. We had no quibble with being shaken from our sleep in such a manner; mistakes of this nature were common because the policy of the day—a good one—was to shoot first and ask questions later. We headed back to our staterooms, still nervous and upset by the rude awakening and the pensive hour in the ready rooms, but happy that nothing had come of it. In another hour, we would all be awakened again, routinely, for our daily predawn General Quarters stand-to.

Unbelievably, the U-boats made no contacts with the invasion armada as we followed a sinuous track to the objective. Naturally, the apprehension over a submarine attack grew as we ventured farther out into the Atlantic, closer to their favored killing grounds and closer yet to their bases. By November 6 we were plodding along within reach of German long-range land-based patrol bombers that might be flying out of the Moroccan bases we were being sent to seize.

On the way, we finally learned what we were facing. The TORCH operation started for us with the study of meager intelligence data pertaining to the southwest coast of French Morocco, particularly the area around Safi, a little port about 65 miles northwest of Marrakech. We were given time to pore over old charts of our objective area, but no aerial photos were available. We had zero data on the Vichy French air forces in the target area, and no clue as to how many, if any, Germans were positioned there or nearby. I do not believe any of us had enough experience or sense to be alarmed by how little we knew.

Everything was to start at first light on November 8. The SBDs and TBFs of our escort air group were loaded with general-purpose bombs and charged with dropping them on call in support of the landing force. Meanwhile, Fighting-29 was to attack the airfield at Safi and destroy any planes found there with our machine guns. Then we were to provide cover for the amphibious task force charged with landing the infantry. After completing our runs on the Safi airfield, my fighters were to report in by voice radio to the amphibious force commander and thereafter "operate as directed" by him.

The night takeoff was hairy, to say the least. To give my first division of six F4Fs an adequate takeoff run in the event there was no surface wind—there was none—and with *Santee* cranked up to her maximum speed of 19 knots, we needed all the deck run we could get. Thus, the seven remaining fighters, their wings folded, were lined up heading aft along the starboard side of the flight deck from abeam the island. The first group of six, which I led off, trundled down the lane between the folded-wing Wildcats and the port edge of the flight deck. When we reached a deck crewman holding a bright light to indicate when we had reached the end of the line of seven waiting fighters, each of us in turn eased over to the right so we could use the whole width of the flight deck—55 feet!—for the remaining 125 feet leading to the black hole beyond the bow. Farther out were two red mast lights, each marking the position of one of the two destroyers steaming 1,000 yards ahead of *Santee* and 30 degrees on either bow. Those lights were our "horizon." All this because safer, surer launch by catapult was deemed too slow.

Shortly after liftoff each of us turned on his running lights so we could rendezvous at 1,000 feet and about 5 miles ahead of the task group. It soon became apparent that only four of my clutch of five chicks had made it. After orbiting as long as we could, I doused my lights, and the others followed suit. Then we test fired our guns and turned for the coast.

We were at 10,000 feet and 10 miles north of Safi when the clear dawn broke. From there, we could easily see the landings in progress as well as the heavy fire from our surface warships and the light counterbattery fire from the Vichy French coastal guns. The airfield we had been sent to neutralize did not exist. We saw no antiaircraft fire nor any evidence of hostile air action. Thus, as ordered, I placed a voice-radio call to the task force flagship, but there was no response. I kept trying, but it eventually became apparent that something was awry, perhaps with my radio, perhaps with theirs. So we circled and observed the action, contributing nothing. It was a dreadful disappointment, and in brief radio exchanges with my formation I gathered we were all as angry as we were frustrated.

When our appointed time on station ran out, we headed for the barn. I had not kept notes of courses and times on the way out to our orbiting station because I anticipated no strain in spotting the ship and getting back aboard quickly and safely. However, by the time we quit our station, the weather had deteriorated from perfect to low overcast and numerous rain squalls. I could not see the carrier, but I did have another proven means for finding her and guiding myself and my fighter formation to sighting distance.

In bad weather and at night, we routinely relied upon the YE homing gear, more popularly known as the "hayrake" because of the shape of its antenna. Simply put, the YE transmitted a different signal—one Morse letter—in each of twenty-four directions, one letter to each 15-degree segment of a 360-degree circle. All a lost pilot had to do was hear a particular letter to know in which direction he should turn to find the ship. If a new letter came up, he had passed the ship and needed only to turn back. In addition, the signal grew louder as one closed, so that the pilot could approximate the distance to the ship. It was not a precise system, but it was nearly foolproof and by late 1942 it had brought many a plane back to our ships.

In addition to the YE receiver, each of us also had a four-channel VHF radio aboard, with frequencies accurately preset and automatic self-keying from transmit to receive modes and vice versa. Also, by late 1942, all of our ships had surface search radar and larger vessels such as carriers all had air search radars as well. Thus, the airplane's radio and the carrier's YE transmitter, combined with the air search radar, was a potent combination for bringing planes and ships into roughly the same area so that recoveries could be made. If there were a lot of planes in the air, and a ship's controller was not sure which was his, a particular pilot or pilots could stand out from the crowd by flying an expanding-square pattern while increasing altitude, a maneuver known as a "square dance."

When I turned my fighters for home—where I thought home should be—the hayrake signal was coming in loud and clear; I thus knew exactly which way to fly. However, long after the estimated time of arrival, we still saw only empty ocean. Also, the hayrake signal had changed to one that did not seem possible. Time for the radio.

"Romeo. This is Shillelagh Leader. Over."

"This is Romeo. Hear you five by five. Over."

"This is Shillelagh Leader. Do not have you in sight. If you hold me, request a steer. Over."

"This is Romeo. Do not have you on my gadget. Commence square dance and stand by for steer. Acknowledge."

"Shillelagh Leader. Wilco."

So we commenced the expanding-square pattern, climbing all the while. I was not completely relaxed, but I was still far from clutching.

At last, "This is Romeo. Hold you. Steer two-five-oh. Acknowledge."

"Shillelagh Leader. Steer two-five-oh. Wilco. Out."

At this point I had about thirty-five minutes of fuel left. I guessed that my four wingmen had less because they had been using more keeping station on me, a typical outcome of any formation flying. I gave it ten minutes on course 250, but no ship appeared. It was safe to bet that the fighter director had seen another target on his radarscope and had jumped to the conclusion that it was us.

"Romeo. This is Shillelagh Leader. I do not have you in sight. I am setting course for the beach. Over."

"This is Romeo. Roger. I no longer hold you. Good luck. Out."

As we swung to the northeast, my mind flashed to a bit of history from the Spanish-American War of 1898: Lieutenant Hobson stands alone on the deck of the burning collier *Merrimack,* which is fast aground in the channel of Santiago de Cuba harbor. Spanish artillery is zeroed in and the shore is lined with hostiles firing small arms. What to do? Stay aboard the ship and burn or swim for shore and be shot? Thus, Hobson's choice. (He swam, survived, and was acclaimed as a hero.)

We had about as attractive a choice. We could ditch in the frigid Atlantic though no one knew where to look even if they had the time or resources. Or we could try to get over the beach and make forced landings in or bail out over hostile territory.

For me, there really was no choice; I ran out of fuel before the others, which was unusual. As soon as my engine coughed, I patted the top of my head, pointed to my wingman, made a vertical chopping motion in the direction of the formation's heading, blew my wingman a kiss, and peeled off to head into the surface wind. The hand signals meant, "You have the lead, continue on your present course, good-bye."

As my four companions swiftly flew out of sight to the northeast, I went through the busy, hurried routine of preparing for a water landing: crank open the cockpit, unsnap my parachute harness, check the life raft lanyard fastened to my Mae West life jacket, cinch my seat belt and shoulder harness as tight as they would go, fully lower my landing flaps, drop my tail hook. I wanted to splash at minimum speed while heading straight into the wind, nearly at the top of an oncoming swell. The tail hook was down to help me find the surface; as soon as I felt it drag in the water, I let the nose drop slightly. And in we went.

Before the spray subsided, I tripped the seat belt–shoulder harness release, stood up, and dived straight over the windshield. My Wildcat, 29-GF-1, rapidly reared her tail up and sank. By then, I had already set the unconfirmed world's record for the 10-yard dash, freestyle, to avoid getting bashed in the head or taken down by the vertical fin as the fighter flipped over. I shucked off my chute, pulled the raft in front of me, and pulled the toggle hooked to the carbon dioxide bottle. As soon as it inflated, I climbed aboard. My watch said that it was 1030, November 8, 1942. My first thought was that I had racked up a brief, ignominious war record. Then I assessed my performance in terms most of my students at Opa-Locka had heard from time to time: "Dumb, dumb, dumb."

I took stock of my situation. I was clad in a lightweight summer flying suit over my skivvy pants, a lightweight flight jacket, Marine field shoes, thin leather gloves, a leather flying helmet with goggles, and a life jacket. There was thus precious little between me and the elements, and none of it was waterproof. I had a .45-caliber automatic pistol with seven tracer rounds, a large hunting knife in a leather sheath, a small flashlight, and two dye marker packets. The life raft's survival pack yielded a pint of water sealed in a soup-type can, two 3-inch by 12-inch "paddles," and nothing else. This was the standard issue of the day.

I estimated that I was 60 miles from the coast on a northwest-southeast line; the wind and swells were out of the northwest. As soon as I had inventoried my meager possessions, I tied a glove on a crude lanyard and dropped it over the side so I could clock the seconds it took the looped lanyard to extend fully. This old-time "speedometer," borrowed from the days of sail, gave me an approximation of my drift rate. If I was right about my position, I would reach shore in about six days. If the raft stayed afloat. If the wind held. If hypothermia did not kill me first.

I quickly hit rock bottom. I was lonesome and frightened and, the more I turned it over in my mind, overwhelmingly depressed by a stupid outcome to my big chance as a fighter-squadron skipper. I also knew that there was zero probability of anyone launching a search-and-rescue effort in my behalf; the forces were not available. As I plumbed the underside of self-pity, I conducted an internal conversation: Why go through an agonizing, futile effort to survive; why not just stick the pistol in my mouth; no one will ever know. But I lacked the courage.

Thankfully, the days were bearable, mostly sunny. The nights, however, were cold and wet, and they seemed of interminable length as I watched Cassiopeia and the Big Dipper inch their way across the cosmos until the sun's first warming glow appeared in the east. The little raft, which was snug at the hips and just long enough to sit in with my legs only slightly bent, perpetually had several inches of water in it. The freeboard of about 6 inches did little to stop the annoying spray kicked up by the blessedly steady wind that was propelling me toward the faraway shore.

After a long time at sea, as I was thinking about the baby goat I would slaughter and whose blood I would drink upon reaching shore, a grouper—three feet long—cruised up, looked me over, and decided that the flimsy raft was a good place to scratch his back. Things were not bad enough; now I stood to get my raft punctured by an itchy fish! What to do? Stab him with my knife? What if I only wound him; will he thrash around angrily and swamp the raft? If I kill him, will his blood attract a shark? Will waiting him out suffice? I have no idea how long he stayed around; my sense of time was gone. But he eventually left me and my good ship, *Lollipop,* making a leisurely, final, and welcome departure without causing any damage. His stay was the most agonizing part of the painful ordeal.

I spotted *Santee* and her two accompanying destroyers on November 10, hull down to the east. Several SBDs were tooling around in the distance as well. I knew damn well they were not looking for me; there were not adequate forces to undertake any searches. In any case, only the other four members of my formation had any clue as to my location, and their news was over two days old—assuming any of them had been rescued.

Santee and her consorts remained beyond sighting distance of me for the rest of the day, though maddeningly close. On November 11, after a pensive night, the task force came into sight again, dead to leeward. One of the destroyers came alongside the carrier to refuel while the other snaked back and forth ahead looking for the feared plume of a submarine periscope. It so happened that the second destroyer was heading straight for me. I silently coached him on, fearful of upsetting the balance of nature that had brought him this far along. Don't hurry, I pleaded, just hold your course and you'll steam right over me.

The tension was unbearable. I knew that from a destroyer's bridge a man in a raft can be seen—if the observer is looking for him—a mile away at most. If, as was the case this day, there were 10-foot swells running, then the raft was in sight of the ship only about 10 percent of the time, only when it was on a wave crest. I knew that the refueling operation would be rushed because the carrier and the refueling destroyer were extremely vulnerable as long as they were obliged to hold a steady course side by side in a straight line. While tethered by the refueling lines, they were a submarine skipper's dream target.

I saw the patrolling destroyer's bridge erupt in furious activity when she was still a half-mile from my position. Then signal searchlights started flashing messages among all three ships. Well, this was it; they had found me or they had found a submarine. Before I could wonder more, the lead destroyer swung toward me, backed down hard to check her way, and dropped a motor whaleboat. I even found it in my heart to admire their smart seamanship.

The pickup was anticlimactic. I was hauled into the whaleboat and motored back to the ship. I was a little shaky getting aboard; my legs and butt were cramped after three full days of sitting half-crouched in the watery bottom of the life raft. I had no feeling in my feet, but I declined proffered assistance. I am proud to say that I still had my whole pint can of water when I was picked up. I had kept my mouth moist by chewing a cud of chamois cut from the liner of my flight helmet. The water was for a *real* emergency. A smiling bluejacket gave me a little drink of water on the main deck of the destroyer and led me below for a divine hot shower. I sort of faded out and came to later, aware that I was buried in blankets and undergoing a gentle, continuous foot massage while the ship's doctor superintended the wolfing down of heavenly hot broth. My first words: "Doc, the foot rub hurts. More soup, please."

"No more just now. Soon, if you keep it down. You have an advanced case of immersion foot—prolonged soaking in cold water. I think we can restore the circulation, but another day of it and gangrene would have set in. You'd have at least lost your feet if that happened."

The news just made my sense of the pickup by my own little task group—by anyone—seem all the more miraculous.

With occasional awakenings for more light fare, I slept through a solid fourteen hours. I neither needed nor wanted the free medicinal booze that was offered at each awakening, a fact not everybody believed when I mentioned it.

Having gone into the drink while in top physical condition, I rebounded quickly and was "back to battery" the following day. I was thus transferred back aboard *Santee* by high line, riding in a coal sack. Having made such an ass of myself, I arrived feeling very hangdog. To my delight and amazement, the ship's exec was on hand to warmly greet me and present the skipper's apology for not being able to do so himself, what with the press of business on the bridge. However, I was invited to see the captain on the bridge as soon as I felt up to it. All this as well as the large welcoming committee of cheering shipmates which turned out to greet me.

As soon as I got my breath back, I asked about the four other members of my formation. Glum-looking countenances told me before words arrived that there was no news yet. There was still hope, but very little, even in spite of my own miraculous reappearance.

The next day, November 13, Brink Bass was scheduled for a solo flight to the Vichy French base at Marrakech to drop messages of amity along with cartons of American cigarettes. I quietly told Brink that I was taking the hop, and I suited up. At "Man planes," I proceeded to the flight deck by interior passageways and climbed right into the Wildcat positioned on the catapult, which was on the port bow of the ship. By boarding the plane from the port side, I was able to get into the cockpit unobserved by the skipper or anyone else on the bridge.

As I was getting hooked up and strapped in by the grinning plane captain, who of course had figured out what was going on, the flight deck bullhorn blared, "Do not launch that plane till Lieutenant Bass is in the cockpit. Lieutenant Commander Blackburn, report to the captain on the bridge immediately."

Skunked! It turned out that our dedicated and enormously competent flight surgeon had come topside looking for me so we could watch the launch together, and so he could see how I was doing on the psychological front. When he found Brink instead of me, he hotfooted it to the bridge and spilled the beans to the captain. I was extremely angry over being found out, and when I learned that the doctor had turned me in, I nearly alienated his friendship by calling him "Doc Fink" for several days, until I cooled down.

Summaries of our invasion efforts brought out that the amphibious part of the operation had been superbly run and totally successful, but that air ops had been a near disaster. Dive-bombers and torpedo planes, as well as fighters, had ditched because of the problem with the hayrake antenna, which had been jarred loose on October 26, when the bomb had gotten loose from the SBD. In all, VGF-29 lost five pilots missing in action—the four members of my formation and one out of Brink Bass's formation, the extra pilot we had picked up with the extra Wildcat in Bermuda. The latter flew into a cloud and was never heard from again. Against that sorry score, one of our pilots, Ens Bruce Jacques, shot down a Vichy fighter on November 10, the same day one of the *Santee* Dauntlesses got a Vichy dive-bomber.

The French soon capitulated and *Santee* was released to head west, for Norfolk. Almost as soon as we left station, good news caught up with us; all four of the strays from my D-Day formation were alive. They had barely made it to the beach near Cape Blanco, well north of Safi, and had all made dead-stick—powerless—landings on fields and roads. Every one of the planes was totaled, but none of the pilots was injured. Astonished and irate locals rounded up the four at gunpoint and incarcerated them in the local bastille until the armistice was signed. They were turned over to the U.S. Army and started on the road back to Norfolk, where they arrived in early December, none the worse for wear and possessed of vivid sea stories.

Following a brief period of R&R—rest and rehabilitation —we reopened for business at NAS, Norfolk, in early December. We were just getting revved up, in fact, when orders for me arrived out of the blue: "As soon as relieved as CO of VGF-29, report to Commander, Air Force, Atlantic Fleet, on 1 January 1943 to form and commission Fighting Squadron 17 as commanding officer."

I was not entirely pleased with this unanticipated and unasked-for news of my rising fortunes. Obviously, it was a terrific assignment; I was to be the CO of a thirty-six-plane fighter squadron, part of the air group of a new first-line fleet carrier. But VGF-29 and *Santee* were going concerns that would certainly face new adventures long before the new carrier and her air group. Moreover, VGF-29 and *Santee* were congenial, happy outfits which had transitioned through the sweat and agony common to new organizations and their shakedowns.

I came up with a great idea and presented it to the people at ComAirLant: Wouldn't it be dandy to incorporate VGF-29 in toto as the working nucleus of VF-17? Unspoken: Let somebody else do the dirty work of setting up and starting a new outfit from scratch.

"Tommy," a senior AirLant staffer replied, "you must be out of your skull. Not only 'no,' but 'hell no!' The remaining VGF-29 people will remain there. However, we'll consider, but not promise, to get you the key pilots you request for VF-17."

I did succeed in getting Brink Bass fleeted up to skipper of VGF-29, even though he was considered very junior for the assignment. He filled the job with distinction and success. VGF-29 was expanded and became VF-29 toward the end of 1944. In Pacific combat under LCdr Bill Eder from November 1944 to April 1945, the squadron scored a highly commendable 113 kills, many of which were credited to the nucleus I had formed and trained.

PART II

. . . .

Fighting-17

5

New Year's Eve, 1943, was more enjoyable than I had anticipated so I did not find my way home from the Norfolk Officers' Club to the Bachelor Officers' Quarters until 0500. Precisely at 0800, wearing my best blue uniform, I was standing tall before ten ensigns and eight bluejackets, reading from a piece of paper in my hand. Fighting Squadron 17 was born.

I made no inspirational speech that first morning of 1943; just, "Report for duty at 0800 tomorrow. Dismissed."

The AirLant staffers had promised to try to fill key squadron billets with people I requested by name. Unfortunately, I was a little late in drawing from the pool of extremely qualified instructors with whom I had served at Opa-Locka a year earlier. LCdr Jumping Joe Clifton had recently commissioned Fighting-12, and he had thus beat me to the same talent pool. Nevertheless, I was able to snag LCdr Roger Hedrick as my exec, and some other Miami talent was said to be on the way.

By the end of January, we had two combat veterans aboard, Lt(jg) Johnny Kleinman and Lt(jg) Sunny Jim Halford. Both had served with carrier-based fighter squadrons early in the Pacific War and then, in September and

October 1942, land-based at Guadalcanal's Henderson Field. Unfortunately, their squadron, Fighting-5, had been right at the forefront—literally the first line of defense—during its tour at Guadalcanal, and the experience had been brutal. Though Kleinman and Halford each had had ample home leave and time to recover, both proved to be a little shaky still when they reported aboard Fighting-17. In truth, neither was overjoyed with the prospect of going out again.

Six lieutenants joined us from various elimination bases, where they had been instructors at the most basic level of the Navy's pilot-entry program. They were all good pilots, but none had any combat experience nor even any time in high-performance airplanes. We got one more lieutenant, who, along with a passel of new ensigns, had only just completed advanced training. I was shocked to learn that none of the newly bewinged pilots had any time in fighters; the final phases of their flight training had been done, perforce, in trusty, undemanding SNJ trainers.

Blackburn, Hedrick, Kleinman, Halford, and Lt(jg) Timmy Gile, one of my Miami plowback instructors—we were the only pilots in VF-17 who had ever set foot in a combat-type airplane. Everyone else had flown only trainers of various and sundry types.

When the dust settled, VF-17 totaled forty-two pilots—and no fighters. In addition to merely forming a new squadron, we were to receive and evaluate a hot new fighter type, the Vought F4U-1 Corsair. I quickly learned that the F4U was an airplane the Navy's own flight-test activities regarded with much trepidation and whose characteristics were cloaked in mystery and, to some degree, misinformation. Nevertheless, the squadron's lead pilots would have to get everyone checked out in the new fighter so we could oversee the transition by all hands. At the same time, on the run, it would be left to us to work out the bugs so the F4Us were ready to go into combat when we were. From this hodgepodge of raw material—new pilots, new fighter type—I had to weld a fighting machine of my own and then get it meshed with the two other squadrons of Air Group 17 —another horde of grass-green pilots flying the Grumman

TBF Avenger torpedo bomber and the new and unevaluated Curtiss SB2C Helldiver scout-bomber. As if this were not enough, the air group then had to be merged with a brand new fleet-type carrier, *Bunker Hill,* CV-17, which was still abuilding at Quincy, Massachusetts.

Our estimated time of arrival in the Pacific war zone was August 1943, a scant eight months hence.

The icing on the cake was the location of our training activities. There could have been a worse place to do them than NAS, Norfolk, in the winter, but choosing it would have been difficult.

I had been through most of this before, with Fighting-29. I had learned a thing or two about creating a new squadron, by doing things right as well as wrong. On the day Fighting-17 opened for business, I knew precisely what I wanted to do, what *had* to be done.

The first consignment of new Corsairs was not even *promised* until early February because the first batches of production F4Us were properly bound for Fighting-12 and several Marine squadrons that were scheduled to make their combat debuts in the hotly contested Solomon Islands, at Guadalcanal, in the spring. Thus, my first order of business was to get some airplanes—fighters and several advanced trainers—so my eager tyros could log as much flight time as possible while we were waiting. I knew only too well that all pilots—especially fresh-caught pilots—lose their touch very quickly if they do not fly regularly. Moreover, I had to evaluate each pilot's abilities while there was still time to weed out the weak sisters and snatch good men from the pipeline leading to squadrons throughout the Navy's rapidly expanding fighter forces. I still had some good connections at the force material command, left over from my Fighting-29 days, and I went right to work latching on to ten SNJ trainers and eight F4Fs.

Transitioning inexperienced pilots from trainers to fighters is not as simple as it sounds. The wing-loading—the ratio of the area of the wings to the weight of the aircraft—is vastly different. Fighters, with their high wing-loading, are inherently more dangerous to fly than trainers. The difference manifests itself most obviously when the power plant shuts down; a lighter trainer will glide for a long distance while a heavier fighter tends to drop like a brick.

We started everyone off in the SNJs. Rog and I, who had learned many tricks of the trade at Miami, first wanted to see how each man handled himself aloft. The early flight time was equally important to the new men because many of them had not flown for several weeks, what with time off for Christmas and long leaves following graduation from flight training, plus the time it took us to get the SNJs. All we did at first was bore holes in the sky and shoot landings. This was time well spent in that it brought all hands up to speed.

As each pilot completed fifteen or twenty hours in our SNJs he was considered ready to transition into the F4Fs. Except for its egregious ground-handling characteristics, the Wildcat was really the ideal high-performance fighter of the day for transitioning new fighter pilots. It was a very nice, honest airplane to fly, an excellent intermediate step on the way to the Corsair.

We managed to stagger through the transition into the Wildcat without killing anyone. Working overtime in these welcome handouts, in lousy, cold, wet weather and operating from an extremely overcrowded field, Hedrick, Halford, Kleinman, Gile, and I went at it hammer and tongs. For the moment, I was not interested in training my pilots to fight in the Wildcat, merely to fly in it. By the end of January, everyone had at least soloed in the Wildcats. In addition to giving the troops needed experience, it allowed the squadron's front office to discover the standout pilots as well as to learn of the shortcomings in various people, those that could be corrected and those that could not. As a result of our early evaluations, five of the tyros were reassigned elsewhere, replaced with five new unknowns who then had to be brought through the entire process and fairly evaluated.

One gain from the transition period was the early tentative identification of candidates to lead sections and divisions within the squadron. Seniority usually played a role in such decisions, but there was no reason to adhere strictly to the rank criterion for there were natural leaders and better fliers of every rank. At this early stage, however, everything of the sort was tentative and everyone started even. If nothing else, the possibility of prestigious assignment as section and division leaders gave the youngest, least senior officers something to shoot for.

Training and evaluating aside, I let it be clearly known early on that I wanted no reluctant dragons in Fighting-17, that my door was always open to anyone who felt he could not cut the mustard or otherwise wanted out. I let it be known right away that anyone who asked would be transferred without prejudice, nor with even a pejorative entry in his record book. I am sure that every pilot who ever was in VF-17 while I was the commanding officer must have taken the time to think about whether he *really* wanted to be a fighter pilot. My open-door offer was meant precisely to make everyone think about whether he was tough enough or adventurous enough—or brave enough—for the job. There were pilots who did come in and discuss their doubts and second thoughts. If Rog Hedrick and I concurred, we eased the man out—hopefully without anyone else being the wiser. If the solution was less apparent, Rog and I had no qualms about consulting with the flight surgeon or other key older members of the unit.

This policy left me with a solid band of aggressive eager beavers, but I also had to make two exceptions in the cases of Johnny Kleinman and Sunny Jim Halford. Though both expressed their reluctance to relive the horrors of their Guadalcanal experience, the squadron would have been ill served by my allowing our only two combat veterans— Halford had 3.5 kills, including 1 at Midway, and Kleinman had a kill and a probable—to go elsewhere; the need to leaven the vast majority of tyros with experienced combat veterans overrode all personal considerations. Balancing their desires and interests with the needs of the squadron, I promised to release them from the squadron at the conclusion of our first combat tour if they still wanted out. This deal with them was agreed to by Rog Hedrick as well, in the event I did not make it to the conclusion of our first tour.

From the first day, Fighting-17 was not destined to be a spit-and-polish outfit. I had acquired a horror of the super-structured military unit in which the brass sets itself up as a corps of infallible *patrones* and treats the junior officers like *peones*. I made it as clear as I could from the outset that I was concerned not with form but with substance, that the accent was on self-discipline rather than the externally applied variety. I perhaps tolerated a little more spiritedness than did other unit commanders, but the troops learned my limits in very short order; anyone who could not operate at the required level of self-governing needed to go through what we all faced together was as good as gone. My experience was that can-do pilots do not require rigid formalities; the ideal is the easy personal relationships formed in countless ready-room bull sessions, where a free exchange of ideas and comments move up the chain of command as well as down. And this is what I fostered.

My own days as a red-assed ensign in a battleship had started a decade before I formed VF-17. In *that* world, age and experience equated with brains. Furthermore, the Old Navy philosophy was, if it wasn't invented here it couldn't possibly be any good. Old Navy—that is exactly what the professional officer corps had to put behind us if we were to absorb and make proper use of the many thousands of wartime officers, the very best of whom found their way into the burgeoning air establishment. These were smart young men, many with degrees from great schools. Who could work with them and fail to notice that behind the temporary facade of youthful exuberance were the minds that would run the machine of our society, of our economy, indeed of our own Navy once we had won the war?

All this is not to say that I did not firmly establish my authority as Fighting-17's CO. When I made a decision, that was it; debate was done, over. I also made it clear that, as exec, Rog Hedrick was my alter ego, and that I would back *his* decisions to the hilt. Though Rog's natural reserve precluded overfamiliarity, he was soon simply "Rog" to all the pilots. I allowed only "Skipper" or "Mr. Blackburn," the traditional greetings. When our prince of chutzpah, Ens Mel Kurlander, tried "Skip" out on me, he was quickly and firmly put back on the track by a few curt words and the cold stare our troops called the "inspection look."

We were military, but not *that* military. We started each work day promptly at 0800 with all hands mustered at quarters and dressed in clean, complete uniforms—khakis sans tie—faces groomed, shoes or boots shined. Hung over or healthy, everyone was expected to stand tall, ready to go. My predilection for half-Wellington "fighter boots," mirror shined, was soon emulated by most of the young tigers. Punctuality for all events was taken as a matter of course, and woe betide the man who was late for a scheduled flight. Other than that, and very little else, we saved our heavy discipline for work in the air, where it really counted for something.

I left nothing to chance in getting across to my men that VF-17 was a *fighter* outfit, charged with engaging the enemy and blowing him out of the sky. The trick, then, was to hone aggressive—indeed, predatory—instincts while building loyalty to the group and to the precepts of military discipline. I was facing nothing new in this regard; it had been part of the process of inculcating fighter pilots from the earliest days of the trade. I had been through the same program myself, and I had already run VGF-29 through the program, with good results, I think. What we needed were high-performance men to fly and fight in high-performance airplanes, to mesh the man and the machine and then to mesh both of them into cohesive units—two-plane sections of section leader and wingman, four-plane divisions of two two-plane sections each, flights of two four-plane divisions each, building to a complete squadron of up to thirty-six airplanes. I needed to make every man feel and act as a part of the team while instilling in each of them the sense that his personal contribution was vital. I needed to make every man interchangeable with every other man in such a way as both to hone individual skills and self-reliance *and* curb an overabundance of individuality.

To do the job, I was not above using any and all corny gimmicks to raise and maintain morale. We got to work early trying to stand out, a means for instilling group spirit and élan into the rough admixture that formed through January. We all flew with flight scarves for sensible reasons of comfort, particularly in cold weather. But while everyone else wore the beautiful standard issue white nylon items, Fighting-17 pilots sported flaming red ones. I also had to tolerate the odd personal totem because I had one of my own, albeit for practical reasons. I had learned upon reporting aboard my first Fleet squadron, Bombing-2, that the standard issue flight helmet was not tailored to my oversize, knobby head. Thus, since then, I had slit the center seam as needed to provide a reasonably comfortable fit. The result prevented headaches, but what the observer saw was a blond-plumed helmet.

More than red scarves and a few bland personal totems, VF-17 needed a squadron insignia around which a sense of group pride could coalesce. Striking eagles and pouncing tigers had long since been preempted and overworked. The anthropomorphic designs copying the Disney world were in vogue, so armed, threatening animals abounded. To us—me—they smacked of being too cutesy and thus utterly inappropriate for a tough combat fighter squadron. Flaming sword, flaming spear, sheaf of arrows, battle-ax, mailed fist—these were all tried in various combinations, but none really pleased me. My thought was that since we were to be a Corsair squadron we should have a piratical theme. Since I was the boss, my views took precedence over everyone else's. In short order, someone worked up a sinister black flag emblazoned with a stark white skull-and-crossbones insignia. Whoever approved such items up the line approved this one, which was a good thing inasmuch as it had appeared on our engine cowlings by then. Furthermore, the standard practice of painting insignia on the fuselage below the cockpit was not for us; we wanted that space reserved exclusively for flags denoting kills.

Once we had our Corsairs in possession, I ordered that the propeller spinner and first 18 inches of each blade be painted in bright colors to denote the part of the squadron to which that airplane was attached. For example, red denoted the two four-plane divisions of my flight, white denoted Rog Hedrick's flight, and so forth.

To help instill unit pride and create personal relationships, we had happy-hour get-togethers every afternoon. There was a lot of singing in addition to a lot of drinking— mostly beer. We were very fortunate in that we did not lack for talented and enthusiastic musicians. We had an excellent pianist in Ens Brad Baker, a great trumpeter in Ens Teeth Burris, and Lt(jg) Duke Henning and Lt(jg) Timmy Gile had been whiffenpoofs at Yale. I was known as the one who could not carry a tune but always remembered the words.

We always went to happy hour as a group and remained apart as an island within the ebb and flow of other enthusiastic drinkers, singers, and talkers. When the Corsairs arrived, we were further set apart by the fact that we were the only F4U squadron in residence at Norfolk, a rather telling distinction when we began encountering dangerous bugs that appeared not to quell our boisterous off-duty activities one iota. I quite consciously fostered the mystique of being a unit apart.

While working on the things that set Fighting-17 apart from other—run of the mill—squadrons, I was also quite concerned lest my fledglings miss a good grounding in the heritage of courage and devotion to duty that stood as the foundation for the U.S. Navy's fighting arms. It was my solemn duty and privilege to teach the uninitiated that, from the ancient days of sail, seafaring men have known that their lives and fortunes depend upon the bonds formed among shipmates. The teachings were embodied in oft-repeated aphorisms like "Never let your shipmate down," and "Never flee in the face of the enemy."

Our young pilots learned from the small cadre of professionals about all the brave men who had gone before them and why and when and where they had said, "Don't give up the ship; fight her 'til she sinks," and "Give me a fast ship, for I intend to go in harm's way." I wanted them to be especially mindful of the heroes and heroics of naval aviation, of LCdr John Waldron and his Torpedo-8, a squadron of slow, vulnerable, obsolete torpedo planes that, unsupported and in broad daylight, had bored through Japanese antiaircraft fire and Zero fighters to attack the Japanese carriers at Midway. Waldron and all but one of his pilots died in that attack, but they established with their blood and their lives a nonpareil precedent of devotion to duty. I did not expect my youngsters to die as the Torpedo-8 pilots and aircrewmen had died, but I did expect them to go down facing the enemy, if indeed they must go down. More important than merely dying with their boots on and thus providing us with an example of courage and devotion to duty, Torpedo-8 had sucked down the Japanese fighter cover and had thus allowed our dive-bombers to score numerous hits that started the decline of the Imperial Navy's hitherto unbeatable carrier air arm. *That* was the real contribution, the real lesson of Torpedo-8, the one I did expect my squadron to emulate—making our positive contribution to the final victory.

6

. . . .

The long-awaited word arrived in mid-February—one new F4U-1 Corsair fighter was ready for delivery at Floyd Bennett Field, New York. I chose this auspicious moment to throw my rank around and so caught the first available flight. I was still clutching the pilot's handbook when we landed so I could get right down to the business of cockpit familiarization and checkout.

The airplane was huge, far bigger than any fighter I had ever seen. Most of it seemed to be engine. As soon as possible, I fired up the big bird and began going through the pretakeoff checks the moment the 2,000-horsepower engine was warm. At length, I gingerly taxied forward, cursing the extremely poor ground visibility of this and all Navy fighters of the day; with its long nose stretching an unprecedented 12 feet in front of my windshield, the F4U was the champ of champs in this regard. Sinuous forward movement was an absolute must if I wanted to see anything out ahead.

"Navy oh-two-three-oh-three cleared into position and cleared for takeoff."

"Oh-two-three-oh-three. Roger."

I went through a last-minute cockpit scan and pushed the

throttle forward to the stop as I began to roll. Habits die hard; I applied right full rudder, a must with the Wildcat. A snowbank on the right side of the runway loomed large, and then my overcorrection threatened to plow the Corsair into the left-hand snowbank. My zigs and zags, highly erratic at first, gradually damped out and I managed to lift off the center of the runway. The thermometer stood at 25 degrees, but I was bathed in sweat. I had already learned a few valuable lessons that needed to be imparted to my eager beavers at Norfolk.

By then, the Corsair had already earned a servicewide sobriquet. After finding the F4U more responsive to persuasion than dominance, Dog Ears Coleman, an ole country boy serving with VF-12, had remarked, "This plane is as cooperative as a hog on ice." Thus, the F4U was known for a long time as the Hog—a nickname the folks at Vought eventually worked through to replace with their favorite, the rather meek U-Bird.

As a crowd of the committed gathered in Norfolk's dank cold, ground crewmen nimbly painted the first Hog's official designator—17-F-1—on either side at midfuselage. Then the skull-and-crossbones insignia was painted on either side of the engine cowl. Finally, "Big Hog" went on the vertical tail fin. I had been caught napping once; I would be ready the first time someone asked for my call sign this time around.

The early work in Wildcats paid handsome dividends as we received more Hogs. By mid-March, when we had a full working complement of thirty-six Corsairs, all hands were fully checked out. By then, also, we were well along in our carrier training.

The first step in getting all hands carrier qualified had been a thorough classroom indoctrination—or refresher, if that applied—for all the troops, many of whom had only a vague sense of what they were facing and how best to overcome it. Then it was off to begin field carrier training, the vital precursor to actual work aboard a ship. The exacting fieldwork required all hands to get "aboard" a simulated flight deck marked with flags on a portion of a much longer concrete runway. The work was by no means a breeze even for experienced hands like Rog Hedrick and I were; we had never done the job in Corsairs.

After about a dozen sessions of field carrier landing practice with our Landing Signal Officer (LSO), Lt(jg) Shailer "Catwalk" Cummings, I was ready to try Big Hog on the real thing. Of course, the Navy, in its infinite wisdom, had not seen fit to share any of the vital information gleaned from earlier activities conducted by Joe Clifton's VF-12. It was thus up to us to develop our own techniques from scratch.

My first actual carrier landing in a Hog went off on March 1, 1943, when I caught up with faithful old *Charger* in Chesapeake Bay. I rolled out of the approach turn about a hundred yards astern of the training carrier, hanging on the prop, indicating about 90 knots. Except for a lot of cold water, all I could see was Catwalk Cummings; the little ship was completely hidden by the Corsair's huge nose. Catwalk was giving me a "Roger"—both arms holding his colorful paddles straight out at shoulder level. This means, Okay, keep coming just as you are. Then I saw the paddle in Catwalk's right hand slice smartly across his chest and then back across his throat. This was the "Cut"—chop the power and land.

I dropped Big Hog's nose to get a view of the flight deck, but I went too far and set up a fearsome sink rate. I honked back on the stick and rotated the nose up so the Corsair would be in the perfect three-point attitude when it impacted —not landed, *impacted*—on the deck. The plane bounced what felt like a good 20 feet, but the tail hook caught the Number-1 arresting wire, and we slammed back into the deck. Both main tires blew as the Corsair and I came to an abrupt stop, both of us vibrating like harp strings. I shut down and climbed from the cockpit to go over the plane with the mechanics. Miraculously, we could find no structural damage; all we had to do was replace the wheels and tires.

My next four touchdowns and arrests—all I needed to

qualify for carrier ops in a Corsair—were not as exciting. Indeed, each was progressively smoother. This was cause for some extra celebrating with Catwalk that night at Boys' Town, as we called the Norfolk officers' club.

VF-17 got through carrier qualifications with no personnel casualties. We busted a lot of wheels, blew a lot of tires, and totaled several of our airplanes, but everyone eventually made his five qualifying landings aboard *Charger*. When Ens Jack Chasnoff bounced higher than *Charger's* masthead on his first landing attempt, he gave his Hog full power and flew the 35 miles back to Norfolk with wheels, flaps, and hook still down. It was a miracle that we suffered no personnel losses. In addition to working with a remarkably temperamental bird, most of our pilots had never seen a steamboat when they joined the squadron three months earlier. Moreover, *Charger* hardly qualified as a carrier; that spitkit rarely produced the 25 knots of relative wind over her flight deck that was considered the standard minimum for safe landing operations.

Even recognizing the remarkable performance of my grass-green tyros—they kept their cool and drove like old hands—most of the credit for our zero casualty rate must go to Catwalk Cummings. An LSO is not unlike a golf pro who can see what a student is doing right or wrong and who can coach the fledgling into fully utilizing his abilities. The typical flag-waver suffers enormous stress getting even experienced pilots aboard a carrier; our qualification program was as tough as it gets.

The Corsair appeared to be a superb fighting machine, but it was overengineered and thus hard to maintain. At the start of a typical day's ops, only about half of our full complement was safe to fly. By "secure," half of those could be expected to be "down."

The 2,800-cubic-inch engine was a monster to fire up after it had sat in subfreezing weather overnight. First, it took two strong men pulling on a prop blade to slowly accomplish the minimum revolutions needed to clear the lower cylinders of oil so the start-up could be accomplished in safety. Next, the engine had to be primed with raw gasoline. This touchy enterprise had to stop short of flooding and thus drowning the spark plugs and evade the obvious fire hazard while getting enough vaporized fuel into the cylinders to get the engine to cough to life. Some genius had equipped the Corsair with a shotgun starter in lieu of the heavy electric starter. When all was in readiness, the shotgun shell was fired. Sometimes it went *bang* and turned the prop through three or more revolutions. Mostly, however, it just went *poof* and the prop just twitched. Four abortive tries generally overheated the starter, and that resulted in a fifteen-minute stand-down for cooling. So much for geniuses.

Each of fourteen cowl flaps had its own baby hydraulic cylinder to open and close it. These tended to leak. In addition, until the maintenance crews became expert, the big radial engine tended to throw a lot of oil. The combination rapidly coated the windshield and seriously decreased the airplane's inherently limited forward visibility. We all became expert at quickly locating rain showers through which we could fly in order to wash away the oil.

The landing flaps had a protective device to prevent extension at airspeeds high enough to cause overstressing. This was a dandy feature—except that the flaps could and often did retract fully and without warning during the final stages of a landing approach. Of course, this resulted in a horrendous loss of lift and a rapid sinking. The pilot, ever alert for such mishaps, had to slam on full power to evade disaster. After too many narrow escapes, we got the "flap blowup" removed, it being our decision to risk tearing off a flap as against losing lift in this terrifying, dangerous manner. To my knowledge, no one ever did tear off a flap.

The Corsair's storage battery, which was located in the cockpit, had an unhealthy habit of boiling over. In one case, a battery exploded while the airplane was in flight. We later determined that it had been excessively overcharged, but the incident gave us one more in a long line of potential life-threatening problems to bear in mind while we were also trying to fly—and eventually, fight—our irascible Hogs.

The enormous task of absorbing a new type full of hidden, potentially fatal, bugs was in no way enhanced by the Navy's decision to centralize repair and maintenance efforts. Through the first full year of the war, each Navy aviation squadron had had its own ground crew organization. However, as we were forming VF-17, the system was radically altered. A large, permanent carrier aircraft service unit (CASU) was established at each major base to perform the major portion of maintenance needs for all units flying out of that base. Similar, scaled-down versions of the CASUs were established for each carrier, organic to each ship's company and *not* organic to the air group or specific squadrons. This system certainly provided more flexibility to cope with the habitual steady flow of squadrons on and off bases and carriers, but it also adversely affected ground crew esprit de corps. The trade-off resulted in a general decline in the daily availability rate of aircraft in all units.

Fortunately, each squadron did retain a small cadre of senior petty officers, each a specialist in his field or in the specific aircraft type deployed with the squadron. Our little cadre, which was an organic part of the squadron, knew all there was to know about our Corsairs. They became infected with unit pride and, as much as possible, they rode herd on the less-senior pool maintenance people to whom our machines were consigned.

We lost four pilots killed in accidents during the early phases of our training at Norfolk, but none to the vagaries of the airplane. Two died in a midair collision while making simultaneous gunnery runs on a towed target. The other two died because they were unable to fly "basic instruments" when they became disoriented. The latter tragedies made Rog and me fully and painfully aware that our squadron's overall flying proficiency was poor, that the fledglings had received inadequate training in instrument flying in the press to get pilots out to Fleet squadrons.

Disorientation is a hazard that can overcome a pilot even on a perfectly clear day. Haze makes the surface blend in with the sky so that there is no apparent horizon. The pilot must lock his attention on the gauges. In its basic and most elementary form, this is "needle, ball, and airspeed" flying. The needle is the gyro-actuated turn indicator, an utterly reliable instrument that shows any turning movement proportionate to its rate; if the needle is centered, the airplane is holding to a steady heading even though the pilot's senses have him absolutely convinced that he is turning. The ball, which rides a curved path, infallibly tells the pilot if he is slipping or skidding; if the ball is centered, the plane is in balanced flight. The airspeed indicator tells the pilot whether the plane is in level flight or climbing or diving; fundamental familiarity with the airplane automatically tells the pilot what airspeed to expect at a steady power setting in level flight. So, if the pilot is at all unsure of his orientation, he only needs to center the needle and ball, then nose up or down to get the airspeed stabilized. Then, to figure out what is going on, he needs to check the view outside and the status of other instruments, such as the altimeter.

The unfortunate alternative to utilization of these basic flying skills and aids is the "graveyard spiral." The nose drops and the plane is turning even though the pilot's basic senses convince him that all is well or that the plane is turning the other way. Typically, when the disoriented pilot in the graveyard spiral sees the altimeter unwinding, he comes back on the stick. But instead of pulling the nose up, this merely tightens the turn. Conscious that the speed is building up, the disoriented pilot will whack off the throttle. But when the plane is already heading for the water or the ground, this action fatally increases the rate of descent. The pilot in such a predicament might hit the silk. If he does not, he will panic or black out. In all cases except the first, the next of kin need to be notified.

After the second incident in which both plane and pilot were lost in safe flying weather, with no "Mayday" or other transmission, we deduced that the problem was disorientation. This led to an intensive course in the six two-seater SNJs the squadron was allowed to retain after the introduction of our full complement of Corsairs. The "students" were placed "under the hood"—in the SNJ's rear cockpit, literally shrouded beneath a lighttight canvas canopy. There, they were utterly dependent on the clocks, albeit while being monitored by the safety pilot in the front seat. This added training paid enormous dividends; not only were there no more losses from disorientation, our guys got so good that we were able to fly day or night in weather so dirty that the multiengine lads were "aborting because of bad weather."

While it was not evident from my sorry display on D-Day in North Africa, I was a real enthusiast of fuel-saving techniques, which had been assiduously practiced by Lt(jg) Bill Eder when we were forming and training Fighting-29. Fuel conservation was an important part of Fighting-17's syllabus, and particularly so as word of my experience afloat off Morocco filtered through the squadron. It would be safe to describe my post–North African attitude toward fuel consumption as downright niggardly. The results of the intensive training were extremely satisfying and bound to stand us all in good stead when we started flying combat ops in the Pacific. In fact, we did so well that our techniques became the overall standard for all the Navy and Marine squadrons equipped with the F4U.

7

· · · · · · · · · · · ·

Our job in Fighting-17 in early 1943 was to train the squadron to be thoroughly proficient in fighter-versus-fighter combat, to be able to defend friendly airfields and flight decks from enemy bombers and fighters, and to escort and protect friendly bombers and torpedo planes charged with attacking enemy ships and ground targets. It soon became apparent that Norfolk was not filling the bill as the ideal place to be learning our trade.

Of necessity, the NAS field operations people were conservative souls, to put it mildly. If the ceiling or visibility from the control tower was not above the prescribed minimum in *all* directions, the field was closed to landings or takeoffs, or both. It was frustrating to be obliged to sit on the end of the runway, wait-wait-waiting when there was bright sunlight in all quadrants except for a low-lying fog bank two miles to the east. If one landed before the plane ahead had completed its rollout and turned clear, there was hell to pay. Similarly, cutting in ahead of an airplane making a landing approach or passing someone on "final" was a rigidly enforced no-no. We seemed perpetually on the phone either hearing a bitch or pleading to get flight ops under way.

I did nothing to encourage grab-ass games in the operating areas—I did not need to!—but I did not frown on them either. My standard reply to some aggrieved squawk that an "F4U appeared from nowhere" to dust off a patrol plane or some such was, "Look, Jack, take an even strain. We're providing excellent training for you guys to keep a sharp lookout as well as an excellent practice opportunity for your tail gunners." For some reason, this reasoned response did not go over well with our brethren in the multiengine squadrons.

Instances of low-level flying—"Hey Ma! Look at me!!"—were not unknown. Needless to say, we aroused a great many beefs about our "flat-hatting," as this generally proscribed technique was known. No beef was ever as long or as loud as the one that resulted from Ens Teeth Burriss's encounter with a truck driver who aroused his ire. The road-bound miscreant in question was barreling down a two-lane road, forcing passenger cars to take to the shoulders or otherwise evade injury or death. Teeth flipped his Hog inverted and came at the big truck head-on below treetop level. The semi took evasive action right into a ditch.

What finally took the rag off the bush was an incident involving a dogfight between Ens Ike Kepford and an Army Air Forces P-51 right over Norfolk. The Army pilot was as enthusiastic as Ike, but not so the citizenry when the two inevitably got below 500 feet. ComAirLant himself, VAdm Pat Bellinger, had me on the carpet.

"Blackburn, I've been hearing reports on your squadron for some time, but this is *too much*. Either you get those hellions of yours squared away and stop this or I'll find someone who can. Is that clear?"

"Yes, Admiral."

"I want a written report from you by tomorrow telling me what you've done about it."

"Aye, aye, sir."

Ike was put in hack for ten days—grounded, forbidden to go ashore or even to Boys' Town. The pilots were assembled, and the riot act was read to them along with the sincere threat that the next one caught getting out of line would be banished to the limbo of a flying-boat squadron.

There were no tears shed—on either side—when we escaped or were banished from NAS, Norfolk, in early April. Our destination was Naval Auxiliary Air Station, Manteo, in the outermost boondocks of North Carolina, just southeast of Kitty Hawk.

It would have been difficult for the Navy to have found a more desolate place than the sand dunes just north of Cape Hatteras and 50 miles from any place bigger than a village. Quonset huts were the base's only structures. There were no fleshpots around Manteo either. Recreation consisted of listening to the radio and playing our deluxe model jukebox in our minimal O Club.

Together with our well-deserved reputation around Norfolk, the enforced isolation of Manteo brought us closer together. It also made for some serious, unobstructed attention to training.

Our gunnery range was available as soon as we reached altitude, for the station was immediately adjacent to the open Atlantic Ocean. We flew whenever we wanted to, in virtually any weather and at virtually any altitude, at whatever landing and takeoff intervals we decided to establish. The many uninhabited islets that dotted Currituck Sound had no wildlife and were thus ideal targets for our ground-strafing practice. There was almost no one else flying in our area; we had it virtually to ourselves and were thus free to undertake unlimited air-to-air dogfights and other grab-ass without worrying about other people and without the constraints of collision hazard.

On the other hand, night ops were difficult because the field lighting was inadequate, to say the least. That, however, did not stop us from doing a lot of night work. In fact, doing so appreciably increased our instrument proficiency.

The skipper of the station was an aged, conservative World War I retread who soon despaired of our wild ways and gave us a free hand. The locals were the uncorrupted descendants of the Elizabethans who once had lured passing merchantmen onto the shoals with lanterns hung from the necks of their horses—hence Nag's Head. They could not have cared less what we did as long as we minded our own business.

Most of our gunnery training and practice was conducted against flat banners 15 feet long by 3 feet wide. These were towed at 115 knots or more, flat to the ground or vertical, depending on the type of run we were working on. Of course, all the shooting had to be deflection from the side, above, or below to avoid hitting the tow plane.

We did an enormous amount of low-level work, over the water, at minimum altitude. Much of this work was in formations of from two to thirty-six airplanes. Many detractors said we were just showing off. This was true to a degree, but my real purpose was to make all hands comfortable with working at high speeds at extremely low level so we could do this type of flying, day or night, with impunity. The ultimate objective was to allow us to achieve surprise against ship or shore targets. Such hair-raising—and eyebrow-raising—efforts off the North Carolina coast paid handsome dividends in the Pacific.

We also got into high-altitude flight ops and vigorously pursued them in order to reassure all hands that their oxygen equipment would keep them alive for long periods at and above 30,000 feet. This work also made everyone aware of the marked changes in performance characteristics the airplanes experienced at various altitudes up to 30,000 feet and beyond.

Another of the many things I stressed was target acquisition. All of the great fighter aces of World War I and the early part of World War II agreed that half the battle of being a successful fighter pilot is seeing the opponent before he sees you. The needed technique—habits, really—could be learned. Though it is axiomatic that some people have sharper eyes than others, it was important for me to get across the fact that the man who masters the basic target acquisition techniques could be a higher scorer than the man with the inherently better shooting eye. The technique is simple: The fighter pilot simply blocks off a small section of the sky, meticulously searches it with horizontal sweeps, and then moves to the adjacent section of the sky to do the same, and so forth. This simple technique needed to be absorbed as an invariable habit.

I also imparted a simple philosophy based on action. I encouraged all my pilots to try new things whenever possible, albeit within the constraints of the guidelines that had been clearly set forth. More to the point, all hands learned very early that a wrong action was much preferred to no action at all.

Further, I made it clear to all hands that the experienced people in the squadron—initially myself, Hedrick, Kleinman, and Halford—were available at any time to discuss any of the professional aspects of our job. In VF-17, there was no such thing as a dumb question. Nor was there a dumb idea; everyone's ideas were heard through and treated with respect. In fact, many ideas floated by the novices found a place in our standard procedures.

At the heart of it all was the task of getting these young men to have faith in themselves, to make their own moves when they were on their own with reasoned judgment and not too late—certainly not after wasting precious seconds trying to recall some instruction they had heard weeks or months earlier. It takes the utmost self-discipline for young men used to being subordinates to act on their own. Aside from the acquired mental and physical skills needed to fly a high-performance fighter in combat, it takes self-motivation, self-confidence, and self-discipline to survive and win.

In May, as part of a self-generated graduation exercise, we sent the following dispatch to all the squadrons in the Norfolk area: "Combat air patrol will be airborne over Manteo from 0800 until 1200 each weekday. Visitors welcome."

The response was marvelous. The poor, beleaguered CO of NAAS, Manteo, nearly flipped his wig. Fighters, dive-bombers, torpedo bombers, even a few patrol types, swarmed in from all directions for some legalized grab-ass.

I have a vivid mental picture of a section of dive-bombers pulling out of their attack on the treetops at 300-plus knots with Corsairs, wingtips skyward, making 90-degree deflection attacks at their level.

We were busy. We never had more fun or better training.

The enormous amount of time we spent aloft was leavened with ample ground school opportunities focused upon every part of the airplanes; what all the surfaces were, why they were shaped the way they were, why they were constructed the way they were, their weaknesses, and their strengths. We put a lot of emphasis on power plant operation since it is the heart of the airplane. I made it a particular point to convince my young birdmen that the abused power plant sooner or later dumps its abuser into the drink, and that treating a high-power engine with tender loving care pays off in the clutch. Aircraft recognition was another course we ran all hands through at length. We had slides, silhouette books, and models aplenty, and we demanded perfection—for the sake of friends as much as anything else.

A great deal of our ground school effort was based on the things the more experienced pilots remembered needing in past jobs or whenever we noticed particular deficiencies in our tyros. The effort was not, alas, as comprehensive as it might have been, nor as thorough as it would become under organized auspices as the war progressed. We simply made do with what we had, and that prevented us from being as thorough in some areas as we would have liked. We were also facing a more or less finite deadline; the length of training time at Manteo would be determined by the availability of our ship, which was nearing completion in Massachusetts.

Our time at Manteo was when I really began to get a feel for the stronger characters and more talented pilots—when the squadron's distinctive personality began to emerge. Several of the conditional leadership appointments I had made early in the year were overturned, several by death and transfer, others based on talent and skill.

Our air combat intelligence officer (ACIO), a real gem, was Lt(jg) Basil "Duke" Henning, a 1932 Yale graduate and former history professor. Our only nonflying officer, Duke knew nothing about airplanes and hated even to be a passenger in one. Slim, dark, aristocratically handsome, Duke was low-key, highly intelligent, loved and respected by all. A good listener as well as very calm, very mature, and very discreet, Duke filled the bill as our father confessor. The young tigers got into the habit of unloading woes on Duke that they could not bring up to their CO or exec. He counseled them and, when necessary, brought certain matters before me or Rog Hedrick. He was a key asset from the start. In time, Duke's presence in the squadron was nearly as important as mine or Rog's.

Our senior lieutenant was Chuck Pillsbury, an AvCad whose only operational flying duty before he joined the squadron had been as an elimination instructor. As the senior officer after Rog and me, Chuck was assigned duties as the squadron operations and scheduling officer. Fortunately for us all, Chuck was a smooth coordinator and a strong leader. He also directly oversaw a flight of two four-plane fighter divisions, as did Rog and I.

Lt(jg) Butch Davenport emerged from the pack to take on duties as the squadron maintenance officer. His interest and aptitude for engineering were marked. His duties as maintenance officer brought him into a close relationship with Russ Clark, a talented civilian F4U project engineer, and with Ray DeLeva, our Vought Field Service representative. Between them, Russ and Butch developed and installed a small airflow spoiler which sharply decreased the Hog's nasty tendency at low speeds to stall without warning with the left wing whipping down. The benefit was that, at stall, the wings stayed more nearly level and thus more manageable. In refined form, the field expedient fabrication wound up being installed on all later production Corsairs.

Every military unit *needs* a scrounger if it is to stay in business. Fighting-17's chief scrounger—officially our material officer—was Ens Hal Jackson, a shrewd Texan and a formidable poker player. Hal never seemed at a loss in winning needed parts and spares from the Supply Corps misers. Frankly, I never dared inquire too closely into how that was done, lest I be hauled in as an accessory after the fact.

I had little curiosity regarding the backgrounds of my subordinates; other than their professional credits, I knew little about them. I was the product of a Navy household and my own years of service, and I had certainly followed the tradition of snobbishness and bigotry that characterized the prewar service. However, somewhere along the line—I am not sure where or how—I concluded that it literally took all kinds to forge a national war effort and that the only things that really counted in a combat fighter squadron were skill and desire.

Some of my pilots, like Lt Chuck Pillsbury and Lt(jg) Timmy Gile, came from backgrounds of wealth and prominence, though certainly neither had attained either in his own right. Others, like Lt Lem Cooke and Ens Ike Kepford, had outstanding records of athletic prowess. But all that cut no ice with me. I was not about to run either a democratic or an elitist military organization, but I did realize the truth of Napoleon's dictum that there is a field marshal's baton in the knapsack of every soldier. If this dictum is followed, the results can be astonishing. My watchword was "loyalty from the top down," and strict adherence paid handsome dividends throughout my tour as VF-17's CO.

Ens Danny Cunningham was short and stocky, strong and tough. He was shanty Irish, his face the map of Ireland, and he had all the traits—quick laughter, quick temper, affection, and loyalty nearly to a fault. He also had a classic fondness for spirits that cleanly wiped out all after-duty inhibitions. Danny was a handful. When the new Hogs had arrived in February, it had become obvious to all that Danny Boy could barely see over the cockpit coaming or reach the pedals with his feet. The Hog had a huge cockpit, and Danny was a small man.

After seeing him give it a try, I called Danny in to my office. "Dan, you're a good man, and we'll need scrappers like you, but that bucket just isn't built for you. I'll have to get you transferred. I can set it up so that you can go to a Hellcat squadron, or wherever you want. You can be sure you'll get a strongly favorable recommendation from me."

Tears welled up. "Skipper, give me a chance. I'll rig up with cushions and pillows—whatever it takes. This time tomorrow I'll demonstrate to you, statically and taxiing that jewel, that I can reach and operate anything and everything."

And so he did.

I did not take to Lt Lem Cooke, a 1939 Annapolis graduate who came across as a slow Southern good ole boy, content to follow the path of least resistance, still riding high on his reputation as an outstanding Academy football star. I grudgingly assigned Lem as a section leader following the division and flight lead of younger pilots junior to him in rank. Was I ever wrong. I was glad to "walk back the cat" in the combat area.

Ens Bobby Mims was our *enfant terrible*. Five-eight and with a classic middleweight's wide shoulders and trim hips, Bobby was a handsome man in the macho mold. The spoiled scion of a wealthy Dallas household, Bobby was perpetually belligerent. With a few drinks under his belt, which was about any time they were available, his ferocious temper all too often manifested itself as he erupted into a cloud of fists. Withal, Bobby Mims was a gutsy man and an outstanding pilot. Hedrick and many others in the squadron wanted no part of him. Once, after I had bailed Bobby out of yet another pointless scrape, Rog said to me privately, "Tommy, you're nuts to put up with him. Get rid of him before he gets you in a bind." I usually heeded Rog's levelheaded advice, but I had a feeling about Bobby, who was fiercely loyal to the squadron and who really thought the sun rose and set on me and his fellow Texan, Hal Jackson, our chief scrounger. Once all hands knew about

Bobby, Hal or I could count on getting a storm warning as soon as Bobby got drunk and often before a brawl developed.

One fine morning, as my lead division swung back toward the field to complete the routine rendezvous with my flight's second division, we were horrified to see an orange ball of flame and a plume of black smoke near the end of the runway. On landing, I learned that Ens Sam Carlton, a very capable and promising pilot of whom we expected great things, had apparently lost power shortly after liftoff. Instead of continuing straight ahead with no greater problem than ditching in the swamp or Currituck Sound—more than doctrine, an ironbound commandment—Sam had tried to save the plane. As he honked back around, turning to try to get back to the field, he ran out of airspeed and spun in. Sam, our premier radio technical expert, was well liked and highly respected; his death was keenly felt.

One of the most distressful aspects of squadron command was following the chaplain in consoling the bereaved. It is tough enough to handle the loss of close friends—an occupational hazard to which I never became inured—but it is even worse to lose a youngster who has been cast in the role of a son. Inevitably, the painful process of getting over Sam Carlton's death, and others, was tinged with feelings of guilt and the unending mental litany, What did I fail to teach him?

8

• • • • • • • • • • •

Though our time at Manteo was Fighting-17's halcyon days of independence, we were not entirely on our own while training there. Fighting-17 was one of three squadrons comprising Air Group 17, and we were obliged to coordinate our training with the others so that we would go aboard *Bunker Hill*, when the day arrived, as an integrated combat air group.

The air group commander, or CAG, was Cdr Michael "Bags" Bagdanovich, a 1929 Annapolis graduate who had been Joe Clifton's immediate boss at Opa-Locka. Bags, a giant Nordic type, had plenty of carrier squadron operating experience, but he fell into the trap of treating his position in Air Group 17 as a sinecure. This attitude was a holdover from prewar days, and it unfortunately ruined a lot of potentially useful CAGs during the war. Bags exercised only superficial supervision and did not even deign to master all the aircraft types employed by the group. He did not even check out in the F4U, nor, to my knowledge, in our dive-bomber type, the SB2C, but only tooled around when he had to in the TBF command plane assigned to him. We seldom even saw Bags in our squadron areas, which I felt was a mixed blessing since it provided the squadron COs

with virtually complete freedom of action. On the other
hand, there were times when Bags's experience and clout
would have been useful in dealing with superior officers
who did not quite see things our way. Word from the
Pacific already warned us that the Navy carrier air groups
had had a bad time during all the early carrier battles
precisely because they had been unable to launch coordinated, mutually supporting group strikes. Indeed, a coordinated strike by as few as two groups had never come off.

Bombing-17's thirty-six Curtiss SB2C Helldiver dive-
bombers were commanded by LCdr James "Moe" Vose, a
1934 Annapolis graduate. Moe was an extremely skilled
combat flight leader who had led nearly two squadrons of
SBD Dauntless dive-bombers which severely damaged a
Japanese carrier in October 1942 during the Santa Cruz
carrier battle. Now he faced the unenviable task of forging
a new fighting force out of tyros like my own with the
misbegotten Helldiver, which was known universally and
unaffectionately as The Beast. Moe elected to undertake
Bombing-17's training work at Norfolk, a decision that was
influenced in large measure by his proximity to the supply
center, good shops, and, most important, the aircraft overhaul and repair facility. The Beast was that bad; it required
no end of changes and modifications to remain operable.

Moe's Academy classmate, LCdr Frank "Silver Fox"
Whittaker, an immensely imaginative and capable pilot and
leader, jumped at the chance to train his eighteen TBF
crews at NAAS, Chincoteague, Virginia, 50 miles north of
Norfolk on the seaward side of the Delmarva Peninsula.
Chincoteague was as isolated as Manteo. The Grumman
TBF Avenger type with which Torpedo-17 was equipped
had made an unsatisfactory debut in very limited numbers
at Midway, but it subsequently proved itself a superb airplane. It was still experiencing some growing pains in early
1943, but it and its virtually identical successor, the General
Motors TBM, was so good that, after Midway, it was the
only torpedo type deployed by the Navy and Marines in the
war. The dynamic Grumman people remained right on top
of any problems Torpedo-17 encountered during its training

cycle. The Silver Fox worked his batch of nuggets hard and well, establishing a tough standard for later torpedo squadrons to emulate. Early on, this lifelong innovator begged, borrowed, or stole several airborne radars, which he used to develop foul-weather and night-attack techniques that eventually won fleetwide acceptance in early 1944.

Air Group 17's composition—40 percent fighters, 40 percent dive-bombers, and 20 percent torpedo bombers—reflected the painful lessons of 1942. The ratio at that time—25-50-25—had resulted in high losses among the bomber types and extremely spotty fighter cover over the carriers. The quandary of the planners was and remained how much bomb- and torpedo-delivery capability needed to be endangered or sacrificed in order to maintain an adequate combat air patrol over friendly flight decks while protecting the strike aircraft. The attempts at answering this basic question in four carrier-versus-carrier battles between May and November 1942 had had disastrous results wherever the fighters had *not* been committed. The 40-40-20 ratio appeared to be the best solution in 1943, particularly inasmuch as more and somewhat better carriers were coming on-line. Even in mid-1943, we were able to foresee that decisions would be more easily reached as we were able to mobilize larger carrier task forces and learned to coordinate the efforts of multiple carrier air groups. However, there were no assurances as we awaited *Bunker Hill;* we had to assume that Air Group 17 would have to attack enemy targets and defend our own carrier without support from other air groups. We had to be independent and self-sufficient, just as many of the earlier carrier air groups had been.

As a senior fighter pilot, I was painfully aware of the shortcomings of the fighter squadrons in the early Pacific battles. This lesson was driven home with some force during a routine cocktail party and dinner hosted by Bombing-17 in March. One of the young wives, whose husband had been one of my favored students at Miami and who had gone on to fight some of the early battles, buttonholed me late in the evening and delivered a heartfelt plea. "Tommy," she started, the directness of her tone no doubt stiffened somewhat by alcohol, "I know that a lot of these guys, maybe my Joe, aren't going to come home from the war. We wives have to accept that. But I want you to promise me that your outfit will do its damnedest to see that they do."

Already mindful of the stories of early Wildcat units flying uselessly hither and yon, like Jeb Stuart's Confederate cavalry at Gettysburg, while the bombers fell prey to unchallenged Zero fighters, I did indeed promise what she asked, and I held to the pledge as I trained and inculcated my Fighting-17 troops. Thus, in addition to honing their predatory instincts, I had to instill in them a loyalty to the air group which might oblige them to stick scoreless with the bombers they were escorting rather than allow themselves to be sucked away by the allure of easy kills.

The entire air group was scheduled to be on target at 1000 one April day to make a simulated attack on a group of Amphibious Command transports and a new command ship boasting the latest in air search radars. The target ships were anchored in Chesapeake Bay at the mouth of the Potomac, about 100 air miles from Manteo. The weather at our base was marginal, and it got even worse as twenty-four of us stooged up the beach line. The cloud base dropped to about 200 feet, with occasional pockets up at 500 feet, and there was plenty of patchy fog as a result of lots of shower activity. As we flew north, it became obvious that Norfolk would be shut down, that the CAG and VB-17 would be grounded. Nevertheless, we closed up tight and forged ahead through the muck—taking advantage of the welcome opportunity to clean the oil from our windshields.

At 1002, as we finished dusting off the task group with pull-ups over their masts at the conclusion of our strafing runs, the Silver Fox led in all of his VT-17 Avengers from Chincoteague and simulated a perfect coordinated torpedo attack. The black shoes were crimson-faced as they scrambled topside from the flag mess and their various wardrooms. They had all been imbibing hot coffee, safe in the illusion that the brown-shoe fly-boys would never attempt the simulated attack in such weather.

For a change, ComAirLant was pleased with Fighting-17.

PART III

Bunker Hill

9

· · · · · · · · · · ·

Bunker Hill cleared the shipyard at Quincy, Massachusetts, in early June 1943. As the spanking new carrier arrived off the Capes on her way to Norfolk, Fighting-17 greeted her with a tridirectional strafing attack from steep dive angles that carried our Corsair flights right across her flight deck with only seconds of separation.

The long hours of practice and rehearsal paid a handsome dividend; the swish and roar of the first division arriving from out of the sun was the ship's company's first inkling of the mock attack. *Un*rehearsed was the follow-up by Lt(jg) Teeth Burriss, who roared straight up the flight deck from bow to stern at 25 feet—inverted. From that moment on, I was told, as far as *Bunker Hill*'s captain was concerned, Fighting-17 was *in*.

Following slow-paced, weeks-long warm-up operations in Chesapeake Bay, in which the ship and air group took each other's measure, Air Group 17 was hoisted aboard on July 15 and *Bunker Hill*'s bows were pointed south for a shakedown in the Gulf of Paria, west of Trinidad. By then, I had long since reported directly to the new carrier's skipper, Capt John Ballentine, the same officer from whom I had conned the extra pilot on Fighting-29's way out to North

Africa. At our first meeting on *Bunker Hill*'s bridge, Captain John gleefully reminded me of the incident—as if I needed reminding—and thereby hinted that my quick ascension to the command of Fighting-17 might not have been a matter of luck, or even of skill.

Shakedown is an apt term for the always-difficult early operations of any new ship, but particularly during a war. The difficulties seem to increase in geometric proportion to the size of the ship involved. Learning the vagaries of a huge and complex physical plant is only one aspect of honing a cohesive crew from a body of more than 2,500 officers and men, 95 percent of whom have never been to sea. For *Bunker Hill*'s crew and Air Group 17, the added pressure of getting ready to go into action by a fixed date too near in real time was virtually unbearable at times.

The interaction between the air group and the ship in the basics of aircraft launch and recovery was vital, but it represented only a small part of the teamwork required of the pilots. The air department was a huge organization overseeing, among many other things, the maintenance and operation of the arresting gear and catapults, the fueling and arming of the airplanes, flight deck fire fighting, crash removal and salvage, and inspection and maintenance of the aircraft. Moreover, essential as it is as the heart of a carrier, the air department was only one of many large and complex departments that must work as a team. Engineering moved the ship and, among numerous other duties, maintained the airplane elevators. Navigation got us from place to place. Supply kept us stocked up. Gunnery was charged with defending the ship against attack in the event enemy warplanes fought through the fighter umbrella. Communications kept us in touch with the rest of the world. And so forth. The carrier was an immensely complex machine that was run by an immensely complex human community.

The transformation of a new ship with a raw crew into a cohesive operational unit, almost from scratch and virtually overnight, is an enormous undertaking. Schools ashore were

essential for sending *Bunker Hill* the trained human material, but intensive practice at sea, painstakingly meshing the
whole, was the only way to get the job done. Thus we faced
days and weeks of intense drill and practice—endless, repe-
titious practice. In the end, the enormous responsibility for
every detail of the transformation fell to the shoulders of
the skipper. Possessed of the dedication of Saint Paul and
the patience of Job, John Ballentine did a superb job. He
was tough and uncompromising but always fair. Somehow,
as we all stumbled along, he never lost his cool.

In our case, the "typical" insurmountable shakedown
problems were disproportionately increased by Air Group
17's need to work the bugs out of two new, untried, and
extremely recalcitrant types of aircraft, both entering Fleet
service for the first time.

Our most basic need was to undertake enough daytime
landings and takeoffs to teach all the air group's pilots to
safely get on and off the steamboat in smooth and expedi-
tious fashion. At the same time, we had to merge with and
work out and perfect the symphonically complex evolutions
of the air department.

Once the group was hoisted aboard, the plane handlers
had to learn how, with tractors and human plane-pushers,
to "spot" the airplanes in a "takeoff spot" on the hangar
and flight decks. The primary tool of the trade is the "Ouija
board," a scaled diagram of the hangar or flight deck on
which are positioned flat cutouts of the various aircraft
aboard the ship, one set of cutouts modeling planes with
wings folded and the other with wings extended. The flight
deck officer and the hangar deck officer are the key men,
the conductors who must orchestrate positioning of the
aircraft on the flight and hangar decks *and* the smooth flow
of aircraft between the decks by means of the ship's three
aircraft elevators. The trick is for the two supervisors to
arrange and rearrange the cutouts on the Ouija board so
that there is at least enough open deck space, particularly
on the flight deck, to move other planes. A final requirement
is for the flight deck officer to leave at least 415 feet of clear

deck for the takeoff run of the first plane. Follow-on aircraft need enough room to taxi forward to the takeoff position, and that means their wings and propeller arcs must remain clear of all obstructions. A taxiing accident will not only inevitably destroy aircraft and possibly kill people, it will shut down the flight deck, which is literally the last thing anyone aboard or aloft above a carrier desires or needs.

With ninety airplanes aboard, the deck-spotting permutations were virtually infinite. However, once the most commonly used spots had been worked out, the various results were photographed and one-to-one-scale prints were made available for reference. The spotters, most of whom were school trained but new to the job, had to study the standard spots, committing each to memory. The trick was to be able to perform flawlessly in the dark or in the rain—perhaps even under enemy attack.

As the pilots are being briefed in the squadron ready rooms, the plane captains are running up the engines, checking them and other systems for proper operation. When the plane captains are satisfied that all is well, the engines are shut down. After the order "Pilots, man planes" is sounded in the ready rooms and throughout the plane-handling areas, the flight crews strap in and the engines are restarted.

The flight deck officer takes position off the right wingtip of the first plane to go, holds up his left hand with one finger extended, and rotates his checkered flag slowly in a circular motion with his right hand. The pilot of the lead plane revs up to half power, checks his gauges and indicators, makes sure all the control surfaces can move freely, and, if satisfied, gives the flight deck officer a thumbs-up sign. The flight deck officer then holds up two fingers and rotates the flag more rapidly. The pilot applies full power while holding his feet on the brakes and the stick in his belly, the former to prevent a premature rollout and the latter to prevent a nose-up. When the pilot nods to signify "Ready," the checkered flag is swung out and down to point at the bow of the ship. Properly executed, all this happens in a matter of seconds. As the number one airplane starts its run, the flight deck officer is already signaling the number two into takeoff position.

The flight deck officer's chief assistant, the yellow-jerseyed director, moves with the grace and precision of a ballet star. His basic hand signals are universal: both hands held high with the knuckles toward the pilot gesturing "come on" to indicate "taxi straight ahead"; one hand held so and the other hand pointing toward a wheel means "keep moving and hold the brake indicated to turn"; hands with palms facing the pilot means "stop temporarily"; both fists clenched means "stop and hold the brakes locked until further orders." The director using these signals, with the pilot following them precisely, can move the plane with only a few inches of clearance if need be; he will be able to position the plane *exactly* where he wants it. The director's hand-signaled commands are mandatory. However, if a pilot does not understand a signal or feels that there is danger lurking—that he might swing his tail surfaces into the arc of the propeller behind him, for example—he stops dead in his tracks until the problem is resolved. While the airplane is taxiing to the takeoff position, the pilot extends and locks the wings and sets the wing and cooling flaps to their takeoff positions.

When the number two airplane is in the takeoff position, the director gives the pilot the hold signal, pats the top of his head, and points with both hands to the flight deck officer. Control of the airplane is thus passed. The flight deck officer, who has visually checked to see that the number one airplane has cleared the flight deck, turns and begins the final run-up sequence with number two. The desired takeoff interval is twenty to thirty seconds—less time for the faster-accelerating fighters, more time for the heavily laden bombers. This leaves no time for dillydallying. The entire sequence, including the rendezvous of various fighter and bomber units, was developed and standardized during the 1930s.

* * *

Once sent on his way by the flight deck officer's checkered flag, the pilot gets extremely busy, though all his motions from that point on are ingrained and should be automatic and smooth. Basic takeoff techniques include bringing the tail up enough to allow adequate forward vision, but no more than that; tail too high makes for extra drag, but it had to be well up in our long-nosed Corsairs. The pilot needs to hold a steady course right down the center of the flight deck—and he must do so using only the rudder and *never* the brakes. As the plane nears the bow, the pilot eases the tail down—that is, rotates the nose up—so the plane flies itself off the ship. The instant the plane clears the bow, the pilot turns smoothly 45 degrees to the right so the next man will not have to battle his slipstream *and* so he will not be in the ship's path in the event he loses power and has to ditch. Once airborne, the pilot promptly gets his wheels up—hydraulically, thank goodness, in the Corsair—and reduces to climb-out power (which causes the black exhaust smoke to disappear). Then it's a smooth, steady climb with no settling as the landing flaps are "milked up" to the fully retracted position.

During the shakedown period, every VF-17 takeoff was monitored by a two-man team of pilots, one to observe the takeoff and the other to keep detailed notes, including times and intervals. At the start of the work, Rog Hedrick or I usually monitored the monitors.

The monitors watched the performance of every move and noted any lapses while logging the minutes and seconds from the "go" signal. A group critique in the ready room followed every flight. The monitors' merciless comments in front of all hands had a salutary effect. As time went on, we shaved seconds from each takeoff and, thus, minutes from each takeoff evolution. In combat, those seconds and minutes could mean the difference between survival of our ship or others at the hands of a surprise enemy air strike. In all cases, seconds saved on the flight deck meant minutes more in the air, and more time in the air translated to more range or more time in a fight.

My personal refinements, while not made mandatory for

the others, were naturally observed and sometimes imitated. Just before full-power turnup, I retracted the landing flaps to achieve a more sensitive rudder response and to decrease drag for optimum rate of acceleration. I extended the flaps again as I neared liftoff and applied light back stick pressure. Halfway through the takeoff run—daylight only—I angled toward the starboard corner of the bow, thus completing part of the needed clearing turn before becoming airborne. As the ailerons became effective, I rolled the right wing down to the horizontal. This resulted in no net loss of lift while the added pressure of the right wheel on the deck obviated any tendency to be drifted by a crosswind. In addition, a small start was made into the right clearing turn. I had developed these minutiae flying the Navy's first monoplane dive-bomber, the Vought SB2U-1, from *Lexington* in 1939.

Once airborne, the flight followed the rendezvous patterns and practices that had evolved in the Fleet before the war. This was all old hat for VF-17 since we had been using the carrier-type rendezvous from the day we arrived at Manteo.

Following the clearing turn, the flight leader resumes the original launch heading while holding at 1,000 feet of altitude at 150 knots for thirty seconds multiplied by the number of aircraft in his flight, up to a maximum of eight. He then makes a standard rate—gentle—left turn to reverse course. Succeeding members of the flight formate so that as the flight passes abeam of the carrier, heading downwind, it is comfortably joined up, ready to orbit to await following units or ready to proceed with the task at hand.

To routinely land aboard, a flight arrayed in right echelon passes abeam the carrier's starboard side at 1,000 feet of altitude, tail hooks down. After thirty seconds on this course, the flight leader breaks left to take the downwind heading. (The carrier always operates with her bow into the wind during takeoff and recovery operations.) Followers likewise peel off at thirty-second intervals. During this phase of the recovery, the landing checklist is followed by the pilot so that, when abeam of the ship's port side, he is ready to start the 180-degree turn into the final landing approach. Once in the final "groove" approximately 200 yards astern the ship, the plane comes under the control of the LSO, who passes inviolable instructions by means of a pair of colorful paddles. He does everything from correcting the speed and altitude of the approaching plane to holding it steady on course or transmitting news of an oversight, such as an undropped tail hook. At the last instant, the LSO either executes the cut, in which case the aircraft lands, or the wave-off, in which case the pilot must—absolutely must—apply full power and clear the area without landing.

Exceptions to the basic pattern are many. For example, a critically low fuel state or damage or mechanical trouble will get a particular plane cleared for an immediate landing—if the flight deck is clear and the ship is not under attack. If there is a problem, the pilot sets himself up to arrive in the groove by any means necessary—dive, right turn, whatever is quickest. In an emergency, all other airplanes in the landing circle must fend for themselves while maintaining the obligatory thirty-second intervals.

After touchdown, the plane decelerates rapidly as the tail hook picks up one of the eight arresting wires stretched tautly across the full width of the after flight deck. As the plane comes to a stop, power off, the alert pilot flips the hook control to the up position while two green-shirted deck crewmen come out from the edges of the deck to clear the wire from the hook. The yellow-shirted landing-area plane director appears ahead and to the right of the airplane and signals the pilot to stop the plane's backward roll with his brakes and to start revving up to taxi forward. As a matter of course, the director holds his left hand out with the palm down and jabs into it with the upraised thumb of his right fist. This means "hook up." As the wire drops clear, the director signals the pilot with an agitated "come ahead" signal to use full throttle to start rolling. Control is then passed to a second yellow jersey 100 feet forward along the flight deck. The director signals the pilot to continue ahead fast or—hands out at waist level, palms down with a patting motion—"come ahead, but slow down." As soon as the plane is out of the landing area and forward of the crash barriers, the throttle is set to idle, the brakes are applied lightly, and control is assumed by a third yellow jersey, who guides the pilot to the "landing spot" or sends him to an elevator to be struck below to the hangar deck. Done properly, the elapsed time from "hook up" to clearing the barrier is twenty seconds or less.

While watching the yellow jerseys, the pilot works the throttle with his left hand and, because the control stick is of no further use, his right hand accomplishes various housekeeping chores with practiced precision by feel alone. These include opening all the cooling flaps to wide, raising the landing flaps, unlocking the wings, and setting the wing control to "fold." All this while controlling the airplane with brakes and throttle, watching the yellow jerseys, and instantly responding to their commands.

Fighting-17's merciless monitors were at their posts for every landing, having positioned themselves so as to have a clear view to port and especially aft of the barriers right on up the groove. This system's net gain for all, in addition to making all hands sharp, heads-up carrier pilots, was the rapid buildup of the squadron party fund. In addition to often stinging criticism, an elaborate system of fines was imposed, no alibis accepted. It cost a dollar for a pilot-caused wave-off and fifty cents per second for a cut more than thirty seconds later than the preceding cut. Every second over twenty seconds between "hook up" and "clear deck" cost two bits. Lesser goofs cost less, but the standards applied to every move. Only perfection was free.

The ultimate fine was five dollars if guns were not set on "safe." This dumb error had killed innocent people on the decks of other carriers, but it did not happen on *Bunker Hill*. The threat was real. We almost always flew with ammunition aboard, and quite often with rounds in the breeches and gun switches on. It was to be expected that a pilot would inadvertently squeeze the trigger switch while clenching his hand during the tension of an arrested landing. The five-dollar fine was levied only once, and that without an accident. Amusingly, the culprit was our squadron gunnery officer, Lt(jg) Timmy Gile, who, characteristically, turned himself in.

10

· · · · · · · · · · ·

The Gulf of Paria is a 70-mile-by-30-mile expanse of deep
water bounded on the east by Trinidad. The only deep-
water entrance is the Dragon's Mouth, at the northeast
corner, while the only other pass, to the southeast, is through
the foul ground of the shoals of the deltas of the Orinoco
River. The passes were heavily mined by mid-1943, and
meticulously patrolled by numerous surface vessels and
aircraft. For *Bunker Hill,* the gulf was the perfect locale for
a shakedown away from the danger of German submarines.
For Air Group 17, the cruise to and in the gulf was the
perfect opportunity to practice group and squadron tactics
and to learn to mesh with the ship's company. We worked
hard and played only aboard ship. We saw lusty, lively Port
of Spain, home of "Rum and Coca-Cola," only from the
air. Once embarked, it was all business. We got in an
invaluable period of intensive operations without let or
hindrance.

Air Group 17 flew seven days a week, undertaking simulated coordinated group strikes, bombing and strafing a
towed sled target. No towed target sleeves or high-speed
banners were available for Fighting-17, so we in the fighters
got no opportunity to practice our aerial gunnery. How-

ever, the spectacular tridirectional coordinated strafing attack we had launched on *Bunker Hill* off the Capes was repeated unto perfection with all guns blazing a frothing, tracer-lit path on the surface of the gulf and enveloping the target sled at the rate of 1,600 .50-caliber rounds per second. Alas, when we started finding wing damage from spent shell casings ejected from the planes which had just crossed ahead of the target, Captain Ballentine reluctantly ordered, ''Knock it off; save it for the Japs.''

The most valuable work we did was in learning to coordinate our intercept work with the ship's Fighter Direction Officer and the Combat Information Center staff. As part of the intercept work, competition was keen among my eagles in the area of eyeball target acquisition. All hands vied to be the first one to holler, for example, ''Tallyho! Eight bombers, two o'clock, down twenty degrees.''

Despite the immense progress all hands were making on all operational fronts, our beloved Hogs were giving us and *Bunker Hill* fits. As if we were not sufficiently beleaguered by oil-coated windshields, exploding batteries, and other general cussedness, our Corsairs were beset by a series of mysterious barrier crashes following what appeared to be perfect landings. After touchdowns with not unreasonable bounces, several of our planes surged ahead undecelerated instead of being arrested. Hog after Hog, deployed in perfect three-point attitude, pranged into the barrier cables at around 60 knots. Almost every time, the runaway went up and over in the barrier, strewing expensive debris in all directions, often as not breaking in two at the engine mount. Miraculously, there were no pilot injuries.

At length, a sharp-eyed green-shirt spotted the problem. The F4U's arresting-hook point, for reasons known only to the Naval Aircraft Factory, had a cross section like an ax blade. Combined with the unseasoned and unweathered soft fir of *Bunker Hill*'s deck, the hook dug in and cut a furrow—something it had not done on *Charger*'s use-toughened planking. In most landings, the hook engaged an arresting wire, which lifted the hook clear off the deck.

However, in those instances where the hook remained in contact with the deck, the hook point snagged on contact with a steel cross-deck drain channel and snapped off, typically flying over the stern. The plane continued undecelerated, of course, and the missing hook point was unnoticed in the twisted scrap pile of the totally demolished machine.

Urgent dispatches to the Bureau of Aeronautics produced the required information and approval. In short order, the supply system coughed up replacement hook points. The siege of barrier crashes was lifted as soon as the hook points were switched. But that was only one problem among scores that we got behind us.

Toward the end of the shakedown, Cdr Bags Bagdanovich and I were summoned to Captain Ballentine's sea cabin. Grave-faced, Bally showed us a dispatch from ComAirLant which offered to replace our troubleprone Hogs with new Grumman F6F Hellcat fighters. The question was whether we three felt comfortable deploying to the Pacific forward area in a fighter that many thought had not been suitably designed for carrier work. The dispatch indicated that we needed to make an immediate decision so that new Hellcats could be ready and waiting for Fighting-17 as soon as we returned to Norfolk.

The query was not unexpected. Vought had been heaving around to get numerous needed changes into the production line. These included, among many others, raising the cockpit, providing a semibubble canopy, perfecting zero-bounce oleo struts—shock absorbers—finding ways to get the tail higher in the three-point attitude, perfecting and installing our homegrown right-wing leading-edge spoiler, perfecting nonspray cowl flap actuators, and on and on. Russ Clark, the boss of the Vought civilian crew aboard ship, had kept messages flying to the factory with problem identifications and recommended solutions. The company clearly saw what was at stake, so promised, scout's honor, to have not less than a dozen F4U-1As waiting for us dockside at Norfolk upon our return on August 10. The balance of the thirty-six fighters allowed the squadron would be in our hands, they swore, by August 20.

Bags, who had not troubled himself with keeping abreast of our difficulties, begged the question. I had spent a great deal of time on the bridge observing flight ops and thus had had many opportunities to talk with the captain. I knew him pretty well, and he knew me. Above all, I knew that he kept himself well informed and was decisive to boot. He clearly expected the same of his subordinates, so Bags's waffling did not sit well. At length, Bally got fed up and turned to me. "Well, Tommy?"

I had done my homework. "We both know that Captain Eddie [Clexton, the AirLant material officer] is no dummy, that he has a real handle on the validity of Vought's replacement schedule. He concurs with you and me that the Hogs we have aboard are by no stretch of the imagination carrier ready. So, he's telling Admiral Bellinger, 'We can go either way. If Ballentine figures the better performance of the Corsair justifies the risks and operational nightmares, I recommend we go along. He knows he'll have to live with them.' "

Bally was all ears. He merely nodded into my break, so I went on. "What you're asking me is, do I believe these fixes for the Corsair are going to give us a combat-ready airplane. Right?"

"Right. I'm listening."

"Skipper, I'm so convinced, and so are my pilots, that I recommend in the strongest terms that we go forward with the Corsairs. Fighting-17 could make the switch to the F6Fs without even breathing hard. But we believe that that would be a cop-out and a serious mistake. The F4U is the better combat airplane."

Bally smiled. "I expected that answer, but not put in such positive terms."

"Captain, we'll be doing a lot of operating during the trip from Norfolk to San Diego. In addition to the crack-ups we've had, we've averaged one blown tire in every three landings. I'll bet you ten bucks that we'll not only have zero crashes, but we won't blow ten main mounts on the jaunt to San Diego—provided, of course, we're not demoted to the Hellcat."

"You've got a bet, Tommy. I'll tell ComAirLant that *Bunker Hill* strongly recommends deployment with the F4U."

It was my practice to cut all hands—enlisted as well as officers—into whatever I could tell them about dealings with outside commands and agencies. Needless to say, everyone had expressed vital interest in the resolution of the what-do-we-deploy-with question. Scuttlebutt—rumor—was rampant in the small-town environment aboard *Bunker Hill,* as in any ship, and I well knew that bum scuttlebutt can be damaging to morale.

The troops were delighted to know that Captain Ballentine had concurred with us and had gone up the chain of command with his pitch to keep us in the Corsairs. When I was able to announce a few days later that we had an unequivocal statement from on high that Fighting-17 would be deploying with F4Us, the cheers were long and loud.

Before the euphoria wore off, however, I put the truth to them in the bluntest terms possible: "This puts the heat on us when we get back to Norfolk. We'll have a month at the most before we shove off again. We've got a hell of a lot of work to do. There'll be intense bounce drill until Catwalk Cummings and I are satisfied that every man is completely ready to land aboard. There will be maximum gunnery practice on banners at two hundred knots. Intercepts and grab-ass at twenty-five thousand feet or more will be routine. I well know that you guys are way behind in your drinking and screwing—so am I. I expect you to play hard, but, by God, it better not interfere with getting this squadron's job done."

I let that last sink in, then went on. "We'll work a six-day week, from first light until dark. Then we'll do night-flying. Anybody who puts in for leave for anything other than a dire, *provable* emergency can expect to be put in hack. If you're not prepared to heave around flat out, let me know now and I'll see that you are promptly sent on your way to a patrol outfit."

I noted that not everybody smiled as I went on to the finale. "There's no knowing how much chance we'll have after this for training before we get into combat. It might not be much. The group, Captain Ballentine, and the ship are counting on us. They believe that you're as good as I think you are. We will not let them down. To paraphrase Henry the Fifth at Agincourt, we'll say to our grandchildren, 'I was there. I served with Fighting-Seventeen!' "

The Vought people proved as good as their word. As soon as *Bunker Hill* arrived at Norfolk, the new Hogs were picked up at Floyd Bennett Field. As I was making my check hop in the first of them—my new Big Hog—I got a radio call, "Corsair out of Floyd Bennett. This is LaGuardia Tower. Over."

"This is Big Hog. Go ahead La Guardia."

"Big Hog, we've got very little traffic. Can you make a low pass by the tower? There are a lot of people who'd like to see that thing."

Would I! Do fighter pilots like girls? "This is Big Hog. Can do. I'll come by downwind. I'll call you one minute out in case you need to wave me off."

"This is La Guardia. Roger. Standing by."

I pointed her down from 5,000 feet and came by, full bore, close aboard the tower at window level indicating 350 knots—403 miles per hour. I pulled up in a 45-degree climb, slow-rolled to the right, slow-rolled to the left, and leveled out at 10,000 feet from the half loop and half roll of the Immelmann, which put me on a heading back over La Guardia.

"Big Hog, this is La Guardia. Wow! I say again, Wow! Thanks."

"This is Big Hog. My pleasure. Any time. Out."

I did not tell the troops about this incident until we were safely on the way south from Norfolk a month later. Based on our past experience at Norfolk, all hands had been sternly notified that we would be ultrarespectable while concentrating on our transition work into the 1A Hogs; no unauthorized grab-ass with other fighters, no dusting off the heavies, and no—repeat, no—flat-hatting. We did not need any trouble with the front office.

Lt(jg)Tom Killefer—TK—had been one of my star pupils at Miami, a bright-eyed youngster with whom I had shared an extremely close father-son-type relationship before he was sent to help form a new escort fighter squadron. Tom's ship, escort carrier *Bogue*, which had been dedicated to antisubmarine work for nearly a year, happened to be in Norfolk when *Bunker Hill* returned from her shakedown cruise in the Gulf of Paria. Thus, Tom was on hand to waylay me almost as soon as I set foot on the beach.

As soon as our first round was set before us on the Boys' Town bar, TK launched into his prepared speech. "Boss, I want to go out with you guys. This pushing a Wildcat around looking for subs is important work, I know, but I got some Hog time in with Jumpin' Joe and it won't take me long to get refammed. My CAG and I don't operate on the same wavelength, so he wouldn't be desolated to see me go elsewhere."

It was a masterful sales pitch. In just a few brief sentences, TK had volunteered responses to every objection I could possibly raise—had I had a mind to.

"Okay, Tom, let me see what I can do."

It just happened that one of our new ensigns was newly married and, while competent, he was no ball of fire. His reluctance to part with his buddies—and me—was tempered with a considerable urge to remain on the East Coast, where he would be able to see his new bride occasionally. He agreed to being part of a swap if I could set it up with *Bogue*'s CAG, LCdr Howard Avery, an AvCad I had known since he came to the Fleet in 1938.

Howard was a very competent, conscientious officer, absolutely straight-arrow, eternally serious, with no use for blithe spirits. After plying him with a few beers at Boys' Town, I opened my pitch. "Howard, I hear that you've got some trouble with Killefer. You probably don't know that he was a student of mine at Miami. I think I can straighten him out. We happen to have a very good pilot who just got spliced, and he would prefer Atlantic duty. He's car-qualled in the U, and he has some Wildcat time, too."

By this time, *Bogue* and her little air group had set a superb pace in pioneering hunter-killer operations against Nazi submarines in the central North Atlantic. Howard's pilots had sunk four U-boats and damaged three, so Howard, who was quite properly riding high, could afford to be magnanimous. "Killefer," he responded, "is a fine pilot. I like him personally, but I find he's not my cup of tea. He's a bit much, if you know what I mean."

"I sure do, Howard. You've probably heard around Norfolk that VF-17 has a lot of prima donnas, including me. Killefer would fit right in. I think I can keep him pointed in the right direction. I'll be glad to take him off your hands."

"Thanks, Tom. I appreciate it."

"It's a deal. I'll fix it up with AirLant tomorrow."

The staff guys were cooperative, Howard was happy, the ensign and his bride were happy, TK was delighted, and I was smug. What I did not then realize—what I could not then have known—was that I had set the stage for VF-17 to become awash in castoffs from other squadrons. TK was the first of a boatload of extremely talented, albeit restive, chargers prone to partake of personality clashes, but hot to trot if the promise of battle was in the air. Why not? Having them aboard suited my spirit.

I updated Captain Ballentine almost daily on Fighting-17's status and progress. Capt Eddie Clexton's AirLant material office and Jack Hospers, the boss of Vought's service reps, could not do enough for us. The CASU maintenance people gave us top priority even though they were still wrestling with the bow wave resulting from the January shift from squadron maintenance units to the CASU's own centralized garage service. Notwithstanding the CASU's Sisyphean task of trying to satisfy the urgent demands of numerous temperamental squadron COs, they really came through for us. I suppose it helped that the CASU's skipper, LCdr Daniel "Dog" Smith, a top-notch naval aviator, was my old friend and long-standing golfing companion.

We went on getting acquainted with our new 1As with vigor and enthusiasm. Raising the cockpit and replacing the antiquated bird cage canopy with a bubble wonderfully improved the pilot's field of vision. Contrary to the gloomy predictions of some aerodynamicists, performance was not impaired. In fact, we noted a slight gain in maximum velocity with no ill effect, thus demonstrating once again that aircraft design is more an art than a science. But we did encounter new problems.

As part of our familiarization syllabus, each pilot had to climb to 30,000 feet, half roll to inverted, and let her go straight down. After checking out roll rates and control forces, the pilot was to level out at 20,000 feet. Lt Chuck Pillsbury, our operations officer, returned badly shaken from one of the first of these maneuvers. He told us that he had experienced some loss of elevator control and was thus unable to level out at anything like the expected rate. When we looked, we found that most of the fabric from his flippers—elevators—was gone.

I was alarmed, but I thought that Chuck had experienced an isolated failure ascribable to poor fabrication of that one new airplane. Nevertheless, I went up and repeated his maneuver in Big Hog, something I had already done with no ill effects. I was terrified when I felt the stick force lighten when it should have become heavier, and when I saw that I was only pulling two gees when I should have been pulling as many as four. As had Chuck, I arrived on the runway with my elevators tattered. I was not happy.

In bull sessions with flight-test people we had heard vague tales of "compressibility" and the magic numbers Professor Ernst Mach had developed with regard to flying at and above the speed of sound. As it turned out, portions of our 1As had been subjected to supersonic airflows. We eventually learned that several Army Air Forces P-38 fighters had been seen disintegrating in steep dives. In those cases, we were told, the dive angles had *increased* at the points pullouts had been programmed. Each time it happened, things got out of control so fast that the hapless pilots had not even been able to transmit, much less bail out. It would be some time before the scientists discovered that the compressibility phenomena were producing control reversal or "tuck-under."

We did not know what we had gotten into, but two deep scares—including my own—were enough to get me to ban vertical dives above 20,000 feet from that day on. Everyone who had completed the maneuver in the 1A had been just plain lucky. Other men in other Corsair squadrons died learning the lesson.

The intensive training period of bounce drill, gunnery, night ops, and other tactics and skills went forward without other notable incident. The Fighting-17 tigers were models of discretion in flight ops, and so there were no unpleasant sessions on ComAirLant's carpet, a fact that I am sure relieved him nearly as much as it relieved me.

On September 8, 1943, we taxied down to the Naval Operating Base's carrier pier and were hoisted aboard *Bunker Hill*. We shoved off to join the Great Adventure in the Pacific on September 10.

Well clear of the Virginia Capes, the big carrier swung into the wind and launched a small flight composed of all types aboard to begin refresher work for some of the air group and for the ship's company. I was on the bridge with Bally, who, pleased with the smooth takeoff, gave orders to start landings as soon as the flight deck was ready.

Because this would be Tom Killefer's first attempt at getting aboard a carrier in a Hog, he was first in the pattern in case he needed to go around more than once. With hook, wheels, and flaps down, Tom came up the groove, hanging on his prop at 90 knots. Catwalk Cummings picked TK up with a Roger and held the "okay" signal until it was time for the cut. The Corsair, which bore its typical resemblance to an old lady with her skirts at half-mast ready to go potty, touched down on three points without even the hint of a bounce.

Bally turned to me and answered my grin with one of his own. "He's qualified." Then the skipper turned to his phone talker, who had a hot line to all the essential stations in the ship. "Tell Pri Fly to have the pilot of that Corsair report to me as soon as he's parked."

Shortly, TK reported with a snappy, "Lieutenant Killefer, Captain. You sent for me?"

"Well done, Killefer. Any problems?"

With an absolute straight face, TK responded, "Thanks, sir. No sweat. It was like stabbing guppies in the toilet with a three-prong fork."

Captain John rolled his eyes heavenward as he turned to me. "Jesus, Tommy, are *all* these guys as outrageous as you?"

I was first aboard the next day and was pleased to be chalking up a smooth approach and landing when I heard and felt the right main tire blow out. Startled and horrified, I taxied forward, Big Hog thumping and clanking its way across the barrier to be parked by grinning directors who knew of my boastful bet with the captain regarding blown tires. As soon as I got to the bridge, Bally gleefully rubbed more salt into the wound with a lusty, "Looks like I'll have to buy you a drink with your ten bucks when we get to Panama." For a change, I had no rejoinder. I must say that the captain was as gracious as he was gloating, for he paid off the bet as soon as I put my hand out while we were tying up at North Island, in San Diego. My blowout was one of only five we sustained all the way from Norfolk to the West Coast, half the wagered number.

Transit of the Panama Canal was fascinating and effected with minimal damage to the ship. Some farsighted soul had decreed more than four decades earlier that the locks be 1,000 feet by 110 feet, even though battleships of the era stretched a mere 500 feet with an 85-foot beam. All of our fleet carriers were designed with the Canal in mind, so all could be shoehorned through. There was ample clearance fore-and-aft, but much squalling of tortured steel and scraping of unyielding concrete on both sides. While the waterline of the *Essex*-class carriers was under 100 feet, and the starboard side was nearly a flat vertical, the horizontal span at flight deck level exceeded 140 feet. Outboard of the fore-and-aft access and shelter catwalks were safety nets, which protruded another 8 feet. The port side bulged at frequent intervals with 20mm and 40mm gun tubs, and the deck edge elevator and its supporting structure protruded 20 feet even in the vertical, folded, position. Thus, concrete lampposts well clear of a lock's sides were regularly mowed down like tall weeds with each Fleet carrier transit.

We got in eight full days of flight ops between Norfolk and San Diego, a wonderful opportunity to prove out our new 1As and our ability to operate them. All hands were extremely pleased with the results. Captain Ballentine went out of his way to make sure that Washington, ComAirLant, and, especially, ComAirPac were fully apprised of our progress and ongoing success. We were all fully aware that there would be no further opportunities for training operations once we sortied from San Diego, bound for Pearl Harbor and the forward area. Carriers departing San Diego were filled to the gunwales with spare aircraft, trucks, and personnel—*Bunker Hill* carried four thousand passengers—so the decks were locked.

The sortie from San Diego on September 28 was exciting. We were on our way at last.

11

•••••••••••••

One evening, only a few days out of San Diego, I was summoned to Captain Ballentine's cabin. Something had to be wrong.

"Tommy," he began, right off, "I just received a message I think you ought to see right away."

Oh God, I thought as he handed me the message flimsy, which read, "Upon arrival at Pearl Harbor, VF-17 detached from *Bunker Hill*. Proceed by first available transportation to Espiritu Santo and report to Commander, South Pacific, for duty. VF-18 will replace."

Typically, no explanation was given. I looked up at Bally, but he just shook his head with a beaten air of finality; there was no sense trying to squawk our way out of this one, the decision from on high was obviously final. Bally and I had talked about the possibility of something like this happening, and we both thought we knew why. As the Navy's *only* carrier-based Corsair squadron, our place in the supply system was ambiguous, to say the least, and troublesome. All the other carrier-based fighter units were equipped with F6F Hellcats or, in the case of smaller ships, F4F Wildcats. The hard realities of the supply system, we guessed, had simply overwhelmed the front office's authentic desire to see us operating Corsairs from the carrier. I suspected that the decision had been made without emotion at AirPac headquarters, for they, after all, would be the people who would have had to jump through hoops to keep us supplied. Bally was later told by AirPac staffers at Pearl that this was indeed the reason we were relieved, and not—definitely not—because the front office thought the airplanes were unsuitable for carrier work. The decision and news, however, were truly shattering. The fact that VF-18 had been formed by my fellow Miami instructor, the redoubtable LCdr Sam Silber, was a meager consolation. I wished Sam well, but I also wished he had not found a berth aboard a carrier at our expense.

I called all hands to the squadron ready room as soon as I got back from the bridge. I wish I could take back the words I had to use to convey the situation to my mates. One moment, they were fidgeting and fooling around in their seats, the next, they were looking up at me with rapt attention, trying to determine if this was yet another feeble attempt to put them on. And, a moment after that, they were all sitting up in their leather-upholstered chairs with terrible expressions on their faces. It was as if I had told them that a bus containing all their relatives had gone off the road, killing everyone aboard.

Suddenly, one of them demanded of me, "Where the hell is Espiritu Santo?"

Good old Duke Henning waded right in to field that and a dozen more questions concerning the hunting possibilities in the South Pacific. Ah, the elasticity of youth; I am sure that they were dreaming of new worlds to conquer.

We were off-loaded from *Bunker Hill* the day we arrived at Pearl, October 2. Our first order of business was to bid farewell to a mate. The night before we reached Pearl, the ineffable Bobby Mims awoke with the granddaddy of all bellyaches. By the time the ship's senior doctor could be persuaded to look, Bobby was in severe pain and uncontrollably discharging from both ends. The medicos who misdiagnosed Bobby's ailment and refused to operate, appeared happy to see the last of him as he was rushed to Tripler General Hospital aboard an ambulance that had been summoned to meet us as the ship docked. Bobby was operated on at once for a ruptured appendix. Of course, I closely followed Bobby's ordeal and soon had word that he would not be returned to flight status for at least a month. Sadness in the squadron was not universal when he was permanently transferred. However, this was not the last VF-17 saw of this scrapper.

As the squadron's gear was being off-loaded, I told our yeoman to discreetly pack the typewriter that had been on loan to us from the ship. After all the troops and impedimenta were ashore, I started on my way up to the CO's cabin to bid Bally a fond farewell and a regretful adieu. I was crossing the quarterdeck when I ran into the exec of the ship, Cdr Swede Ekstrom. As I launched into a syrupy good-bye, I could see that the genial Swede had gone all flinty eyed. "Tommy," he interrupted with a peremptory wave of the hand, "can it. You aren't leaving just now."

"Sir?"

"You will not leave the ship until that typewriter is back aboard."

"Typewriter?"

But Swede was not buying what I was trying to sell. In the end—it was a quick end—I had to send word to the dock to unload the stolen machine and return it to the exec with all possible speed. The squadron would have to make do with a flimsy portable on loan from one of the pilots. Of all the things we needed to run the squadron, a good office standard typewriter came in only one step behind aviation gasoline.

I had only just walked into the temporary quarters assigned to me at Ford Island when Lt Johnny Kleinman appeared at the door. "Skipper, I'd like you to meet two old friends of mine who just showed up. They'd like to talk to you."

The two impressed me at first sight. They were both

smartly turned out in tropical worsted khakis, and their fighter boots gleamed as if ready for a Marine parade. "Sir," Johnny introduced, "Lieutenants March and Innis."

"Yes?" I decided not to fool around; I thought I knew why they had arrived at my door, and I was right.

There was no sparring, no time frittered away on inconsequential pleasantries. Characteristically, March was the spokesman: "Sir, we want to go back out with Fighting-Seventeen."

Even before I knew March's and Innis's credits, I was willing to give them any benefit of the doubt. "Any friend of Johnny Kleinman's starts with a strong recommendation."

The pair had been in Wildcats off carriers and land based at Guadalcanal—during the "dark days," as everyone who was there rightly called them. As a fresh-caught ensign, Don "Stinky" Innis had bagged a Zero before being shot down and painfully burned on D-Day at Guadalcanal, August 7, 1942. Also an ensign on D-Day, flying off *Enterprise* with Fighting-6, Harry "Dirty Eddie" March had killed a Val dive-bomber, a feat he repeated at the Eastern Solomons carrier battle on August 24, 1942. Who wouldn't jump at the opportunity to get two blooded veterans aboard an unblooded fighter squadron? Both had lots of carrier time in Wildcats and Hellcats, but neither had ever set foot in a Corsair, a minor, eminently correctable flaw.

So what were they doing trying to get into Fighting-17? Like Tom Killefer, they did not march to the pace of their present CO's drum. Their visit with me was strictly aboveboard; their CO knew they were looking for a new home, and approved of the transfer if they could wangle it with me. We got the paperwork started through channels that afternoon. The two were on the flight schedule the very next morning.

They were a real Mutt-and-Jeff combination. Dirty Eddie March was tall and rangy, with the build of a track-and-field star. Despite his opprobrious nickname, he was extremely fastidious, a good-looking young man in the John Wayne mold. Stinky Innis was about five-eight, of medium build, and darkly handsome. Though warm and friendly, Stinky was by no means the effervescent extrovert his sidekick proved to be.

If not on personality alone, Dirty Eddie's popularity with his fellow pilots was quickly established. He had been at Pearl for some time and had made connections among the young ladies who manned the plotting boards at the Honolulu Aircraft Plotting and Tracking Center. To cap this enormous vote-getting asset, Dirty Eddie had the keys to a huge antique Buick touring car left behind by some departing pilot and thereafter passed from one transiting fighter squadron to the next.

We faced a busy week at Pearl. In addition to flying the socks off March and Innis to get each of them at least forty hours in the Corsairs, we all put in a full schedule with intercept practice at 25,000 feet, generally honing the sharp edge of our fighting abilities, for first combat could not be far ahead.

Meantime, we wasted no time establishing a beachhead in a suite at Waikiki's Halekulani Hotel. This magnificent, generally staid landmark adopted us with a live-and-let-live attitude. The open, honest approach of the Hawaiians toward sex had long stood in refreshing contrast to the hypocritical Victorian or absurd puritanical preachments that anything enjoyable was, ipso facto, sinful. This was, after all, the end of the second full year of the war, and Hawaii was the last jumping-off point for many thousands of sailors and airmen bound for life-threatening duty in the forward area. We were not vulgar or sloppy or brawling, but we sure were not angelic either. We all had wallets made fat by our days of isolation at Manteo and aboard ship, and these were matched by compelling urges and enthusiasms, all of which could be bought or otherwise paid for in the Hawaii of the day. We never had it so good, nor in such quantity. Bacchus and Eros beamed.

We left Pearl on Columbus Day, October 12, 1943, aboard the jeep carrier *Prince William*. The "Pee Willie," as she was universally tagged, was chockablock with our thirty-six

Corsairs and an entire squadron of Army Air Forces P-40 fighters, miscellaneous other planes, trucks, jeeps, and blue-jackets and Marines bound for the forward area. We plodded along at 15 knots under escort of one dinky little destroyer, which, we agreed, was present only so someone would witness our demise at the hands of Japanese submarine wolf packs. In fact, only six weeks later, that is exactly what happened to the Pee Willie's sister ship, *Liscome Bay*.

The passage was no joy. Only the small wardroom was air-conditioned, and the hot, sweaty bodies of the many officers aboard threatened to overwhelm the system almost from the first hour afloat. Only two events enlivened the crushingly boring eleven-day passage.

We were a few days out when the forenoon calm was split asunder by the clanging of the general alarm and the blatting of "General Quarters. All hands, man your battle stations," from the PA system. We apprehensively jumped to the conclusion that the tiny destroyer escort ahead had picked up a submarine contact on her sonar. Calm was shortly restored. My summons to report to the bridge soon followed. It turned out that Timmy Gile's maintenance boys had been working over a Corsair on the hangar deck when one of them somehow fired three .50-caliber rounds. The hangar deck was filled with airplanes fueled to capacity with an aggregate of thousands of gallons of volatile avgas. Moreover, the hangar's forward bulkhead was covered with torpedos, each mounting an impact-sensitive Torpex warhead. One incendiary armor-piercing .50-caliber round was thus enough to torch or blow the entire ship and all who sailed in her. Those three ear-splitting bangs echoed and reverberated through the entire rest of the trip. Terror was palpable. Miraculously, the three half-inch bullets harmlessly plowed into the overhead.

The second main event was crossing the equator, which brought with it the traditional initiation of Pollywogs by Shellbacks. Neptunus Rex, complete with a flowing white beard festooned with seaweed, presided over judgment and punishment of all parties guilty of trespassing with our first incursion into his Imperial Domain. The horseplay, rough to a point just short of injury, consisted of a trip on hands and knees through a 30-foot "tunnel of love" which followed and preceded shellacking by torrents of biting salt water sprayed from high-pressure fire hoses. The tunnel was two 3-foot-diameter target sleeves filled with garbage, shredded paper, and malodorous butcher's scraps saved in warm storage for the occasion. Final indignities were meted out by barbers who randomly provided Mohawk haircuts or whacked off half a beard or mustache. The barber chairs had been hinged so as to flip Pollywogs, ass over teakettle, into a seawater tank manned by frustrated fullbacks who ducked and reducked victims trying to make their final escapes so they could be proclaimed Shellbacks. Age and rank were not ignored; seamen second class got the lightest treatment, and officers got the works. The ship's exec, Cdr Dave Young, once my squadron mate in Fighting-2, and the Air Boss, LCdr Sammy Randall, with whom I had played water polo at Annapolis, were on hand to be sure that I got the royal works.

Each day saw all pilots dragooned into very vigorous calisthenics led by me for half an hour following the standard 0800 quarters for muster. The bitching was long and loud, but I was adamant.

Duke Henning filled our forenoons with skull sessions, preparing us for our imminent combat tour. Foremost was geographical orientation. To us, as was the case with most Americans, the Solomon Islands were terra incognita. Only Guadalcanal and Rabaul were by then household words, the former because of the grinding six-month-long first American offensive that had taken place there from August 1942 to early February 1943, and the latter because it remained the center of the Japanese war effort in the region. New Georgia, which the U.S. Army had invaded and seized between June and August 1943, only a few months before our arrival on the scene, was less well known. There were names of places we had never heard before: Choiseul, Kolombangara, Vella Lavella, and Bougainville.

I was astounded to discover that the charts upon which

our charts were based had last been updated by the British Admiralty in 1852. Once I had that vital fact under my belt, there was no longer any need for Duke to explain why a close look revealed topographical information so vague as to be nonexistent. I had been exercised about the vagueness of charts relating to Morocco in 1942, but the meager offerings provided for our trip to this war front exactly a year later won the prize. As we would learn quite soon, for our purposes the key failings of these charts were life-threatening bum elevations and the mislocation of nearly all the peaks and ridges jutting up from those mountainous islands.

For survival purposes, Duke passed out small books filled with phrases in Pidgin, the universal glot of the islanders in the region to which we were heading. Phrases key to the downed pilot were, among others, "Gifim wara bilong dring," meaning "Bring drinking water," or "Balus bilong me im all buggerup," which informs the interested party that your plane had crashed. "Ouse pek-pek ware e stop" is the vital inquiry if one is in search of the nearest facility with a modicum of plumbing—a bush, perhaps.

Except for updates as to the general situation in the air war in the Solomons, I must say that, no fault of Duke's, I came away from the briefings with a sense of having retained my crushing ignorance.

At long last, October 25 found us standing by to be catapulted off Pee Willie, bound for the island of Espiritu Santo, our side's primary supply base in the New Hebrides, within easy one-way fighter range of fabled Guadalcanal. Even then, nearly a year after the air war at Guadalcanal had turned in favor of the thin Marine and Navy squadrons based there, that base was itself only a fighter's flight to the ongoing air battles over the Central and Northern Solomons. The main runway complex at Guadalcanal, Henderson Field, was still occasionally subjected to harassment raids by single Japanese bombers.

Almost everyone was happy to see me take the first catapult launch, just to see if Pee Willie's slingshot worked.

A catapult shot makes for an easy takeoff, but it is not for the fainthearted; you *always* wonder if it is really reliable.

The flight in to the beach was brief. We set up a landing pattern at Bomber-1 and went in to experience a new thrill. The strip was "paved" with interconnected perforated steel plates known as Marston Matting. These provide quite a smooth surface, firm even on soft or sandy ground. The only shortcoming is that it tends to become glassy if wet. What raised goose bumps for us that day—our first time landing on the matting—was the ungodly loud banging and clanging that accompanied each touchdown and rollout. I was sure I had blown both main tires, and I believe everyone else thought the same. Only our four South Pacific veterans, Lieutenants Halford, Kleinman, March, and Innis, wondered what all the excitement was about.

My first official act after parking the planes was to jeep over to ComFairSouth headquarters to report us in and ready for duty. The Fair (Fleet Air) commands were basically support activities responsible for air ops and maintenance outside the combat areas. I had no sooner reported Fighting-17's presence than the ops guys told me, "Take off tomorrow morning for Guadalcanal. On arrival, report to ComAirSoPac for further orders. Your ground echelon and gear will go tomorrow, too." *Wham, bam*.

I quickly learned, also, that Cdr Jumpin' Joe Clifton was temporarily based at Bomber-1. His carrier-based Fighting-12 had recently transitioned under duress from Corsairs to Hellcats. By the time I made it back to the squadron from Fair headquarters, Jumpin' Joe and a bunch of his pilots were on our flight line drooling over our new 1As, the first to reach the forward area. The brightly painted prop hubs and the fierce skull and crossbones emblems on the cowls made a wonderful impression. With Joe leading the way, all hands repaired with alacrity to the O Club to swap lies, tell sea stories, exchange gossip, and so gird for the combat into whose face we were finally about to charge.

While at Bomber-1, I learned of the loss of destroyer *Strong* in one of the many hellish night surface actions that had marked the progress of our forces at Guadalcanal and, more recently, in the New Georgia Group. Among *Strong*'s dead, I learned, was her exec, my Naval Academy roommate and dear friend, LCdr Fred Purdy. So, I was not only headed "in harm's way," I was doing so with a personal score to settle.

PART IV

· ·

Cherryblossom

12

The morning of October 26, 1943, found us killing time at Bomber-1 while the local mechanics tried to revive two sick Hogs. There was no joy there, so I decided to proceed to Guadalcanal with the thirty-four available Corsairs, hoping the other two would join us late in the day or soon thereafter.

Takeoff commenced at 1130. We all joined on the R4D transport, which would serve as our navigation plane while also carrying Duke Henning and some of our small permanent ground crew complement. The gooney bird turned out to be a headache; its cruising speed obliged the fighters to poke along at 135 knots. In fact, it was uncomfortable for the fighters to fly so slow, so what we had to do was set up intricate weaving patterns to, in effect, slow our rate of forward progress. I had to fight the urge to leave the gooney and do my own navigating—I was quite capable of holding a heading over only 500 miles of water—but two things stayed my hand. Our own people were aboard the gooney, and that fat, slow transport was capable of orbiting over one spot for quite a long time in the event an F4U had to ditch because of mechanical difficulties.

Our first sight of the Solomon Islands was when we made landfall over San Cristobal, the first big island at the southern end of the chain, the closest to Espiritu Santo. I was immediately struck by the beauty of the war's venue. From the air, San Cristobal was spectacular—steeply rising green-clad mountains and ridges set out in the cobalt blue of the deep tropical waters. The ridges rose 2,000 to 3,000 feet to greet us, and we saw volcanic cones in among the higher peaks, some of which pierced the sky to elevations in excess of 7,000 feet. The higher peaks were obscured by what were described as permanent cloud cover. It was an altogether breathtaking introduction to a region we had heard was dotted by little more than stinking, swampy, rain-forested hellholes.

North of San Cristobal, and stretching northwest to Bougainville, the northernmost and largest of the Solomons, was a double chain of mainly long, narrow, rain-forested islands. Immediately ahead were Guadalcanal and Malaita, the latter to the east and the former to the west. The next pair were New Georgia, to the west, and Santa Isabel, to the east. Choiseul, to the west, slightly overlaps the northern reaches of the New Georgia Group, which includes Kolombangara, and points the way to Bougainville. The name of the natural sea lane between the double chain of the Solomon Islands appears on the charts as New Georgia Sound, but all the Americans who had fought or otherwise served in the region knew it only as the Slot. Stretching away to the northwest of Bougainville's northern cape is the crescent of the Bismarck Archipelago, with New Britain to the west and New Ireland to the east. Rabaul, the huge port and air-base complex that was the hub of the Japanese regional war effort, was at the eastern end of New Britain, virtually overlooking the western cape of New Ireland. The Australian-held eastern leg of New Guinea is due south of Rabaul.

Our immediate objective that day was fabled Henderson Field, named for Marine Maj Lofton Henderson, who died leading a dive-bomber raid—sans protecting fighters—against Japanese surface warships at Midway. The original runway had been started by the Japanese in June 1942 and was nearing completion when the U.S. 1st Marine Division struck on August 7, 1942. The field fell with little bloodshed ashore, but several tragic oversights combined to set up the surface fleet for a brutal defeat the night of August 8–9. Four Allied heavy cruisers—three U.S. and one Australian—were sunk against no Japanese losses. The tragic Naval Battle of Savo Island resulted in the virtual abandonment of the Marine division by the naval forces charged with protecting and—above all—resupplying it. Even at the time of our arrival little more than a year after the event, the Guadalcanal Campaign had achieved a legendary aura, and Henderson Field was a fitting first stop for modern pilgrims on their way to battle the Japanese only a little farther north.

Four of my lieutenants—Sunny Jim Halford, Johnny Kleinman, Stinky Innis, and Dirty Eddie March—had flown with the only Navy fighter squadron, Fighting-5, to be committed to the defense of Henderson Field during the "dark days." They had told us how it was because we would not let up on them until they did. Each of them had tasted Japanese blood with aerial victories.

The combined U.S. Navy, Marine, and Army force committed to the simultaneous land, air, and naval campaigns associated with the Guadalcanal Campaign had not so much defeated as worn down the Japanese land, naval, and air forces charged with wresting back control of Henderson Field and environs. In a plodding six-month campaign punctuated once a month during the first four months by massive but not overwhelming Japanese combined-arms offensives, the thin American forces had pushed the Japanese from Guadalcanal. In doing so, they had suffered grievous losses, but they had destroyed so many Japanese ships and Imperial Navy warplanes that the Japanese were forced to take a backward step for the first time in the Pacific War. Following the official conclusion of the Guadalcanal Campaign on February 9, 1943, the U.S. forces in the region had been hors de combat, unable to follow through right away. The Japanese used the breathing space to build and fortify several new bases along the Solomons chain.

The Russell Islands, 35 miles northwest of Guadalcanal's

western cape, Cape Esperance, had been bloodlessly seized in mid-February. A fighter strip—Advance Base Knucklehead —was quickly built by Seabees on Banika, one of the two large Russell Islands. However, it took until June 30 for VAdm William "Bull" Halsey's U.S. South Pacific Command to muster a blow against New Georgia, where the Japanese had built up a major air-base complex at Munda. Marine fighter squadrons out of Knucklehead and Army, Navy, Marine, and New Zealand fighter and bombing squadrons out of Henderson had amply supported the June 30 landings at Rendova. In time, as the terribly mismanaged New Georgia Campaign reeled on to victory at Munda, the Seabees built a new advance fighter base at Segi Point, on New Georgia itself.

In addition to supporting the ground effort against Munda and, later, outlying islands, the squadrons based at Segi and Knucklehead spent an increasing amount of their time raiding farther and farther up the Solomons, against the Treasury Islands, the Shortlands anchorages in southern Bougainville, outlying bases on Choiseul, and a variety of targets in and around Bougainville. It was generally held that these raids—none of them very heavy—were designed to soften the way for yet more contemplated landings that would eventually pave the way to Rabaul herself. By the time we arrived on the scene in late October, Munda was a full-going operation, and so were Segi and several new outlying fields scattered through the New Georgia Group. It remained to be seen what the next amphibious target would be, but it was certain that there would soon be one.

We were all stiff as we climbed from our revetted fighters following the 3.5-hour flight from Espiritu Santo. The landscape I had seen during my approach and as I shook out my legs on the taxi apron still gave vivid indications of the savage fighting that had wound up nine months earlier. Several scarred and frondless coconut palms were still in evidence, the ground was amply pocked by shell and bomb craters, and twisted, burned-out airplane carcasses—many of them Wildcats—still littered the edges of the runway.

The usual level of exuberance following a Fighting-17 group landing was muted to the point of sober, dumbstruck—I would even say reverent—silence. I cannot begin to imagine the depth of feeling my four Guadalcanal-blooded veterans were experiencing.

At length a jeep came out to carry me to a meeting with Capt Al Morehouse, the AirSoPac operations officer. After I reported us present for duty, Al escorted me in to make a call on VAdm Aubrey "Jakey" Fitch, ComAirSoPac himself. The admiral was an old friend of my father's, so the welcome was warm and personal, and it extended to a cordial invitation to dinner in the Flag Mess. I welcomed the opportunity to connect early and at a social level with the key players running the regional aviation effort.

AirSoPac, like its boss, Halsey's Noumea-based South Pacific Command, was multinational and multiservice in its staffing and operational components. Present at the first dinner on Guadalcanal were Australians and New Zealanders as well as Navy, Marine, and Army Air Forces officers. The same held for the command responsible for air operations in the Solomons, AirSols; it was multinational and multiservice, truly an Allied and allied effort.

At the conclusion of dinner, Captain Morehouse directed me to have Fighting-17 ready to go at first light. We would be proceeding direct to Ondongo, on New Georgia. On arrival there, I would be working for ComAirSols, MGen Nathan Twining, of the Army Air Forces, through his Fighter Command chief, Col Oscar Brice, of the Marines.

We were airborne and enroute to Ondongo by 0600, October 27. After an uneventful but watchful ninety minutes, I led the squadron into the landing pattern over our new home. Proud of its carrier training, Fighting-17 pulled off a precision carrier-style breakup over the coral strip. Carrier-type approaches were made with standard tight turns with the cross-wind leg over Diamond Narrows, whose half-mile width separated New Georgia from Kolombangara. Three-point touchdowns at thirty-second intervals, we expected, would be the envy of the Army P-39 and New Zealand P-40 pilots already operating out of the place. However, we soon learned that they thought we were merely nuts as we came in low and slow preparatory to stalling out and landing on the first 200 feet of runway. On the other hand, on this and ensuing days, we did not emulate their sorry record of hairy landings and crack-ups from overshoots.

Ondongo—which means Place of Death—was a scenic spot, to say the least. The strip had been carved from a gorgeous coconut plantation and was framed on the west and south by the steep tree-shrouded ridges of northern New Georgia and on north and east by similar ridges of southern Kolombangara. Farther off to the north were Kolombangara's twin extinct volcanoes, each stabbing the sky in excess of 5,000 feet. Kolombangara, roughly circular and 25 miles in diameter, is set like a dark green jewel in the cobalt waters of Kula and Vella gulfs, and is further accentuated, as are all shorelines in the region, by the apple greens and turquoises of shoals, coral reefs, and passes. Placid and beautiful on the surface, Kula and Vella gulfs had been floored by the gray steel of American and Japanese warships and carpeted by the bodies of American and Japanese sailors in a pair of ferocious night naval actions associated with the New Georgia Campaign.

Scenic as this paradise seemed to be at first glance, we soon learned that there were no golden beaches and no dusky, bare-bosomed maidens. The nearest nurse was at Espiritu Santo. What we got was clean, virtually bugless, free of snipers, and, above all, near the enemy.

As promised by AirSoPac, we were met by a complete and extremely competent ground crew organization, that of Marine Fighting Squadron 215 (VMF-215), whose pilot component had just been rotated to Australia for R&R following a full six-week combat tour. Not entirely fair, the ground crew organizations worked straight through each squadron's six-month tour of the war zone while the pilots alternately flew and rested in six-week increments until the tour was completed. This was a boon to the land-based Navy units, of which Fighting-17 was merely the first Corsair entry, in that there was no CASU operating this far forward. The superb VMF-215 ground crew adopted us as their own literally from the moment we taxied off the strip following our first landing. Indeed, it is difficult to tell if they considered themselves part of VF-17 or us as part of VMF-215. Whichever the case—perhaps both—we meshed gears perfectly from the first moment.

After we were chocked and shut down in the revetments, we made our way to the good-sized Quonset hut that served as the ready room and squadron office. As soon as I stowed my flight gear, I got on the hand-cranked field telephone and negotiated my way through the manual switchboard to Fighter Command. "This is Lieutenant Commander Blackburn at Ondongo. May I speak to Colonel Brice?"

After a brief delay, "This is Colonel Brice. Welcome."

"Colonel, Fighting-Seventeen reporting for duty with thirty-four F4Us. Two more will be in tomorrow. Taussig Nineteen-Seventeen."

"We're glad you're here. What the hell is 'Taussig Nineteen-Seventeen'?"

"Sorry, Colonel, that's an old Navy catchphrase. When someone asks when you'll be ready to go into operation, it signifies 'we are ready now.' "

In April 1917 Captain Fightin' Joe Taussig commanded the first group of U.S. Navy destroyers to reinforce the valiant, weary British antisubmarine forces at Cobh, Ireland. Mindful that the spitkit American destroyers had just weathered a stormy North Atlantic crossing, the British admiral had signaled, "How many days do you need to refit for sea?"

Taussig had instantly responded, "We are ready now."

The good colonel took us at our word, for our phone jangled after only a brief wait following the end of my reporting-in conversation. The word was that a reinforced brigade of the 3rd New Zealand Division had begun landing in the nearby Treasury Islands at daybreak. Thus, Fighting-17 was ordered to launch a flight of eight Corsairs to patrol over the beaches. I claimed the honor of leading off Fighting-17's first combat mission, which launched at 1315. The flight lasted ninety minutes; we were back on the deck by 1445. Results were negative; there were no contacts. Eight more Corsairs were aloft from 1400 until 1625, with the same negative results. And the third mission of only four Corsairs made a similar dry run between 1545 and 1810.

The Japanese made only one effort to get at the American flotilla and New Zealand landing force, but it was headed off well to the north by Army Air Forces and New Zealand fighters out of Munda. The scrap happened while one of our flights was on station, but the ship-based fighter director did not even tell our combat air patrol (CAP) there was a fight going on, and we did not learn of it until the following day.

During the squadron briefing that evening, I made two policy statements I probably should have announced earlier. First, I wanted official news only of enemy planes positively shot down; "probable" and "damaged" claims would not find their way into the Fighting-17 War Diary. Second, pilots returning from combat missions were not—repeat, not—permitted to execute victory rolls or other low-level aerobatics; violators would be relieved and sent to the rear in disgrace. My reasoning was that too many fighter pilots had bought the farm while performing stunts in airplanes that had suffered unperceived structural damage from enemy fire.

That evening, our first at Ondongo, we settled into our spartan permanent housing, a pair of large Quonset huts. We also had the dubious pleasure of our first meal at the Hotel Ondongo Mud Plaza, the Army-run officers' mess. When we heard that our own ground echelon was coming over by boat from Munda at 1845, four of us jeeped down to the dock to greet and assist them. As they debarked, Condition Red was sounded and everything blacked out as streams of red tracer filled the sky immediately overhead. We all bolted for cover while the Marines and boat crews remained in the open, cackling with laughter over our discomfiture. As we tried to recover our dignity, a lone Japanese twin-engine Betty medium bomber tooled around overhead and dropped the odd bomb into the jungle as searchlights tried to fix her meandering course. One of the boat crewmen muttered "Washing Machine Charlie," the generic name coined by Marines at Guadalcanal for such goings-on. Shortly, the lone Betty departed, the lights came on, and the All Clear was sounded.

The following day, October 28, Fighting-17 flew forty-four combat sorties, but we did not get shot at nor get any shots off. On October 29 several of our pilots were titillated by ground fire while escorting B-25s and PV-1s on a pair of morning strikes against the Buka-Bonis airfield complex at the northwest tip of Bougainville. No damage was sustained and no enemy aircraft were seen in a pair of what the AirSols Strike Command bomber boys aptly called "milk runs."

Our warm-up continued through the afternoon of October 29 when sixteen of us relieved tension with a barge-busting mission. Heavy, armored barges had become the Imperial Army's chief means for getting troops and supplies from place to place in the Solomons. This was a legacy of the Guadalcanal Campaign, when so many Japanese transports and surface warships had been lost or severely damaged trying to lift troops through waters dominated in daylight by our land-based fighters and bombers. Barges were cheaper, there were lots of them, and they were relatively more difficult to detect as they lay beached along tree-shrouded shorelines during the day.

The October 29 operation began as a support hop for a P-38 photoreconnaissance flight to the Shortlands anchorage, incorporating the Shortland Islands and southern Bougainville. However, when the P-38 failed to show at our rendezvous, I led the other Corsairs to Bougainville and approached Tonolei harbor from the north. In repeated strafing runs, we destroyed three 80-ton cargo vessels and four landing barges full of troops. The AA was light and ineffective, though they got several rounds into each of several Corsairs. Not what we expected, but Fighting-17 had finally drawn some blood.

On October 30 we launched twenty-four Corsairs, but

one had to abort. Thus, twenty-three of us joined with forty other fighters of various types to escort seventy-two SBD dive-bombers and twenty-four TBFs, the latter being laden with four 500-pound bombs apiece. The target, the airfield at Kara, also part of the Shortlands complex, put up no resistance, and no Japanese fighters appeared from anywhere else. Thus, with full loads of machine-gun ammunition still aboard, Fighting-17 once again beat up on Tonolei on the way home.

That afternoon, twenty-four VF-17 Corsairs and a dozen Ondongo-based P-39 fighters again shot up everything in sight at Tonolei. This attack was the charm, for we never again saw a worthy target at what had been a major Japanese anchorage until it fell within range of our fighters. This result more than justified all the low-level work the squadron had undertaken at Norfolk and Manteo. Despite the opinion of all the cookie pushers at the former base, low-level fighter ops were clearly a key part in our matrix of victory in the Solomons. That last week of October 1943, my pilots were comfortable and skillful while executing high-speed firing runs at negligible altitudes.

That evening, we got a real demonstration of guts under fire. Sunny Jim Halford led off a flight of seven F4Us assigned to cover a PBY on a "Dumbo" mission, as air-sea rescue ops were called. The twin-engine Consolidated PBY-5A Catalina flying boats were very slow and extremely vulnerable, but the Dumbo crews nevertheless routinely kited straight into the teeth of enemy installations to pluck our downed pilots from danger. As Sunny Jim and the other Corsair pilots strafed the beach to suppress the enemy fire, the seemingly nerveless PBY driver made a straight-in approach and stopped while his crewmen reeled in an Ondongo-based P-39 pilot who had had to ditch during the afternoon strafing run. All this was done within range of shore-based weapons that would have blown the PBY away had they not been engaged to the hilt by the Corsairs. The fighter pilots knew, as did the PBY crew, that the whole operation was a dream opportunity for a high-speed diving bounce by Japanese fighters who could surely cream the Catalina and knock down one or more Corsairs. *We* would not have neglected such a silver-platter presentation. It was a keen lesson for us; we knew that there were people on our side who were willing to risk death to bring us home alive.

October 31 provided a series of what proved to be warm-up operations that resulted in no bloodletting whatsoever. Despite the raids on Tonolei, there had been grousing in the ranks because we had yet to be placed in a position to engage enemy aircraft. Little did we know that the curtain was about to ring up on the next major Allied landings in the region, at Bougainville. Fighting-17 was about to climb aboard the gravy train.

13

• • • • • • • • • • •

We knew there was to be another landing, but that is all we knew. We *assumed* it would be somewhere on Bougainville, which was obvious to anyone with access to a map of the region. But we had no idea as to the precise location of the effort, nor the exact date, nor the size and composition of either our forces or the enemy's. Our briefing on the evening of October 31 simply told us that the landing was to be made at dawn, November 1, at Cape Torokina, about midway up Bougainville's southwestern coast. VF-17 was directed to provide overlapping high-cover missions over Empress Augusta Bay—code-named Cherryblossom—with eight-plane flights on station as follows: 0730–0930, 0845–1045, 0945–1145, and 1345–1545 and a four-plane division at 1545–1745.

I led the first flight off at 0640. I had Lt(jg) Doug Gutenkunst on my wing, and Ens Jim Streig led my second section with Lt(jg) Tom Killefer on his wing. Lt Thad Bell led the second division with Lt(jg) Earl May as number two and Lt Ray Beacham as number three leading Ens Don Malone.

Adhering to our standard practice, we test fired our .50-caliber wing guns as we turned northwest well out over the Solomon Sea—a short *brrrp* from each pair of sequence, then a short burst from all guns together. Gun switches and reflector gun sights were left on. When we were 10 miles southeast of our assigned patrol station, I reported in by radio to the FDO—Fighter Direction Officer—who was aboard the command ship *George Clymer:* "Cocker Base, this is Gem One. Eight F4U, twenty-five miles southeast, angels twenty, climbing to twenty-five. Over."

I heard no reply. Since I had broken radio silence anyway, I decided to check in with my companions. I learned right away that my transmitter had malfunctioned. I could hear Cocker Base, however, and some other chatter, which turned out to be Joe Clifton's characteristic perpetual yakking. As it turned out, Jumpin' Joe's VF-12, off Fleet carrier *Saratoga,* was getting its baptism at Buka-Bonis along with the remainder of Air Group 12 and light carrier *Princeton*'s Air Group 24.

We went into a 10-by-3-mile racetrack orbit pattern at 25,000 feet and 10 miles north-northwest of the landing area. All throttles were set for "fast cruise," a relatively high setting from which we could go into action without delay. While we were orbiting, far from our sight, Navy transports were landing two reinforced regiments of the untested 3rd U.S. Marine Division at Cape Torokina. Unbeknownst to us, the Japanese had already begun launching their first aerial counterstrikes of the day. Over the past three or four days, the first Imperial Army fighters to enter this thus-far private Imperial Navy air war had staged into several of the Rabaul airfields, and the complete air groups of Japanese light carrier *Zuiho* and Fleet carriers *Zuikaku* and *Shokaku* had also arrived for land-based duty.

At about 0745, Cocker Base transmitted, ". . . Many bogies, course one-eight-oh, angels fifteen." I immediately sighted a good-sized formation about 15 miles to the east-northeast and about 10,000 feet below. They were heading south, directly toward the landing area. I fired a short burst to alert the flight, bent on full combat power, took a heading to intercept, and tried to convey by sign language that we were going in on an attack.

What a moment! First combat! The tension and concentration were almost corporeal. Thank God, I exulted, no buck fever. While we were in a great relative position to attack, the Val dive-bombers in the formation were perilously close to the pushover point above our transports. There was not an instant to lose.

The sun was at the ten o'clock position relative to them, elevation 45 degrees. This was the ideal spot for a high-cover group of Japanese fighters to be on station to clobber an attacking force—us—preoccupied with the main formation. The targets were eighteen Val dive-bombers at 14,000 feet escorted by a dozen Zeke fighters at 16,000 feet. This was a scant fighter force to protect so many vulnerable dive-bombers drilling into an area that simply *had* to be infested with U.S. fighters. The whole setup fairly screamed, Mousetrap! It wasn't.

We flew into the Japanese formation from five o'clock at a shallow dive angle, indicating 350 knots. I set up to shoot at the fighter leader. When I was 1,000 yards from my prey, all the Zekes dropped their belly tanks. Instantly, the leader, followed in quick succession by his three wingmen, honked his Zeke around in a tight, tight right climbing turn. This was a duck hunter's nightmare, the toughest shot in the book, nearly head-on with the flight direction rapidly changing. I opened fire at 500 yards and held the trigger down until I had to flick Big Hog's nose up to clear him as we roared past one another. I am sure I got rounds into him, but I sure did not nail him with the 220 .50-caliber bullets I fired.

Recovery from the run was in the form of a steep left chandelle into the sun, back up to more than 20,000 feet. Time had become meaningless, a typhonic Technicolor blur. I suddenly found myself coming up fast on the tail of a Zeke, holding fire until he filled my windscreen. The next thing I knew, I was flying through a fireball, emerging with a coating of his oil and hydraulic fluid. Wow! What a sensation!

As we made our initial run in, Doug Gutenkunst spotted a Val as it bugged out of the main formation to head back toward Rabaul. Doug left his position on my wing to go after the Val, and he fired at it from long range until he realized that he was being dragged farther and farther from help of his own. He wisely gave up the chase and turned back to the fight. He found me tooling around alone following my kill. We rejoined, but he left again when he saw a Zeke below us. He opened fire, and the Zeke shot back, during a head-on run. Suddenly, tracers from an unexpected direction alerted Doug that a second Zeke had joined the duel astern of his Corsair. Doug took violent evasive action and managed to duck into a cloud before sustaining any damage. After he stopped twitching, he climbed to 25,000 feet, from which he searched for the rest of us. After a fruitless twenty-minute search, Doug headed home alone.

Streig and Killefer, who initially trailed Gutenkunst and me, fired on the first pass, but also without success. They leveled out together at 17,000 feet and headed east before turning back into the fight. The pair next executed a highside run on a Zeke on the left flank of the formation. The Zeke flamed and exploded and Streig and Killefer zoomed back to regain altitude. They spotted yet another Zeke as it headed north against the volcanic smoke plume of Mt. Bagana. Fire-walling their throttles, they caught up and opened fire simultaneously at 250 yards. The Zeke started burning and the Japanese pilot hit the silk. Certain that there was more prey ahead, the two continued northward and inconclusively fired at a third Zeke near Buka. With that, they wisely decided to turn back south while they still had some bullets left. By the time they returned to the scene of the fight, the sky was empty, so they flew straight back to Ondongo.

Thad Bell's entire division followed mine, but neither element—Bell and May followed by Beacham and Malone—spotted the Japanese formation until it was too late to set up and shoot. Swinging back after the chandelle, Bell and May simultaneously fired 45-degree deflection shots at one of the swirl of Zekes. As they broke clear, they saw a flash of flame abaft the target's cockpit. However, the flame died out as the Zeke went into a steep dive and disappeared. A second, quite similar, attack on another Zeke netted no observable results. The two tried to get back into the fight, but the sky suddenly appeared empty, so they returned to the patrol station at 25,000 feet until it was time to head home.

Following the first abortive pass, Ray Beacham spotted a pair of Zeros making gentle S turns below his port bow. A steep high-side attack on one of the Zekes produced no evidence of hits, but the Zeke rolled into a vertical dive. Ray followed in his heavier, faster-diving Corsair and fired a solid burst from 200 yards dead astern. The Zeke blew up at about 5,000 feet. We later determined this to be the squadron's first kill.

As Beacham recovered and headed back east toward the fray, he realized that his gyrations had shaken Don Malone off his wing. He was thus alone and unprotected, passing back up through 13,000 feet, when he was bounced by a pair of Zekes boring in head-on from out of the sun. The leader hit him and held his attention while the wingman headed for the saddle position astern. When Beacham realized that he was in the hands of solid professionals, he kicked his Corsair into a violent skid and flipped inverted. All he wanted was out of there. The Zekes followed Ray's vertical dive, but again the heavier fighter was able to pull away. When he thought he was free, he leveled off, but he remained at full power until he was 100 miles closer to home. A string of 7.7mm bullets and several 20mm cannon rounds had chewed up his right wing beyond repair.

Don Malone and I wound up as a pair as soon as the brannigan broke up. All the time from the moment I had completed my first firing pass until Malone and I suddenly found the sky around us clear of all other airplanes was a swirling kaleidoscope of infrequent and disjointed recollections. The rest was and is a surrealistic stream of intensely vivid sensory memories. Malone and I orbited at 15,000 feet, breathing easier, calming down, looking and hoping for the onset of more excitement. When it was time to head home, we turned south and eased on down to 8,000 feet so we could shed our confining oxygen masks and crack our canopies for some cooling air.

We were just tooling along, still getting our emotions under control, when I spotted, broad on my starboard bow and at only 1,000 feet of altitude, a lone Ondongo-based New Zealand P-40 fighter obviously going flat out to reach friendly skies before the Zeke a mile astern of his tail caught up. Even as we dived to set up on the Zeke, it was obvious that he would catch up with the P-40 long before Don and I could arrive. With nothing to lose, I pulled my nose up a tad and, with Don following my every move, fired a long burst in the slim hope that my tracers would spook the Zeke. We witnessed a miracle. The pursuer broke off into a 180-degree turn for home. As we closed on the Zeke at full bore from dead astern, Don moved out about 200 yards abeam to counter the expected evasive action. However, the Zeke just flew on, straight and level. It was unbelievable; he had to know we were there. I put out a brief burst from 200 yards and sent him flaming into the Solomon Sea.

All eight Corsairs from the initial November 1 mission made it home. Several of the airplanes had sustained varying amounts of damage, but all would be back in commission by the following morning. For no losses of our own, we had scored 5 Zeke kills—2 for Blackburn, 1 for Beacham, 1.5 for Killefer, and .5 for Streig. Unbeknownst to me, and against orders, Duke Henning also scored "damage" to 4 Japanese—2 Zekes damaged by Blackburn, 1 Zeke damaged by Bell, and 1 Val by Gutenkunst.

That evening, a Kiwi flight lieutenant buttonholed me and thanked me for saving his life. The best I could get out was a Jimmy Stewart imitation, "Aw, shucks."

Sunny Jim Halford led his flight of eight F4Us, our second of the day, to 28,000 feet over Empress Augusta Bay at 0845. As he and his companions flew their racetrack pattern, the weather worsened. Typical of many days that dawned bright and clear, the fierce heat spawned heavy cumulus buildups in the muggy air. At 1045, Lt Butch Davenport tallyhoed bogies 270 degrees from Cape Torokina, but the enemy flight apparently spotted the Corsairs coming on and ducked into cloud cover. No contact. Sunny Jim had trouble with his oxygen, so he led his division back to base early while Lt Lem Cooke remained on station with his division until relieved at 1045. On the way home, Cooke led his boys on an ad hoc strafing mission against the Japanese airfield at Ballale. This was well within the directives for fighters returning to base with sufficient ammunition aboard. I was never convinced that we did enough physical damage to warrant the risks, but I am certain our ongoing efforts inflicted deep psychological damage. Still, I am not sure that that was worth the deaths we sustained over the long run at the hands of their antiaircraft gunners.

Johnny Kleinman's flight of eight, which arrived on station punctually at 0945, strained eyes and nerves to no avail. They left at noon and also strafed Ballale.

Rog Hedrick led off our fourth mission of the day, timed to arrive on station at 1345. While still climbing away from Ondongo, Rog heard the shipborne FDO off Torokina report that a large Japanese raid had been reported on its way down from Rabaul. Eager to arrive in time to get a piece of the action, Rog immediately speeded up. On the way, Rog's generator went out, so he took his radio off-line to conserve power—there was no way he was going to turn for home at that juncture!

Once over the Treasuries and within sight of Empress Augusta Bay, sharp-eyed Rog spotted several specks in the distance to the north. Though he was intent upon getting over the Torokina beachhead, Rog felt he had to check out the bogies over the bay; he could not recall any news of friendlies being in that quadrant. Rog figured that the bogies, which appeared to be at 20,000 feet, could only be fighters, so he continued to climb in order to get above them while sweeping out to sea to gain the preferred up-sun position.

At length, Rog made out eight Zekes flying in two four-plane divisions similar to our own. These were the first

Japanese fighters Rog had ever seen, but, even from a considerable distance, he recognized them for what they were.

Rog set himself up in a gentle, moderately slow high-side run aimed at coming down astern of the Zekes. As he progressed, he gave the rest of the flight the visual "Attack" sign by rocking his wings. His target was the leader of the second four-plane Zeke division. Just before opening fire, Rog rocked his wings again to let all hands know they were free to attack. What Rog did not know was that no one else in his formation had yet seen the Zekes, which were by then quite close.

As busy as he was, Rog could not help focusing upon the huge red meatballs on the Zekes' wings and fuselages; he could not help thinking that the path that had led him to this point had begun years before at Pensacola. Like all old naval aviators, Rog had lost good friends to airplanes sporting identical insignia. This was his first opportunity to pay back some outstanding debts, and he did not want to ruin the opportunity.

As Rog fired at the Zeke's wing root—a tactic aimed at flaming the vulnerable fuel tank on that side—the Japanese fighter instantly burst into flames. With that, the remaining seven Zekes all instantaneously snap rolled in split-Ss and streaked earthward in vertical dives. As Rog dived to give chase, and without his seeing it, his first target blew up. The only other member of the entire Corsair flight to open fire on that attack run was Hedrick's wingman, Lt(jg) Mills Schanuel, but with no observable results. Several of the others later admitted that they were slow arriving at the realization that these were enemy planes and thus fair game. Sad to say, this is a reaction to the reality of first combat more typical than Rog's.

The entire flight followed Rog into the dive, all the way to the deck, in hot pursuit of the lighter Japanese fighters. The Japanese pilots were obviously of a superior caliber and undoubtedly fresh. (Their formation of sections and divisions suggested as much, for the Imperial Navy had until then flown in squadrons of nine deployed in three vees of three.) The paired deployment of Hedrick's quarry worked as well as ours. Their basic technique was known as the vertical scissors. As one of a pair comes under attack, he rolls away into a dive. Meantime, his mate executes a tight level turn in the opposite direction and then reverses course to get on the attacker's tail. This maneuver takes guts as well as skill and discipline. It forced our guys into violent evasive action, typically in the form of frantic diving for the deck or into a handy cloud.

All hands in Rog's flight eventually made it home, unscathed but disappointed. In addition to Hedrick's confirmed kill, Lt Timmy Gile, the second-division leader, and Lt(jg) Danny Cunningham shared credit on a damage claim, and Mills Schanuel damaged a Val he dug up along the way. Damage to our fighters was nil.

Sunny Jim Halford returned for a second mission with his division at 1545. The two-hour patrol over Empress Augusta Bay was fruitless, so he led his troops down to strafe Ballale on the way home. For the first time that day, Ballale responded with intense antiaircraft fire. Lt(jg) Johnny Keith's Corsair was hit and, streaming smoke, Keith ditched about 5 miles southeast of the Japanese base at 1810. Keith's wingman, Ens Country Landreth, saw Johnny swim clear of the sinking fighter, but Keith did not deploy his raft. While Halford and his wingman ran for our base at Barakoma, on Vella Lavella, to make a personal appeal to get a Dumbo flight laid on, Landreth circled over Keith. By the time a PT boat and a PBY were both sent north to find Johnny, the sun had set and Country was obliged to head for Ondongo while he still had fuel aboard. The PT boat and PBY arrived in the vicinity of Keith's downed Corsair, but it was much too dark to see a thing and, thus, they had to pull out with no results. A renewed effort at first light produced no sign of Keith. His apparent loss—we were not ready to give up—more than muted the effects of our six confirmed kills that day.

* * *

We learned several valuable lessons on November 1. First, the Japanese were quick to spot and attack singles, so it behooved us to do everything we could to maintain our basic two-plane sections or, at least, for singles to join on other singles. I also had to admit that my personal fetish for absolutely minimal radio transmissions had proved to be counterproductive; I thus decreed that flight leaders *had* to broadcast what they saw, right up to the last instant before an attack commenced. We came up with no easy fixes on countering the newly unveiled vertical-scissors maneuver, but all hands got to work thinking of one, and we passed the word to other fighter units so they could get working. In time, once we caught on, the Japanese maneuver was effectively countered by our getting the second pair of an attacking division latched onto the lead target's wingman, thus breaking up the maneuver before it could get going.

November 1 was not to be Fighting-17's best day—not by a long shot—but it *was* the day we lost our virginity.

14

On November 2, the day following Fighting-17's leap onto the scorecards, I led off my eight-plane division in time to provide high cover over the Bougainville invasion force beginning at 0745. However, on the way, Lt Thad Bell's Corsair developed engine trouble and his entire division aborted with him. As I flew on, I realized that this was at least the second time we had lost the services of a full fighter division because of the division leader's need to abort. I made a mental note to find a solution—to see how other fighter units handled the matter—because I was not about to allow Fighting-17 to get the reputation of a unit that did not fully meet its commitments. (The solution, simple in hindsight, was to maintain a "ready" division on the field, ready to launch for whatever reason.)

I orbited with Gutenkunst, Streig, and Killefer at 23,000 feet, directly over the landing area, trying to make sense of the confused babble among three FDOs vying for space on the single fighter circuit. This was an old problem the Navy clearly had not yet worked out.

At 0815, a strike of eighteen Vals escorted by eighty Zeros went after our destroyer *Foote,* which had been damaged in a wild night surface action only five hours earlier. (The Japanese had lost a light cruiser and a destroyer sunk.) *Foote,* whose stern had been blown off by a torpedo, was under tow and escorted by four cruisers and seven destroyers commanded by RAdm A. Stanton "Tip" Merrill. In the confusion of conflicting orders and information, a mixed bag of only sixteen fighters—eight F6Fs, one F4U, three P-38s, and four New Zealand P-40s—got out from our strong covering force over the beachhead to intercept the Japanese formation. About all those fighters did was draw off some of the escorting Zeros. Fortunately, the heavy concentration of shipborne AA was able to cope. Nevertheless, light cruiser *Montpelier* sustained two bomb hits that wounded several sailors but killed no one. The rest of Merrill's Task Force 39, including damaged *Foote,* was able to evade the remaining Vals' bombs. The Zeros did not attempt to strafe our ship. Several of the Zeroes initially engaged by our fighters were destroyed, and so were several others during the Japanese retirement, but we of Fighter Command were nevertheless frustrated and humiliated by the precipitating communication breakdown.

During my division's routine beat-up at Ballale on the way home, Killefer caught a 20mm explosive round in the cockpit, and it blew up his oxygen bottle. Wounded, burned, and a bit overwrought, TK thought he had bought the program. Remembering the last words of the Royal Air Force hero, Paddy Finucane, TK calmly keyed his mike and muttered, "This is Tom. This is it, chaps." But TK did not go down; he made it home. After our flight surgeon, Dr. Lyle Herrmann, patched TK's wounds and fortified him with a little medicinal brandy, Killefer appeared in the ready room, where he got only a very mild measure of sympathy. TK remained sulky until it came out that the 20mm round had smashed his transmitter and thus prevented his cool, gallant farewell from being heard.

By the time I landed, I learned that the meticulous, thorough search for Johnny Keith had produced no results. I wanted to hold out hope—downed pilots were known to turn up weeks and even months after going in—but I knew that it was not fair to withhold the news from Johnny's family. That afternoon, I wrote the first of all too many heart-wrenching next-of-kin letters from the forward area.

November 2 was a busy but unproductive day for Fighting-17. We launched forty-seven airplanes that clocked an aggregate of 186.9 hours in the air, but we never saw the enemy.

November 3 began with a twenty-eight-plane mission escorting Marine SBDs and TBFs to the big Japanese air base at Kahili, in southern Bougainville, overlooking the Shortlands anchorages. No Japanese fighters rose to challenge us; it was yet another milk run. Next, as soon as our fighters were refueled, Lt Chuck Pillsbury and I led off our divisions for a barge-busting strike through lousy weather at Matchin Bay, just south of Buka, in northern Bougainville. We were all a little frustrated, so we sort of ignored Fighter Command's dictum against jousting with the Japanese AA batteries—that is, to make just one pass and scram. When I pressed the trigger during my second pass, only one of six wing guns responded. In the face of plenty of small-arms tracer and mushrooming 3-inch shell bursts, Big Hog's relative silence was deafening. I considered myself lucky to come away with a wrecked wing panel and a deep gouge in the Plexiglas canopy just over my head and in line with the bullet hole in my wingtip. On the other hand, we believed we destroyed four or five barges and a pair of small coastal steamers. At about the same time, Rog Hedrick's division was setting fire to a 120-ton coaster and a fishing schooner elsewhere along Bougainville's northern coast.

Although the first Japanese surface reaction to the Cape Torokina landings had been soundly defeated by RAdm Tip Merrill's Task Force 39 in the Battle of Empress Augusta Bay, the Japanese were determined to destroy the Allied transport fleet by any means. In addition to ordering the Japan-based 12th Air Fleet to bolster the Rabaul-based 11th Air Fleet, the Japanese had already committed complete air groups from two fleet carriers and one light carrier. Also, Imperial Army squadrons were on the way. Then, over the dire predictions of the admiral who had overseen operations in the Solomons for more than a year, the Truk-based Combined Fleet committed the largest force of cruisers to be sent to the Solomons since the previous November. So, in addition to the local and defeated force of light cruisers and destroyers already at Rabaul, the Imperial Navy committed seven heavy cruisers, one light cruiser, and four destroyers to the job of annihilating the Cape Torokina amphibious force and its covering surface armada.

On November 2, the day the fresh Japanese surface force sailed from Truk, the U.S. Navy had but two battle forces capable of meeting it. The first, Merrill's Task Force 39, was both outnumbered and out of breath following incessant operations beginning with the Treasuries invasion on October 27. The second was a task force built around Fleet carrier *Saratoga* and light carrier *Princeton*. Commanded by RAdm Forrest Sherman, Task Force 38 was ordered by VAdm Bill Halsey to stage strikes against the combined Japanese surface force before it could sally from Rabaul. AirSols—also known as Task Force 33—was ordered to bolster the antishipping strikes and help protect the carriers from Japanese strikes. It was widely held, when the word got around, that *Saratoga* and *Princeton* could not possibly survive the inevitable Japanese countermeasures.

In fact, quite the opposite occurred. At 0900, November 5, Task Force 38 launched two full air groups from a point in the Solomon Sea only 57 miles southwest of Cape Torokina and 230 miles southeast of Rabaul. They committed everything they carried. Of the ninety-seven planes, twenty-three were TBFs, twenty-two were SBDs, and fifty-two were F6Fs. As the strike cleared the ships, land-based fighters from bases around New Georgia arrived on station to guard the carriers.

The carrier strike pounced on Rabaul through breaks in heavy cloud cover and, despite heavy ship- and shore-based antiaircraft fire, they severely damaged three heavy cruisers, two light cruisers, and two destroyers. The Japanese surface battle plan was aborted before it was even launched. In return, the Japanese downed five carrier bombers and five escorting fighters at a cost of fifteen Americans killed or missing. None of the five downed carrier bombers fell to the guns of Japanese aircraft because no Japanese aircraft penetrated the tight fighter protection, a fact duly noted and appreciated by the bomber pilots and crewmen. Altogether, over and around Rabaul, U.S. Navy fighter pilots and bomber gunners were credited with twenty-eight confirmed kills and nineteen probable kills, and they damaged another seventeen Japanese aircraft.

Later on November 5, New Guinea–based 5th Air Force B-24 heavy bombers and P-38 fighters kept the Japanese at Rabaul busy by hitting wharves and other installations.

Japanese reprisal strikes failed to locate or attack Rear Admiral Sherman's Task Force 38. Instead, they claimed a tremendous victory by misidentifying the three warships they did find and attack—a small LCT, a somewhat larger LCI, and a PT boat—as "one large carrier blown up and sunk, one medium carrier set ablaze and later sunk, and two heavy cruisers and one light cruiser and a destroyer sunk."

As far as is known, the PT boat, which shot down two of eighteen attacking Kate torpedo bombers, was the only one of its class ever to rate an aerial torpedo attack. The deadly missile penetrated her light plywood hull, but it did not detonate, and the boat was salvaged. The LCI, which also bagged several Kates, was also torpedoed, but it too was salvaged after being towed home by the LCT. (The congratulatory dispatch to the PT boat closed, "Fireplug sprinkles dog.")

Fighting-17's part in the stupendously successful November 5 action was guarding the carriers. Beginning at 0735 and ending at 1840, we committed three eight-plane flights, each of which was on station over the friendly flight decks for three hours. However, thankfully, there was no joy. The carriers turned south at 1300, after recovering both air groups, and made 30 knots through heavy weather until beyond Japanese strike range.

The next day, November 6, the Imperial Navy's Combined Fleet commander, Adm Mineichi Koga, ordered all his heavy fleet units to depart Rabaul for Truk. These were the last heavy Japanese warships to use Rabaul.

On November 6, while returning from escorting six B-25s to Buka, Lt Butch Davenport's division spotted a lone Betty medium bomber off Cape Moltke. Unfortunately, it took all four of Butch's Corsairs ten runs and 4,200 .50-caliber rounds to beaver the Betty out of the sky. In a way, I felt sorry for the Betty crew, given the prolonged agony those Japanese suffered. So they would never have to stop explaining their crummy marksmanship, I told Duke Henning to award Butch and his boys .25 kills apiece.

15

• • • • • • • • • • • •

The twin Japanese airstrips at Buka and Bonis, in northern Bougainville, remained serious potential threats to the Torokina beachhead throughout early November 1943. Although the Japanese did not regularly base airplanes at either field, they meticulously patched runway damage after each bombing raid, and they maintained heavy antiaircraft defenses around both runways. The danger lay in the readiness of the runways, through which the Japanese could, at any time, stage raids against the beachhead or supporting bases farther south. Moreover, as long as both runways remained operational, Japanese aircraft damaged in fights farther south had a safe haven 165 miles south of Rabaul. A new dimension to the problem emerged as the Japanese worked furiously on a new strip at Chabai, just 5 miles south of Buka Passage near Matchin Bay. In addition, ·Matchin Bay was a large, sheltered, deep anchorage well suited for transloading barges bound for the Torokina area and points as far south as the bypassed but still active Shortlands bases. These facilities—the airstrips and the anchorage—were only 55 miles north of Torokina but 200 miles from our nearest runway, at Barakoma, on Vella Lavella. Rabaul was 165 miles north-northwest of Buka Passage, a night's easy round-trip for troop- or supply-laden destroyer transports or an hour's flight for airplanes out of Rabaul. If the Japanese managed to base Zeros or bombers around Buka Passage, they would be within easy attack range of our air bases.

Similarly, the Japanese air bases in southern Bougainville—Kara and Kahili—and Ballale, in the Shortlands, provided serious potential threats to the security of our rear areas. So did Tenekau and Kieta, midway up Bougainville's northern coast. All five of these bases could be used as staging areas for raids farther south, and, as long as they were properly maintained, all five provided safe havens for damaged Japanese airplanes.

AirSols's main job, in addition to guarding the Torokina beachhead and providing on-call support for our carriers, was neutralizing all of the Bougainville-area air bases and as many barge facilities as we could uncover.

We held our regular evening briefing in the large Quonset hut which served as the squadron office and ready room at 1930, November 7. Lt(jg) Duke Henning, our ACIO, had the floor.

"The first operation tomorrow will be a twelve-plane escort for nine B-25s making a low-level bombing and strafing attack on Matchin Bay. It looks as if it will be essentially similar to the November 6 strike. Primary targets are two medium-size cargo ships and their escort, probably a destroyer but possibly a light cruiser. Time on target is 0700. Air opposition is not expected. As you know, the Japs won't night-fly with Zekes, except for late-evening return to their base. You should be in and out before their CAP gets there from Rabaul, in the event one is sent. For your information, they have not sent a CAP down for about two weeks. Planned approach is straight in from the southwest, on the water. Cross the harbor, then take a forty-five-degree turn and cross Bougainville's northeast tip. Retirement is down the east coast, staying with the B-25s until south of Kahili. Secondary target is the new installation on the beach of Chabai, and, of course, any targets of opportunity. Fighters are to provide cover, in and out. If there's no air opposition, you're free to strafe the ships and AA positions ahead of the B-25s. There is no heavy AA known, just light automatic weapons on the ships and along the coastline. You'll rendezvous with the strike aircraft over Baga at 0600. We'll review this tomorrow morning. Any questions before I turn this over to the skipper?''

There were no questions, so I took center stage. ''Reveille's at 0330. We'll leave the mess hall at 0410. Man planes at 0500. Take off at 0520. Pilot and plane assignments as shown on the blackboard.'' I pointed to the blackboard, which indicated three four-plane divisions with Tom Killefer and Dirty Eddie March as leaders of the second and third divisions. This was to be Killefer's first hop leading a division, a debut he had earned.

''Departure from Baga at 0600,'' I continued. ''Due west of Cherryblossom [the Torokina beachhead] at about 0640. Take close cover position there: March's four thousand feet above the B-25s, Killefer's at two thousand, my division at three thousand. If any Jap fighters show, we'll hold these positions 'til we're well clear on the retirement. If there are no bogies at five miles from the target, March will move out on the port beam and attack shore batteries, left to right. Killefer moves to starboard to strafe straight ahead. I'll swing out to the right on the run-in, above Killefer, and attack right to left, pulling out above March. The B-25s will be making skip-bombing runs and shooting with everything they've got. We need to get in and out fast so we don't screw them up or catch a stray arrow.

''I don't believe this B-25 outfit has done this before, so they'll be skittish as hell. Our cover must be close and tight or they might bug out. No matter how tempting an opportunity you spot, do not break the cover pattern unless you absolutely must. When we're well clear on retirement, we'll resume comfortable loose escort positions. As you have seen, these guys have the nasty habit of leaving any cripple behind to fend for himself. Unless the group is under attack, my division will stay with the wounded bird 'til he either ditches or gets to Munda.

"Surprise is the key element. We'll stay at the B-25s' level until assuming cover positions. As usual, radio silence except for urgent bogie reports or ditching.

"Questions?"

Breakfast was at the Hotel Ondongo Mud Plaza, which was overseen by our Army Air Forces neighbors. As usual, the meal consisted of coffee too long on the fire, grapefruit-flavored battery acid, boxed cereal caressed with milk coaxed from powder, scrambled powdered "eggs," and fried Spam. Capping this luxurious eye-opener was the rainstorm that struck as we were settling in for our final briefing.

Flying with exterior lights set on full bright as we went into the racetrack pattern for rendezvous, we dodged between moderate showers and intermittent heavy squalls. I was on the clocks—instruments—almost as soon as I lifted wheels from the runway surface. It became obvious after ten minutes of orbiting that some of the guys were not going to join up. I was not overly apprehensive about them, but I was furious about what I considered to be a second-rate performance. My hope was that the missing birds—seven of twelve!—would appear when we joined on the B-25s at Baga.

Not only didn't my clutch show at Baga, neither did the B-25s. I waited around in cruddy weather until full daybreak, but no one new arrived to join my five Corsairs. The five of us set course to the north, cruising at 500 feet to remain below the turbulence yet high enough to be relaxed. We had plenty of fuel aboard, so I went to fast cruise, 200 knots. All the stooging around and waiting for no-shows had put us behind schedule and I did not want to throw away all the tactical advantages of an early arrival if I did not have to. We broke into clear skies halfway to the target, and it remained bright and sunny the rest of the way. I could not help thinking—and the others later concurred—that it would have been nice to have had the weather the other way around. CAVU—Ceiling and Visibility Unlimited—over the target could make for a rough show.

At 50 miles out, I led the others down to about 50 feet

and signaled all hands to go to combat-power settings for the run-in. The primary target area at Matchin Bay was empty, so we came left 45 degrees to set up for strafing runs at Bonis and Buka, respectively 6 and 8 miles to the north. Dirty Eddie March and Ens Whit Wharton formed a loose vee with me and Jim Streig and Tom Killefer flanked us well out to starboard. No radio transmissions nor even hand signals were needed as we swung to the right to line up with the runways—my three bound for Buka and Streig and Killefer bound for Bonis.

A light transport plane was in the traffic pattern over Buka, turning on final approach. Dirty Eddie and I fired at the same instant at about 200 yards; we didn't even have to pull up in order to clear the flaming wreckage. The three of us flew straight in, kicking up a lot of dirt mixed with tracer sparks. Wharton concentrated on a parked Zeke and smoked it while Dirty Eddie and I took aim on the fifty-man reception committee still in parade formation for the newly deceased dignitary aboard the flamed transport. As we hauled ass out of there, one AA shell burst vaguely in our direction. Jim and TK were not as lucky; they had to content themselves with shooting up the Bonis tower and sundry antiaircraft emplacements.

We strafed Ballale on the way home, but TK picked up a large hole in his right wing from the 20mm reception. He really laid on a bitch because the students at this AA postgraduate school had blown one up in his cockpit only a few days before. TK theorized they had it in for him, personally.

As I taxied up to the revetments at 0845, I anticipated the Marine plane captain's standard first question by holding up one finger—"One!" As soon as Duke finished interrogating the five of us, he got on the hand-crank field telephone to Fighter Command. When he got off, he told me that the Fighter Command skipper and his ACIO wanted to talk with me, in person, as soon as I could fly down to Munda, approximately immediately.

At Munda, I was quizzed at length by Col Oscar Brice, Fighter Command's Marine skipper. Also in the room were

Brice's ACIO, Lt Joe Bryan, and Cdr Pat Rembert, the somewhat stuffy skipper of a Hellcat squadron based at Segi. When I had finished relating my tale of glory, Pat got in the first word—"Fools rush in." Colonel Brice and Joe Bryan just looked at him. Subsequently, Brice and Bryan laid a lot of static on their opposite numbers at Strike Command and the AirSols Army Air Forces types about the bombers aborting because of foul weather which had not stopped *their* fighters.

My euphoria from the warm session at Munda evaporated as I taxied out to return to Ondongo. A B-25 with a full load of gas and bombs aboard was approaching the runway with one fan feathered. Less than a quarter-mile short of the strip, the B-25 ran out of airspeed and dropped into the rough ground. He bounced once, landing gear sheared off, and he slid on his belly in a great cloud of dust onto the end of the runway. The wreckage stopped less than 50 feet from me and torched off into a ball of flames. I got close enough to feel intense heat and, with Big Hog's tail toward him, revved up full blast in a desperate hope I could blow the flames clear enough for at least some of the five crewmen aboard to get out. As the crash trucks and meat wagons screeched to a halt 200 yards from the inferno, I got the message and had just rolled rapidly to a safe distance when the Mitchell's bombs started cooking off. There were only small bits and pieces to be seen when the smoke finally cleared.

Our second mission of the day was an eight-plane romp to Empress Augusta Bay to provide high cover for the fleet. Johnny Kleinman led off his and Chuck Pillsbury's divisions at 0730, the prelude to two fruitless hours of orbiting at 25,000 feet.

It was by then an old saw that combat flying is hours of complete boredom punctuated by moments of sheer terror. The sort of flying Kleinman's and Pillsbury's foursomes endured on the morning of November 8 was classic. No matter how much natural padding a pilot had, or how much he squirmed about in the relatively spacious Corsair cockpit, the parachute beneath his stern got harder and harder with each passing minute. We complained that our major ailment was Acute Aereo Asserosis.

As the two divisions started for home at the end of two unproductive hours, Torokina's FDO sent them to strafe four camouflaged landing barges. Seeing nothing, all the eight could do was spray lead across the designated tree-shrouded beach. The results, if any, were not apparent, so the mission was logged as "Patrol negative." All planes landed without incident at 1135.

Rog Hedrick led off two divisions, his own and Lt Timmy Gile's, at 0930 to relieve Kleinman over Empress Augusta Bay. However, shortly after the flight formed, Gile's Corsair developed engine trouble, so Rog released him and sent his wingman, Ens Brad Baker, back as escort in case Timmy had to ditch. Thus, Hedrick arrived on station with his four-plane division—himself, Lt(jg) Mills Schanuel, Lt(jg) Andy Anderson, and Lt(jg) Jack Chasnoff—plus Gile's second pair—Lt(jg) Paul Cordray and Lt(jg) Danny Cunningham.

The six spent an hour repeating Kleinman's no-joy mission, but the radio suddenly crackled to life at about 1100: "Gem Three. This is Cocker Base. Many bogies. Vector two-two-oh. Buster. Acknowledge." The meaning of this esoteric verbal shorthand: "Numerous unknown aircraft are on my radarscope. You steer 220-degrees magnetic to intercept them. Proceed at high speed."

To which Rog replied as he fought down the adrenaline rush, "Gem Three. Wilco. Out." Since Rog had no information as to the enemy's altitude, he quickly swung to the assigned heading and went into a high-speed combat-power climb. There were two separate layers of broken cloud overhead, but no solid overcast.

Minutes after turning onto the FDO-provided heading, hawk-eyed Rog spotted the enemy gaggles—two of them—coming on in standard vee-of-vees formation. He also spotted four P-38s coming up on him from astern. Certain the Army fighters were going to join his Hogs in the bounce, Rog decided to attack the far larger enemy formation. However, as it turned out, that one backward glance was the last he saw of the P-38s.

"This is Gem Three. Tallyho. Twenty-four fighters. Angels twenty-two. Fifteen Vals. Angels twelve. Course one-one-oh. Gem Three out."

Fearing that there might be more Zeros up-sun of him, Rog had his trailing section—Cordray and Cunningham—make a 360 to catch any bushwhackers he might not have seen. Then Rog dived away in the lead of his division, thinking all the while, "Well, here's where we learn how good the Hog really is."

Rog was astounded; as soon as he hit the big Japanese fighter formation, the enemy fighters broke up into two huge Lufbery circles. This maneuver, purely defensive in nature, was employed in World War I by small formations under attack by large formations—and not the opposite, as it was being employed in response to Rog's four-plane attack.

As Rog set up his firing pass, he noted with grim satisfaction that all the Vals were turning north for Rabaul without having dropped their bombs. He never considered breaking off to go after them; there were plenty of other fighters in the vicinity to take on that job. Rog's immediate concern was attacking the Lufbery circles. For Corsairs with an initial altitude advantage, it was like ducks going 'round and 'round in a shooting gallery: Pick a target, dive on it, shoot, zoom clear, and set up another run.

Rog picked out a Zeke and opened fire on it from out of a high-side run. However, the Zeke dived straight into a cloud, albeit streaming avgas from a punctured fuel tank. Mills Schanuel, who had followed closely on Rog's wing, picked out another circling Zeke, opened fire from 100 yards, and flamed it.

Meantime, Rog's second section, Anderson followed by Chasnoff, fixed sights on a Hamp, a square-wing Zero variant. Anderson opened fire from 500 yards and bored in to 100, blowing off quick bursts all the way until the Hamp exploded.

The two initial firing runs broke up the bigger of the two circles. Anderson and Chasnoff recovered from the first attack and tried to get their sights on one solid target in the sky littered with Zekes and Hamps. The two stayed together through a total of six firing runs, but their only kill was Anderson's first Hamp. Anderson got full credit for it and for one damaged Zeke.

Meantime, Hedrick and Schanuel chased a loose confederation of six Zeros north toward Buka. The two Corsairs, barreling along at 15,000 feet, finally overtook the Zeros, which were at 12,000 feet, just a few miles southwest of the Japanese air base. Suddenly, quite unexpectedly, all six Zeros reversed course to meet the two Corsairs. For the next few minutes, Rog kept finding himself embroiled in one head-on run after another. Unbelievable to Rog was the apparent fact that, in three consecutive head-on runs, each approaching Zero withheld fire. On two occasions, as Rog pulled up to avoid running into his targets, he was certain he saw large objects fly through the engine cowls of his targets; these were possibly cylinder heads knocked loose by his bullets. Rog also saw at least two Zeros he nailed in tail chases going down streaming what he described as "big buckets" of gasoline from fuel tank punctures. However, neither flamed or splashed. When the dust settled around Buka, Rog found himself all alone. He reversed heading to rejoin his flight over Empress Augusta Bay. He could find none of the others, so he headed for the barn. Schanuel joined up just as Rog passed over Bougainville's southwest tip. Mills's Corsair had sustained engine damage, and he had to make a low-state emergency landing at Barakoma. He got down with only 7 gallons of fuel aboard. Rog touched down alone at Ondongo at 1330.

The fight also led Anderson and Chasnoff away toward Buka. The two split out to take on a group of Zeros they found crossing in front of them. As Andy fired without apparent effect on one Zero that was heading for a cloud, he was in turn jumped from behind by two Zeros. He instinctively flipped inverted and nosed straight down, but the Zeros followed. Chasnoff saw what was going to happen to Andy, so he came in astern of the two Zeros, but he was in turn caught by four others before he could open fire.

The combined fire of the four Zeros on Chasnoff's tail shot away his rudder cable, but he evaded with a desperate vertical dive into a cloud. Anderson also somehow evaded the Zeros on his tail and found Chasnoff. The two tooled around the clouds until the heat was off and then headed southeast at full throttle, their seats all the way down, their shoulders hunched up to provide as much protection for their skulls as they could. They made it home without further adventures.

Cordray and Cunningham had peeled off from Hedrick's division at the start of the action to guard against an up-sun bounce by unseen Zeros. As directed, despite the heavy action below, the two then remained at 29,000 feet, ready to take on high-altitude attackers if there were any. In fact, six Zekes flew by right over their heads, but neither side attacked. Apparently, the Japanese leader did not see the Corsairs, and Cordray coolheadedly did nothing to attract the attention of the larger Japanese flight. With that, Cordray led Cunningham into the free-for-all below. By then, the Lufberys had broken up and there were Zeros everywhere. Cordray's opening dive brought him right down on a lone Zero. He smoked the Japanese bird, but he had too much speed on and had to pull up before the Zeke blew up. As Cordray pulled up, Cunningham opened fire on the smoking Zeke, which disappeared into a cloud trailing thick black smoke. Just as the two rejoined, they were bounced by a dozen Zeros. They went into an immediate, instinctive, and thankfully successful defensive weave, covering each other's tail while trying to get rounds into the attacking fighters. At length, they evaded the Japanese swarm and started for home. From an altitude of 18,000 feet, the pair spotted two Zeros heading by on their port bow and 3,000 feet below. Cunningham led the way down on an opposite-course run. Danny's .50-caliber rounds flamed the lead Zero just as Danny chandelled out of his pass. For no good reason, the two Corsairs followed the flamer down for several thousand feet. Satisfied that it was indeed a dead airplane, they headed for home, arriving just behind Hedrick.

* * *

The initial official tally came to a meager two kills—one each for Schanuel and Cunningham—and five damaged—three for Hedrick, one for Anderson, and one for Cordray. Fellow pilots from other squadrons who were flying low cover beneath the clouds subsequently put in reports that as many as fifteen flamers might have crashed into the water. This number was high, no doubt the result of multiple sightings. Rog was sure he had killed three and pretty sure he might have killed two others, and several of the others were convinced that they, too, had scored uncounted kills.

On the up side, Rog returned with the deep-seated conviction that the Corsair was a wonderful Zero-killing platform. Until that day's series of wing-wrenching actions, he had had his reservations. This fight was the first time any of us had tested the Hogs in maximum combat situations. Rog pronounced the Hog superior to the Zero in every respect except maneuverability.

When we tallied up the reports of all six pilots involved in the November 8 battle, we were universally mystified by the Japanese tactics. For example, we could not figure out why the fighters were stationed 10,000 feet above the vulnerable Vals. Certainly, by this stage of the war, the Japanese had figured out that unescorted Vals were dead meat if our fighters were around. The Val pilots sure knew it; they bugged out the moment Rog engaged the Zeros. And there was no way to explain the Lufbery circles. The deployment into the Lufberys by the main body of twenty-four fighters smacked of rehearsal, but certainly the Japanese trainers did not mean for their pupils to go defensive when they had a four to one advantage in numbers. The only explanation we could think of was that the large fighter formation was acting as a decoy for the six-plane division Cordray and Cunningham saw passing over them. If so, however, we could not figure out why six up-sun Zeros with the altitude advantage had failed to attack the Corsairs.

Even if the bulk of Japanese fighter pilots were rank amateurs—as seems to have been the case—surely they had some combat veterans along who were capable of putting on an aggressive show. Three of them who stood up against Rog Hedrick's determined head-on attacks apparently did not return Rog's fire, which was simply beyond our comprehension.

We knew by then that we were no longer always fighting the Japanese first team. The superb air groups of early and mid-1942 had been ground to dust over Guadalcanal and environs by the end of that year. We also had not yet learned that the fresh 12th Air Fleet was staging in from Japan. Perhaps the Zeros Hedrick's flight engaged on November 8 were just in from the home islands; perhaps that explains their rank amateurism. But hadn't the Japanese bothered to train those kids adequately, or even to tell them what to expect? The only pros in the bunch seem to have been the Val pilots; they knew exactly what to do. They ran.

The last squadron missions of November 8 were a pair of two-division CAPs over Empress Augusta Bay. Long before I led off the earlier of the two missions, I had all available hands on the carpet to "discuss" my feelings about going into action that morning with five of the twelve planes assigned. This sad showing was not repeated; the two divisions I led off—my division, and Killefer's—were fully manned.

We got off at 1320 and returned at 1745 without sighting any enemy airplanes. Similarly, Halford's and March's divisions were at full strength on our last mission of the day. They got off at 1510 and returned without incident at 1820.

By later standards, November 8 was a so-so day. But it was evident that the squadron was picking up the rhythm. The troops certainly seemed to have caught on to what they were supposed to do when they found enemy airplanes sharing their patch of sky.

16

. . . .

Fighting-17 was changing before my eyes. In just twelve days of continuous flight operations beginning October 27, we had matured well beyond any point I thought possible for so short a break-in period.

Among many other matters, the tactical organization of the squadron had been in a state of ongoing flux from the start. The squadron was nominally organized into five flights of eight planes each despite the fact that we initially deployed only thirty-six airplanes for, at first, forty-one pilots. Given our one combat loss so far, plus damage to a number of airplanes, plus ongoing routine mechanical malfunctions, the number of airplanes we had available on any given day was moot. Usually twenty-six to thirty were up. Typically, only four missions of eight planes each would be scheduled on a given day, sometimes only three. This allowed one flight to stand down on a rotating basis, so pilots could get needed rest. Our neat plan of assigning planes with the same color-coded propeller hubs to a particular flight soon became a shambles as airplanes were juggled from flight to flight to meet pilot assignments. Nevertheless, despite maintenance problems and battle damage, our schedulers did everything they could to see that each pilot flew his own, permanently assigned airplane. This was because each Hog had its own quirks, which were best overcome by the man who knew them the best.

I had made no changes in flight leader assignments; the flight leaders were still Rog Hedrick, Sunny Jim Halford, Johnny Kleinman, Chuck Pillsbury, and myself. However, I had been playing around with division leader assignments, both in the face of lackluster performances and to give some of the more junior shining lights an opportunity to try leadership roles. Dirty Eddie March had earned a division assignment before we left Hawaii, and so had Lem Cooke, once I saw beyond my early misjudgment of him. Lt Butch Davenport and Ens Ike Kepford were coming along, though I had only just tried them without permanent assignment.

Tom Killefer was a special case whose abilities were not at first utilized to the fullest. Because of my longstanding personal friendship with TK, I was extremely sensitive to a negative reaction of other pilots if he, as "teacher's pet," got what might seem like preferential treatment. So, early on, he flew as tail-end-Charlie in my division. There was no need for discussion with TK; he knew what was going on and performed in exemplary fashion. However, by the end of the first week, his talents were needed at the head of a division, and we used him as such on a rotating basis.

We had also begun the process of weeding out the weak sisters. I must say that no one knows how he will react to being thrown into combat. Despite all my years of flying fighters, I had no idea how I would really do when faced with the real thing. I was certain I would engage the enemy when the moment of truth came, but not *absolutely* certain. I could empathize with anyone who had doubts, hence my open-door policy with respect to transfer requests. At the same time, I recognized that some people were going to need a little time and trial to find themselves, one way or the other.

It is almost an axiom that units and people entering first combat experience some hesitation having nothing to do with guts or instincts. No matter how intense the training or inculcation, the immediate shift from a lifetime of peace to the first moment of war is accompanied by an instinctive *disbelief*. This was manifested in all our early combat, as when I opened fire too soon at my first Zero target, or when Rog's entire flight, except for Rog, failed to open fire at the Japanese flight of eight they otherwise bushwhacked on November 1. It takes a special concentration to fire at another human being—the first time. This is the well-known "buck fever" of the tyro big-game hunter. I was aware of the possibility that, despite their best intentions, there were pilots in VF-17 who would never fire unless first fired upon. However, I was determined to identify them and get them over the hump or send them home. The funny thing is that there was no way to tell in advance who those people were—mainly because they themselves did not know before the moment of truth overtook them. Given the rather aggressive group ethos I had instilled, I doubted if many of my young men would turn themselves in even after accepting the truth. I had no animosity toward this live-and-let-live attitude; it simply had no place in a fighter squadron at war.

As I pored over Duke Henning's laboriously typed pilot accounts of each engagement—the few we had had—I noted with pride and relief that the ex-nuggets—and the old men—were opening fire at progressively shorter distances from the enemy. This takes awareness and determination. We had trained them to fire at the shortest possible ranges, but doing so against target sleeves and real enemy aircraft are two very different matters. As each pilot gained confidence in his leaders, his airplane, and his instincts, we were getting closer and doing more damage with fewer rounds. In fact, it was standard practice for squadrons to maintain records of rounds per kill, and that became the basis for competition among flights, divisions, sections, and individual pilots. The payoff was building a squadron that typically was able to stretch a finite number of bullets per airplane on more kills per sortie. The best proof we had so far that it could be done was Rog Hedrick's November 8 performance, in which he fired on no less than seven Zeros and might have destroyed as many as five of them. Gun reliability increases with avoidance of long firing bursts.

I also noted with great satisfaction that our two-plane sections were routinely remaining joined, even through some hairy combat episodes. Our early performance in this regard had been miserable; we had too many lone-wolf incidents. During Rog's November 8 engagement, I was pleased to note, every section remained intact throughout the fight.

Attainment of my ultimate goals still seemed to be in the future, but even a casual reading of early reports and statistics revealed that Fighting-17 was already trending toward realizing its potential as a very competent squadron.

Before we deployed to the forward area, Kahili was known as an inordinately tough nut heavily defended by swarms of fighters amply assisted by plenty of competent antiaircraft gunners. Many good fighter squadrons had risen to prominence as Kahili was made untenable for the Japanese by means of the unrelenting daily assaults. By the time VF-17 joined the fray, Kahili's fighters were gone, but her AA defenses were still formidable. Woe betide the eager beaver who opted to throw in a second strafing pass.

"Kahili Knock," as it had come to be known, was a natural phenomenon brought on by overdrafts of the imagination. Pilots bound for Kahili in its heyday often perceived unusual vibrations in their airplanes, brought on, as some claimed, by bargain-basement spark plugs. These and other imagined ailments often led to a steady stream of aborts for "mechanical reasons." After Kahili was more or less defanged, Kahili Knock was encountered by pilots on the way to other tough targets. In-flight malfunctions occurred, of course, but a pilot became suspect when he routinely aborted "mechanical" too often. When one fighter aborted, the flight or division became unbalanced; it was almost better to send an even number home, as Rog Hedrick had done on November 8 when Timmy Gile experienced a malfunction.

By the middle of our second week at Ondongo, one of our young ensigns had experienced more than his share of

Kahili Knock. After his third consecutive abort, I called him in for a little heart-to-heart. The first thing I did was remind him of my open-door policy; if he felt he wanted out, I would grease a transfer in such a way as to save him embarrassment.

The ensign appeared authentically shocked at the mere suggestion that his aborts had been intentional. "Skipper," he pleaded, "you've got me wrong. Honest, it's not my fault. I've had rough-running engines."

While I did not want to encourage bug-outs, neither did I want anyone augering in because they insisted on maintaining face by flying along in authentically malfunctioning airplanes. He could have been on the level, so I decided to give him another chance. *One* other chance.

The next mission was his last with us. He returned early with a "bad engine," which I immediately turned over to the plane captain for evaluation. The Marine mechanic soon reported that the engine was "baby-butt smooth" on run-up. As soon as our squadron engineering officer, Butch Davenport, returned from the same mission, he also test-flew the ensign's Hog. "Boss," he reported, "it runs like silk."

Our reluctant warrior's immediate exit did not end the problem entirely, but I am sure it convinced those of ambivalent attitude to think hard before they succumbed to Kahili Knock.

17

•••••••••••

The next day, November 9, passed with various flights and divisions fruitlessly circling over Empress Augusta Bay and escorting unopposed bombing missions to Kahili and Buka. But the next storm was building, as I learned when Duke and I were summoned to Munda late that afternoon to confer directly with ComAirSols, MGen Nathan Twining, of the Army Air Forces.

As always, Duke's jaunt to the regional command center was attended by wild-eyed protests. No wonder! While I blithely flew down in Big Hog, Duke reluctantly climbed into the tiny passenger compartment of a rickety, antique parasol-wing monoplane transport piloted by a frustrated fighter pilot. Since this gem had lost its passenger access door, poor Duke was obliged to hang on for dear life in the windswept cabin. As usual, following each jaunt, our Yale professor pronounced us and anyone else who flew to be candidates for the Funny Farm.

Major General Twining, who commanded the Army Air Force's 13th Air Force as well as AirSols, chaired the conference at headquarters. Leading off was the command intelligence officer, who gave a detailed brief on our situation at Bougainville and that of the Japanese at Rabaul.

This was the heart of the briefing, and no punches were pulled. According to the best information available, the November 5 air strike by the *Saratoga* and *Princeton* air groups had severely damaged units of the Imperial Navy's 2nd Fleet. However, the Japanese force of light cruisers and destroyers remained a formidable threat to the invasion fleet off Cape Torokina. Moreover, significant other Japanese surface forces were still based at Truk, only thirty-six hours sailing time away. The medium and heavy bombers of MGen George Kenney's New Guinea–based 5th Air Force had been unable to do more than harass the Rabaul-based Japanese surface ships. The primary fear was that the Japanese were still of a mind to mount an all-out surface attack against our invasion fleet. If they did so soon, they could count on the support of whatever was left of the 270 combat aircraft known to have been based in the region on November 1. It was possible, the intelligence officer averred, that the combined strength of Japanese air and naval forces could overwhelm our outnumbered cruisers and destroyers, crush our thin-skinned amphibious force, and thus be in a position to support the defeat of our ground forces on Bougainville.

As all the terrible possibilities sank in, the briefers sprang the master plan. Even as the November 5 carrier-based air strikes were under way, Adm Chester Nimitz, commander in chief of all our forces in the Pacific, was setting the master strategic stroke into motion. Fleet carriers *Essex* and *Bunker Hill,* with light carrier *Independence* and nine escorting destroyers, had been diverted from the upcoming Gilberts (Tarawa and Makin) invasion in response to Admiral Halsey's urgent plea for assistance. Commanded by RAdm Alfred Montgomery, this powerful fresh force was to hit the Japanese surface warships at Rabaul from the Solomon Sea while *Saratoga* and *Princeton* launched simultaneous strikes from due east of the objective. The operation was set to go off on November 11, one full day hence.

Among numerous other records, the combined force of five carriers was the largest thus far gathered by the U.S. Navy for a single mission. If successful, this would be a classic case of the projection of power by means of carrier-based aircraft where horizontal bombing had failed—precisely what the earliest innovators of carrier warfare had envisioned.

The stakes were high. If the powerful preemptive strike did not work as planned, our naval forces faced the possibility of being defeated in detail. While a success would certainly pave the way for overcoming Fortress Rabaul in 1944, a failure would certainly stall our thrust up the Solomons chain toward that essential objective. The worst possible scenario, the sinking of the bulk of our carriers, would undoubtedly set the war effort back, perhaps as long as several years. The tide in the Pacific, which had already turned once, might well turn again.

In addition to mounting a heavy bomber raid against Rabaul, AirSols was charged with providing fighter protection for the carriers while their own fighter squadrons escorted the carrier-based bombers to Rabaul. To accomplish this most effectively demanded supplementing the fighters based aboard the carriers. That task came down to two land-based Navy squadrons, Lt John Kelly's Segi-based VF-33—a dozen Hellcats—and twenty-four VF-17 Corsairs. Twelve land-based fighters were to land aboard each of Admiral Montgomery's three carriers, and all were to be available at his discretion. In addition, thirty-two Corsairs from VMF-212 and VMF-221 and a New Zealand P-40 squadron were to provide overhead protection while our land-based carrier-equipped Navy fighters were refueling aboard the carriers following our initial hop out from our bases.

General Twining turned to face me. "Blackburn, your people haven't been aboard ship for some time now. The word we have is that you were sent down here because the F4U isn't carrier suitable. If need be, we can assign the two other Hellcat squadrons we have based at Segi." He held up his hand when he saw me instinctively lean forward to launch my knee-jerk protest. "Colonel Brice tells me that you're his first team. You now know how vital this mission is. We can't afford a mistake. Can you handle it?"

I was already wound up for my delivery, and I got right

into it. "General, that story that our Corsairs aren't carrier suitable is hogwash. My guys cut their teeth at carrier work with the old F4Us on a little bitty slow escort carrier. An *Essex*-class ship with plenty of wind over the deck is a piece of cake." Then, remembering how our cotenants on Ondongo still laughed about our habitual carrier-type landings, I added, "Every landing approach we make is a simulated carrier pass. My people are good! It'll be no sweat, sir."

The general gave us the nod, so, at the conclusion of the meeting, I flew back to Ondongo to tell our engineering officer, Lt Butch Davenport, to have the ground crew reinstall the tail hooks and check their operating mechanism and antibounce dashpots. As soon as our ground crewmen broke out the hooks—which had been removed upon arrival at Ondongo to save weight and prevent accidents—the pilots began showing up to try to allay their curiosity with eager questions. Duke and I brushed off all the where and when questions; we could not afford a leak in the event someone was shot down and captured before the mission got underway.

November 10 was another nothing day; more fruitless hops to the invasion area, more dry milk runs with the bombers. The troops were doubly put out because they knew a big show was imminent.

Duke and I conducted the squadron brief after supper on November 10. Reveille was to be at 0200 and takeoff was to commence at 0400. Six divisions—Hedrick's, Kleinman's, Pillsbury's, Bell's, Gile's, and mine—were to proceed as one unit at 10,000 feet, set to arrive over Admiral Montgomery's Task Group 50.3 well before dawn. Upon reaching the task group, which was to be 190 miles southwest of Rabaul, we would orbit and do our best to conserve fuel. After landing to refuel at about 0900, we would operate as directed, probably to resume CAP coverage for the carriers and their escorts. Depending upon Japanese activity, we would use the carriers for refueling—and rearming, if necessary—through the day or until sent back to our bases. All this effectively increased the availability of the carrier-based Hellcats, every one of which was needed to escort the bombers on Task Group 50.3's two planned antishipping strikes.

I assigned Hedrick to go aboard *Essex* with a flight of twelve; I would take the other twelve Corsairs aboard *Bunker Hill,* and John Kelly would land with his twelve Hellcats aboard *Independence.* As usual, voice-radio transmissions were to be made only if the information was vital or the situation extreme.

As soon as the brief was over, I sent all hands straight to bed with the reminder that we were all facing at least eight hours of flight time and, probably, stiff combat.

We were on schedule and on course at 0420, November 11, but one member of my flight had to drop out because of a mechanical problem. The night was clear and pitch-black. Running lights were doused as soon as we turned out of the rendezvous, but the formation was maintained through use of the blue lights located atop the wings of each plane as well as the ubiquitous and unavoidable flame and glow from the exhaust stacks, which could be seen only from below.

We were five minutes past our estimated time of arrival over the carriers, and I was already having dank visions of my adventure off Morocco, when Chuck Pillsbury decided to break radio silence. "Skipper, this is Chuck. I hold Judah's hayrake [*Essex*'s homing beacon]. We passed directly over three minutes ago. Out."

Enormously relieved, I silently blessed my operations officer for his sharpness, and for having the brains and guts to speak up. I immediately banked into a gentle turn to get into our holding pattern. There was no need for additional transmissions; the ships had doubtless held us on their radars from the time we were 100 miles out. This was standard; our cruise-out altitude had been selected for, among other reasons, their timely acquisition of us at an altitude at which it was minimally probable that we would be mistaken for an inbound Japanese strike.

We saw nothing beneath our wings, which was to be expected. "Darken Ship" had been passed at sunset, and no exterior lights were showing except for a few dim hooded red ones needed on the bridges and other topside control stations. Even during night flight ops, the carriers remained darkened; only the dimmest lights were used to aid topside activities, and all ships in the force showed single red mast-head lights as clearance markers for the airplanes. Deck-edge lights required for night landings and takeoffs were screened so that they were not visible except at horizontal near distances, generally from one edge of the flight deck to the other.

The breaking dawn brought with it the unforgettable, unimaginably beautiful sight of the two carriers' flashing bow waves and white wakes as they arrowed on parallel headings a mile apart. The light carrier similarly brightened the sea as it brought up the rear, forming an equilateral triangle. The nine destroyers were arrayed in a precise circle two miles from the center of the triangle. The dark blue of the tropical sea was thus ribboned by the twelve brilliant white wakes churned out by the 30-knot run that was taking Task Group 50.3 directly "in harm's way."

We circled overhead in our holding pattern for about an hour. Suddenly, the silence was broken by a call from *Essex*. "Big Hog, this is Judah. Bogey. Angels one-five. Vector three-five-oh. Buster. Acknowledge." (That is, Big Hog from the *Essex* fighter director: One unknown aircraft, probably enemy, is at 15,000 feet. Steer 350 degrees, magnetic, and proceed at high speed.)

"Judah, this is Big Hog. Wilco. Out." (*Essex* fighter director from Big Hog: I understand and will comply. End of transmission.)

We all bent on combat power, swung to the 350-degree magnetic heading (roughly north-northwest), and began climbing to 18,000 feet. Shortly, sooner than I expected, I heard myself yelling on the radio, "This is Big Hog. Tallyho! One Tony, eleven o'clock, twenty degrees down. Out."

If I had not spotted the huge red ball on its wing, I never would have guessed that the airplane I saw was one of the newly deployed Imperial Army fighters. The Kawasaki Ki-61 fighter looked almost exactly like our own P-51 Mustang fighter, and nothing like any of the Zero variants that had dominated Japanese fighter operations in the region from August 1942 onward. If I had not spent long hours beside the troops poring over aircraft identification tables, I never would have known he was a Tony. I might have guessed that he was a Messerschmitt Me-109, a mistake other Allied pilots had made since the Ki-61 had entered combat over New Guinea in April 1943.

Rechecking—for the fourth time—that individual gun selectors and the armament master switch were on and that all my guns were charged, I dived to intercept the lone enemy fighter. The Imperial Army pilot—a completely unknown quantity—saw us coming and desperately slanted for a nearby cumulus head. But he had all the prospects of a mouse at a cat ranch. I flamed him just in time, barely an instant ahead of the enormous and bloodthirsty talent approaching from up my slipstream.

"Judah, this is Big Hog. Splash one Tony. Returning to station. Over."

"This is Judah. Roger. Out."

Well, that wasn't so hard. But neither was it a fair test of what the Imperial Army had to offer in the way of a challenge to our skills.

A short time after returning to the task group to circle overhead, we saw the formation of ships realign preparatory to turning into the wind. Then, with ballet precision, all the ships executed simultaneous turns to begin launch operations. If all went as planned, the carriers would be stripped of all their aircraft, the land-based Marine F4Us and New Zealand P-40s would arrive on station, and we could land to refuel and, in my case alone, rearm.

As soon as the launch was completed, the carrier formation reversed course. This was expected. The surface wind was at 15 knots from out of the north-northwest—bearing roughly from the carriers to Rabaul—so flight ops inevitably carried them ever closer, at 20 knots, to the enemy base. The task force was close enough for our purposes, certainly, but prudence dictated that they get no closer in the event the Japanese surface task force that was our primary strike target sallied to throw in a counterpunch.

At length, the two Marine F4U squadrons arrived on station to relieve us and VF-33, but the New Zealand P-40s did not. When we were set, the carriers turned back into the wind and their signal searchlights blinked out the message we had been awaiting:

- - - - -	. - - .	- . - .	- - - - -	. - - .	- . - .
Attention	P	C	Attention	P	C

which means, Attention, prepare to land aboard.

By then, the twenty-three Corsairs had formed into two flights led by Rog and me. As the searchlights blinked, Rog and I both rocked our wings to acknowledge and rapidly led our flights down to 5,000 feet, Rog's twelve toward *Essex* and my eleven toward *Bunker Hill*. John Kelly's twelve F6Fs were doing the same toward *Independence*. As the ships swung full into the wind, I led my troops down *Bunker Hill*'s starboard side, the three divisions strung out in right echelon formation with hooks down. Before the carrier's lights could flash "Land Aboard" (-.-. or "C"), I was already on my final approach, well into the groove. Dead ahead, Catwalk Cummings was holding his arms and paddles straight out from his shoulders—"Roger"—indicating that I was heading for the stern ramp in perfect attitude, speed, and height. As I crossed over the ramp, Catwalk signaled "Cut." It was 0830, precisely.

Here, as on *Essex,* Fighting-17 provided textbook perfect landings—good tight intervals, no wave-offs, no hairy passes, no blown tires. I was proud. Most of my pilots had never even *seen* a steamboat until nine months before this, and none of us had landed on one for about two months. If ever there was a question about the Corsair's suitability for carrier ops—or ours—we laid it to rest that morning.

We received a measure more than a royal welcome aboard *Bunker Hill*. The flight deck crewmen were beaming as we taxied forward to park, and they gave us ebullient thumbs-up signs or clasped their hands over their heads. I received huge grins and fervent handshakes from Captain Ballentine and his exec, Cdr Swede Ekstrom. I did not even have to put the arm on the air boss, Cdr Kit Carson, to collect the ten-buck wager I had attached to a parting boast that Fighting-17 would see combat before any part of the *Bunker Hill* air group; Kit paid up as soon as he saw me. I doubt if anyone topside or on the hangar deck missed seeing or commenting on the red-and-white meatball flags painted beneath the canopy rails of many of our Hogs. Each flag denoted a kill. My kill of that morning was painted on while Big Hog was below getting checked out and refueled.

Hedrick & Company got an equally enthusiastic but less personal welcome aboard *Essex,* as did John Kelly's troops aboard *Independence.* As soon as Rog landed aboard the flagship, he was summoned to the flag bridge to brief Admiral Montgomery and his staff. His final comment: "From what we've seen in our two weeks down here, you can expect that the Japs will throw everything they can get airborne into a counterstrike. My estimate is that they'll be here at 1300."

As it turned out, the enemy was thirteen minutes late.

We used the interval to lay below for dreamy hot showers, I in the skipper's in-port cabin, which came complete with a steward serving delicious, well-made coffee. Once clean, all hands were ushered to the wardroom for a deftly served repast of fresh grapefruit, steak, eggs (the real thing!) cooked to order, hot toast, and good coffee. All this and sparkling white tablecloths and linen napkins; courteous, smiling stewards; and seconds and thirds of everything. As we stuffed ourselves, ship's officers swarmed in to hear our best sea stories—some of which were even true. As I felt more and more like the country bumpkin just come from out of the hills to visit rich relatives, I found it increasingly hard to believe that I had been part of this friendly, well-off tribe until only two months earlier. Fantasy briefly suggested that some—maybe all—of our pilots would find reasons to stay aboard, and I briefly regretted that only twenty-three of us out of forty had been awarded this delightful respite.

Our fling with the good life came to an early but necessary end as we were ordered to man the fighter ready room. When we arrived, the teletype connected to the Combat Information Center clanked out the first message, a heartwarmer which read, "Welcome home, Fighting-17." Then we got down to business. The teletype hammered out the current tactical situation—clear radar screens, Marine fighters on station overhead, our launch time set at 1030. There was no word yet from the strike group, which we all took to be good news. A yellow-jerseyed flight-deck coordinator arrived with a diagram of our takeoff spot plus word from the flight-deck officer that all planes, which had been completely reserviced, rearmed, and mechanically checked out, were ready for takeoff.

All the ships of Task Group 50.3 were at Readiness Condition II—all battle stations partially manned, guns loaded with live ammunition, and plenty of ready-service ammunition on hand. The ships were also opened up to provide plenty of relatively cool fresh air to internal compartments. All hands who could be spared were eating hot meals, showering, changing clothes, doing what they could to relieve tension. Nevertheless, all the ships were within mere seconds of being at Condition I—full combat readiness, all guns and battle stations fully manned, and all spaces buttoned up tight for complete watertight and damage-control integrity.

The twenty-three VF-17 fighters and twelve VF-33 fighters were launched beginning at 1030. We immediately climbed to 25,000 feet to relieve the high Marine Corsair squadron while John Kelly's F6Fs relieved the other Marine squadron at 20,000. The Marine aircraft shoved off toward their bases in the islands.

I had no sooner gotten airborne than my previously troublesome radio transmitter crapped out again. I desperately wanted to retain control of my flight, but I now had no way to communicate anything except basic instructions by visual signals, and even that only when the formations were close aboard. As soon as we reached patrol altitude, I reluctantly passed the lead of my flight to Chuck Pillsbury. Also, as soon as we got on station, three of our pilots— Tom Killefer from my flight and two others from Hedrick's— reported by radio that they were experiencing mechanical or ordnance malfunctions. Chuck ordered the three back to Ondongo. Thus, together with the Hog that had aborted over Ondongo, we were down to two unbalanced ten-plane flights.

The weather, which had been beautifully clear, remained so in the carriers' operating area. As the morning wore on, the usual cumulonimbus buildups started forming to the north and west. By noon, some topped 35,000 feet with bases as low as 1,000 feet. They did not form a solid front; the gaps were wide open over what amounted to about one-third of the sky.

The friendly strike bombers and fighters began returning well after noon. There was to have been a second strike, as soon as the bombers and carrier fighters could be refueled and rearmed, but at the last minute Admiral Montgomery decided to concentrate on getting his fighters back up to challenge any possible Japanese counterstrike. The task group's Hellcats had been sent on ahead of the bombers as soon as the strike group was well clear of Japanese aircraft activity. Using their superior speed, the Hellcats arrived home early, landed, and were readied for relaunch on an urgent basis.

Meanwhile, we were very much on the *qui vive* for Japanese attack aircraft that might have followed them home, but neither we nor the ship-based radar found anything. Unbeknownst to us, however, Japanese snoopers were almost certainly at work in the cloud cover. These no doubt guided in the expected strong Japanese counterstrike, for at 1300, when about a quarter of our own strike aircraft had yet to land, the routine chatter on the radio was stilled by, "All fighters. This is Judah. Many bogies. Bearing three-five-oh. Angels three to twenty-five. Distance thirty, closing. Vector three-five-oh. Buster.'' Hedrick's estimate to Admiral Montgomery was only minutes off.

Apparently, interference from the thunderstorms had masked the radar returns from both the snoopers and the incoming strike. The counterstrike was right on top of us, only 30 miles out and closing fast at high speed. There was neither time nor adequate information for other than blanket fighter direction, no time to deploy to optimum advantage.

From 25,000 feet, the scene was idyllic, peaceful. A sparkling azure sea accentuated the bright white comet tails left by the twelve toy ships. As we fire-walled our throttles and swung north to intercept as far from the ships as possible, I looked down at the carriers and saw that all three were frantically catapulting fighters at minimum possible intervals. It made me feel great in the face of unknown opposition that the carrier F6F squadrons were top-notch. The three Hellcat skippers were good leaders as well as close friends—LCdr Flip Torrey, my old prep schoolmate, had *Essex*'s Fighting-9; LCdr Sam Silber, formerly of Opa-Locka, had *Bunker Hill*'s Fighting-18; and Lt Harry Harrison, another Miami alumnus, had *Independence*'s VF-22.

Pillsbury led our ten-plane flight to the east of the huge thunderhead that was between the ships and Rabaul, and Hedrick sheered left into the clear alleyway to the west of it. I lost sight of our ships as the first of their Hellcats steered north and slanted up, each trailing the distinctive faint black smoke of an engine running at full bore.

We were only a few minutes out from the carriers when the radio opened up with simultaneous sighting reports from Jim Streig and Teeth Burriss.

''This is Jimbo. Tallyho! Thirty Zekes, angels twenty. Twenty-five Vals, angels eighteen. Eleven o'clock.''

''This is Teeth. Tallyho! Thirty-five Zekes, angels eighteen. Fifteen Kates, angels fifteen. Twelve o'clock.''

These were about the last intelligible transmissions I heard since there was only one frequency in use and it immediately became jammed with other sighting reports, battle cries, war whoops, rebel yells, warnings, boasts, and other assorted junk transmissions.

* * *

I had a fleeting look at John Kelly's Hellcats boring in after the Vals while Pillsbury led our flight into the first enemy formation, a gaggle of about twenty-five Zeros.

As Pillsbury moved to set up a high-side run, I broke my three—me, Gutenkunst, and Streig—to port to gain position over the lead Zero foursome. I half-rolled inverted to start my dive and lined up directly on the formation leader. I was still out of range when he saw me and snapped into a split-S to his left. At the same time, his wingman honked around in a tight level right turn, setting up to nail me with a beautifully executed vertical scissors. The only thought that registered was, These guys are *good!* I kept after my target, ignoring the wingman, who expected to reverse his turn and get on my tail. This time, however, Gutenkunst and Streig peeled off from my wing to go after the wingman. Hah! Jimbo flamed him, our first kill of the afternoon. (Streig subsequently got another kill and damaged a Zeke and a Hamp.)

I was sure that I could easily bag the opposing fighter leader, so I left my wingmen behind and followed the Zeke down. He violently twisted and turned as we screamed out of the heavens. It was dogma that the Zeke's ailerons got unusually stiff at very high speeds, but I saw no evidence of that as the nimble fighter kept a step or two away from my gunsight pipper. To the contrary, at my own high speed, *my* ailerons overbalanced and I needed to maintain a light but firm touch to avoid going into an uncontrollable wing roll. I was making little progress catching up and I thought I might lose him altogether, so I fired a desperation burst from 500 yards. My passing tracer, which was not concentrated enough at long range, caused him to execute an abrupt radical pullout from his dive; his wingtips were streaming water vapor as he pulled six gees or more. I believed I was finally getting some rounds into him as I honked back hard to try to keep my pipper apace of the rapidly increasing deflection. However, his tighter turning circle pulled him out of my sights despite my own gut-wrenching pullout. He disappeared into the cloud, undoubtedly shaken but by no means defeated.

As I flattened out at 2,500 feet, I became extremely angry with myself. What an amateurish performance! Not only had I failed to kill the Zero, I had allowed him to suck me out of the battle, and I was all alone to boot. The old pro had really boobed it.

My windshield and canopy were densely fogged by condensation, a near-constant hazard of diving from cold high altitudes to moist, warm low altitudes. I could see only to the sides and rear. As I could not reach the windscreen to wipe the condensation clear with my hands, I made a beeline for the nearest cloud, opened the canopy, and stooged around in the murk until the moisture evaporated. All the while, my radio receiver gave out an absolute babble: "Look out, Joe!" and "Wow!" and "Where are you, Sam?" and "Jeez, look at that flamer!"

When I finally stuck my nose out of the soup, my head was swiveling in all directions. The first item of interest was a flight of six Tonys at four o'clock. They were 5,000 feet above me and all too close aboard. The leader immediately rolled to his left, starting a dive in my direction. I convulsively flipped Big Hog left into a tight, tight diving turn, a terrified effort to get back into the cloud before he opened fire. I know I hunched my head into my shoulders and pressed hard into the seatback, for I fully expected to hear the impact of a sheet of final bullets. I did not release my breath until I was long seconds into the protecting cloud.

I have no idea how long I circled inside the lovely cumulus, and I cared not at all about who or what might be in there with me. Eventually, I quit shaking and got my heart rate and blood pressure back under control. Eventually, I decided that the Tonys had certainly shoved off in search of another patsy.

Screwing up my courage, I eased the speed back up to 200 knots. Then out I went, hopeful I would find no more threatening hostiles. Indeed! Two F4Us were close aboard at nine o'clock, right at my level, about 300 yards out. At once, I saw gun flashes erupt at the leading edges of the leader's wings.

BAM-BAM-BAM!

Anguish and concern written all over his face, Rog Hedrick pulled up beside me to the left. After closely inspecting Big Hog, Rog shook his head and passed a questioning thumbs-up sign—was I okay? To my right, Mills Schanuel did much the same as I rapidly actuated various controls and scanned the gauges to check for damage. All apparently was okay. Rog later told me that he had shagged an enemy fighter into the cloud seconds before I emerged at just the spot he thought we would find his quarry. Rog's was a beautiful full deflection shot; he had put three .50-caliber bullets just behind the armor plate behind my seat and three through the engine accessory section, between the engine and fuel tank. Fortunately, Big Hog had been inside the convergence distance of his guns. Otherwise, those six rounds would have gone through me.

The view from the surface on up to 25,000 feet was almost beyond belief. The whole hemisphere of sky was polka-dotted with black 5-inch shell bursts interlaced with colorful 20mm and 40mm tracer. Here and there, dark-tailed orange comets marked the passage of burning airplanes as they arced toward the cobalt surface. Around the twisting ships, bomb and shell spouts heaved up spectacular white geysers. Through it all, planes rolled and turned with sunlight glinting off their flat surfaces and contrails streaming off their wingtips as they executed maximum-gee high-speed pullouts, some right on the deck. The scream of overrevving engines and props was punctuated with the *whomp*s of bombs, guns, and shells, plus the staccato *rat-a-tat* of machine guns. It was Technicolor bedlam, and then some.

An exchange of hand signals with Rog revealed that he, like me, had only 75 gallons of fuel aboard. Schanuel had about the same. I signaled that I was heading for home, and Rog signaled his smiling assent. We had tooled around for nearly three hours before the battle and had used up huge quantities of fuel during our high-speed jousting; we had enough for the flight home but too little to get in any more fighting. I had a kill, and so did Rog. Enough was enough.

* * *

As I peeled out of the original flight formation to go after the Zeros with my trio, Chuck Pillsbury had gone in way too fast and had thus thrown the rest of the formation out of balance. He missed his target, but his two wingmen, Ens Hal Jackson and Ens Bob Hogan, each flamed a Zero.

As soon as Teeth Burriss tallyhoed the gaggle of Kates and their formidable fighter cover, Rog Hedrick positioned his division—himself, Ens Mills Schanuel, Lt(jg) Andy Anderson, and Lt(jg) Jack Chasnoff—for a high-side run against the lead Zeke division's port quarter, which was holding course at Rog's ten o'clock. At the same time, Lt Timmy Gile—followed by Ens Danny Cunningham, Lt(jg) Paul Cordray, and Ens Brad Baker—crossed ahead of the Japanese formation to set up for a close follow-on from the enemy's starboard quarter. Also at the same time, Lt Thad Bell and his division—Ens Teeth Burriss, Ens Ike Kepford, and Lt Lem Cooke—slanted in to hit the Kates with a horizontal pass from the targets' port side. This all added up to a nice bit of unrehearsed headwork by the two division leaders following Hedrick's lead.

Hedrick scored an immediate kill against the first Zeke that turned up in his gunsight, and Anderson and Chasnoff—number three and number four behind him—opened fire so close together on another Zero that they were not sure which of them hit it. They thus shared credit for a damaged Zeke.

Timmy Gile's tigers, attacking from the starboard side, met with about the same success. Brad Baker registered a clean kill when his target exploded in midair. Paul Cordray saw his target shedding big chunks of metal, but, when last seen, the smoking Zero was still flying straight and level. Paul got credit for a damaged Zeke.

Of Bell's division, only Burriss connected, a natural follow-up on his early sighting. His target, a Kate, was sent spinning out of control, trailing a huge plume of oily black smoke. Doubtless, our master of unauthorized inverted flight was displaying the toothy, mirthless, nervous grimace that had earned him his nickname.

All the rest of the Kates successfully scrambled into the

nearest thunderhead—still in perfect formation. This obliged Bell's division to reconnoiter for new targets. They headed into the AA show over the carriers and Bell bounced a group of diving Vals well before they released their bombs. Screaming up their tails, Thad quickly bagged one and then dived onto the tail of a second, which he sent skidding out of control. Score two dead Vals.

Burriss missed the Vals but he found a lone twin-engine Betty. He peeled off into an overhead run and blew off the medium bomber's port wing. Shortly, Teeth found a lonesome Kate as it dropped down to begin its torpedo run on one of the ships. As he set up his firing run, a Hellcat zoomed in from out of nowhere and went after Teeth's target. Their combined competitive fire sent the Kate cartwheeling across the surface, and so they each got credit for a half kill.

Lt Johnny Kleinman and Ens Windy Hill, who had briefly joined on Pillsbury's trio, were shaken loose by Chuck's abrupt initial attack, so they got no rounds off at the ample targets. As Johnny and Windy pulled up from this run, they saw the big black puffs of ship-fired 5-inch AA. Reasoning correctly that the ships would not be firing at empty air, the pair dived in that direction to get in on the action. Using the AA as a beacon, they soon spotted a flight of torpedo-armed Kates nosing down and deploying in a fanlike attack formation against one of the carriers—*Bunker Hill*. Kleinman and Hill caught up with the torpeckers just above the water plumes put up by erupting 40mm and 20mm rounds from the ships.

Hill broke away from Kleinman and latched onto the first Kate he could reach. He opened fire as he flew straight up the torpedo bomber's tail and saw flame sprout just before the Kate knifed into the water, torpedo and all. Then Windy wisely decided to remove himself from within the only marginally friendly AA umbrella.

After damaging his first Kate target, Johnny Kleinman also drilled into the welter of AA while chasing another Kate. According to Cdr J. C. Shaw, *Bunker Hill*'s gunnery officer, "I saw a Kate about twenty feet off the water dart by the formation with a Corsair closing fast. Like a cowboy roping a wild steer, the Corsair sent tracers licking out, and the Kate went in with an awesome splash." Johnny killed the Kate, but in the process a friendly 20mm round exploded on contact with his heavy glass bullet-proof windscreen. Blood coursing from many painful facial wounds created a red mist before Johnny's eyes that made flying an extremely difficult chore. He had tiny cuts all over his face, but his goggles had saved his eyes. As soon as he thought of it, he regained his vision by pulling the goggles up to his bleeding forehead. Not unreasonably, Johnny pointed his Corsair's nose for home. And, not unreasonably, his plane captain registered a terrified grimace when first he saw Johnny grinning broadly through the bloody mess of his face. The wounds proved to be superficial, and all quickly healed without appreciably marring Johnny's good looks.

Timmy Gile also bounced the Kates at low level. He caught up with one of them just as it made a bad drop—the fish porpoised and veered sharply from its target. This loner flew doggedly for home just above waves foamed by bullets from Timmy's guns, many of which undoubtedly passed through the Kate. At length, the stubborn torpedo bomber dropped its nose and flew straight into the next wave.

With that, Timmy got his division joined and headed for home. A short distance from the carriers, Brad Baker handsignaled that his fuel state was perilously low, so Timmy set course for Empress Augusta Bay, where there was a chance of finding friendly ships to pick Brad up in case he had to ditch. Timmy was able to raise Cocker Base, the Torokina fighter director, on his voice radio. The FDO alerted the local search-and-rescue forces. Brad's prop started windmilling when the division was still a good 20 miles from the beachhead. Timmy and the others were also getting low on fuel, so they only hung around until they were sure Brad was safely out of the ditched fighter. Within minutes, a PBY touched down and scooped Brad out of the water, good as new. He was flown to Munda, checked out by the medicos, and returned to Ondongo in time for supper.

Like Kleinman, Ike Kepford drilled right on through the intense friendly AA to burn a Kate just as it seemed ready to launch its fish only 1,000 yards from *Bunker Hill*. Unlike Johnny, however, Ike evaded the friendly fire. However, at the same moment he was killing the Kate, and unbeknownst to Ike, a Hellcat blew a Zero off *his* tail.

Ike emerged from the shoreward side of the AA umbrella and decided to call it a day because he was getting low on fuel. He shaped course for Ondongo and cracked his cockpit canopy so he could dry his sweat-soaked coveralls and enjoy a relaxing smoke. He was just lighting up when he happened to see an unchallenged flight of six Vals on course for Rabaul. Ike flipped his smoke over the side, closed and locked the canopy, and went to General Quarters. He flamed three of the slower dive-bombers in quick succession as the virtually helpless quarry stayed bunched together to share the meager protection of their rear-firing 7.7mm machine guns. Ike was scoring hits on the fourth Val when he expended the last of his ammunition.

As Ike broke away from the surviving Vals, he noted that his fuel gauge was bouncing on "Empty." Estimating he had less than thirty minutes' flying time left, and 150 miles from the nearest runway, Ike felt that his only recourse was to get back aboard one of the carriers. Fortunately, by then, the extreme clutter on the fighter frequency had died down, so Ike called the *Essex*-based fighter director: "Judah, this is Ike in [airplane number] Seventeen Fox Twenty-nine. Do you read? Over."

"Ike, this is Judah. Five square. Send your message. Over."

"This is Ike. I'm low state. Request steer and immediate pancake. Over."

"This is Judah. Roger. Steer two-eight-oh. Distance twenty. You'll get 'Charlie' by flashing light from whoever can take you. Acknowledge."

"This is Ike. Thanks. Wilco. Out."

Quick translation: Ike had asked Judah if they could hear him and Judah had replied they could hear and understand him perfectly ("five square"). Then Ike had told Judah he was short on fuel ("low state") and had asked for a course and permission to land aboard ("pancake"). Judah had given him a course and distance to the ship (they had him on their radar) and had told him that he would get a flashed searchlight signal—letter *C* for "Charlie"—from the first carrier that could take him.

As promised, *Bunker Hill* trained one of her signal lights on Ike as soon as the Corsair hove into sight. The Charlie signal (- . - .) was repeated until Ike was in the groove, coming up the carrier's wake toward the stern ramp. When Ike shut down the Hog forward of the barrier, it had 5 gallons of avgas aboard.

Ike was treated to a huge hearty hello and welcome aboard from all hands as he climbed out of his smoke- and oil-stained fighter. As far as *Bunker Hill*'s crew was concerned, he represented all the brave land-based fighter pilots who had helped save their ship from the Japanese attackers. Ike was instantly escorted to the bridge, where a beaming Capt John Ballentine boomed, "Welcome home, Ike. *Bunker Hill* thanks you and the rest of Fighting-Seventeen. I doubt that we'd have made it without your help. Anything we have is yours. What would you like?"

This set Ike back on his heels. It was a real thrill, second only to the realization that he had scored four sure kills. The fact that he, a mere ensign, was getting the royal treatment from this venerable, respected four-striper was almost too much. "Er, I could use some coffee, sir." Seconds later, Ike accepted a steaming cup directly from the skipper's hand. Ike next asked that he be allowed to fly off to the beach to rejoin the squadron. Captain Ballentine eagerly assented and, after enjoying a relaxing half-hour respite, Ike catapulted off in his refueled, rearmed, and fully checked-out Hog. Ensign Kepford clocked the squadron's high score—four kills and one damaged—and the high flight time—eleven hours—for the day.

* * *

In all, VF-17 was credited with 18.5 confirmed kills and 7 damaged Japanese warplanes. However, our evening celebration was severely muted by the mysterious disappearance of Ens Windy Hill.

But Windy was far from gone. After scoring his first kill on the Kate and threading his way apparently untouched through Task Group 50.3's shower of steel, Ensign Hill found himself all alone on the east side of the battle. His gas gauge indicated there was only enough fuel aboard to get him back to Ondongo if he used an economical power setting. As he turned for home, he was pleasantly startled to see Chuck Pillsbury's Corsair overtake him. Both pilots were happy to have company for a long and anxious reach for friendly territory.

Hill's engine started cutting out northwest of the Treasury Islands. He radioed Chuck that he was apparently out of gas and that Chuck should not be a damn fool and stick around. Chuck knew he could do nothing to help Windy, so he sensibly nursed his Hog to Ondongo, where refueling required all but three gallons of his Corsair's total capacity. Chuck reported the coordinates at which he believed Windy had had to ditch.

Hill stayed airborne for ten additional agonizing minutes. His engine kept cutting in and out, but he maintained enough lift to keep him aloft 20 miles farther toward the Treasuries. When his engine sounded its final cough, the islands were close aboard. Following the adventure of ditching and escaping from his rapidly sinking Corsair, Windy took stock of his situation as he bobbed mostly above the surface in his Mae West life jacket.

Windy knew of our October 27 invasion of the Treasuries, but he was by no means sure that the island near him was yet in friendly hands. Thus, he did not yet want to risk greater visibility from the beach by deploying his life raft, which remained reassuringly attached to his Mae West by means of a stout lanyard. Soon, however, he found that he was tiring rapidly from the weight of his survival gear, so he reluctantly inflated the raft and climbed aboard.

Minutes later, Windy saw a ragged-looking figure appear

from out of the bush at the beachline. He was sure it was a Japanese soldier. The stranger spotted the raft and waved, but Windy lay doggo. The potential adversary waved both arms and then sent a message in semaphore: "Help is on the way."

It was, according to Windy, "the only time in my life I was able to read semaphore."

Shortly thereafter, a PT boat roared up and hauled our happy warrior aboard. Windy was turned over to the New Zealanders at Mono Island's Blanche Harbor, where he spent a recreational four days until he was picked up by a PBY on its way from the Torokina beachhead to Munda—with VAdm Bill Halsey aboard.

Somehow, word of Windy's rescue did not reach Ondongo. Of course, intensive searches the next day at Windy's last known position proved fruitless. We had sadly given up long before Windy walked into the squadron ready room. Windy's adventure made for a good story the first time he told it. It was even good the second time. But Windy gummed the tale literally to boredom and death until all hands began giving him a wide berth.

The Battle of the Solomon Sea, as the November 11 imbroglio came to be called, was a bag of mixed results in which the combined might of our carrier- and land-based air groups did more damage to Japanese powers of perception than it did, in fact, to Japanese planes and ships.

The original plan had envisaged an initial antishipping attack on Rabaul's Simpson Harbor by New Guinea–based 5th Air Force bombers, immediately followed by successive strikes from our two carrier task forces, immediately followed by a strike by AirSols B-24s.

Bad weather over New Guinea caused all but thirteen of the 5th Air Force B-24s to abort. The results of the leadoff strike were, if anything, marginal.

RAdm Forrest Sherman's superb Task Force 38—*Saratoga* and *Princeton*—arrived on station at the right time and launched thirty-six F6Fs, twenty-three SBDs, and fifteen TBFs while several land-based fighter squadrons flew CAP over the ships. The strike group flew into bad weather over Rabaul, but that was the least of the problems, for the earlier B-24 strike had fully alerted the defenders. Antiaircraft defenses were at maximum alert. The bombers sighted only one light cruiser and four destroyers through holes in the cloud cover. The attack was conducted under the worst possible conditions; the air was full of antiaircraft rounds and the targets were obscured. Hits were claimed, but the extent of damage inflicted, if any, was neither adequately nor accurately observed.

The 165-plane strike from Task Group 50.3 arrived about an hour after the Task Force 38 strike departed. Once again, the weather at Simpson Harbor was rainy, and the antiaircraft fire was enthusiastic. This time, numerous Japanese fighters were vectored in to engage the attackers. A total of seven of our fighters, three of our dive-bombers, and three of our torpedo bombers were downed, but our bombers claimed two destroyers sunk and several other Japanese warships damaged, and our pilots and gunners claimed thirty-five Japanese aircraft downed.

The final element of the attack, forty-two AirSols B-24s, arrived on schedule, just as the Task Group 50.3 bombers were leaving. As before, the results of the high-altitude drop through heavy clouds were negligible, if that.

A second series of carrier strikes had been requested by Admiral Halsey, but Sherman's Task Force 38 was obliged to withdraw early because several of the escorting destroyers were low on fuel. Montgomery's Task Group 50.3 had been in the process of simultaneously recovering and refueling—and preparing to relaunch—strike aircraft when the Japanese counterstrike arrived. Frantic efforts to clear the carriers eventually got a total of sixty-four Hellcats aloft before the Vals and Kates arrived and obliged the carriers to take evasive action. Also, twenty-three TBFs from the first strike were aloft, their landings having been delayed by the Japanese attack. They merely flew out of range until the action died down.

Aerial combat, particularly over ships firing their own guns all out, is confusing, to say the least. And the results are confusing. Overzealous pilots tend to claim kills for every burst fired, and there is a marked tendency by each of the crews of competing warships to count shared kills as their own. For whatever reasons, claims of kills over embattled warships are usually inflated and, at best, should be taken with a degree of skepticism. In all on November 11, over Rabaul and over Task Group 50.3, our planes and ships turned in claims for 111 confirmed kills. Postwar searches through Japanese records turned up confirmation for less than 50, including several torpedo-laden Bettys knocked down by Task Group 50.3 Hellcats after dark. I nevertheless stand behind Fighting-17's claim of 18.5 kills.

Despite the mixed and questionable physical results of the November 11 raids and the wild defense of Task Group 50.3, the Japanese regional high command was severely shaken. Whether the losses they suffered in ships and planes were as high as we claim or as low as they recorded, the fact that we had five carrier air groups, numerous heavy bombers, and so many artfully employed land-based fighter squadrons to devote to a spoiling raid on their fortress-like main base came as an awesome shock. Their resolve fell away, utterly. Far from reinforcing Rabaul, the Japanese *withdrew* their carrier air groups, which had been all but obliterated in two weeks of constant action. The Imperial Navy also withdrew their Rabaul-based warships to distant, safer Truk Lagoon. The enemy never again used Rabaul as a base for his men-o'-war. Thus, the November 11 strikes, serving as the culmination of a two-week struggle for hegemony over the Torokina beachhead, resulted in a decisive capitulation of the Japanese to the will of the Allies. A step taken at great peril to our own forces and long-range plans resulted in the virtual evaporation of the means by which the Japanese could reverse the trend of defeat followed by defeat in the Solomons campaign. Moreover, the total price we paid in ships, airplanes, and lives for so complete a psychological victory was astoundingly, gratifyingly low. This was of major strategic importance, for it opened the way for the Allied thrust westward into the Marianas and beyond.

In all, between October 27 and November 11, the Japanese carrier squadrons based at Rabaul lost forty-three of eighty-two Zekes, thirty-eight of forty-five Vals, and thirty-four of forty Kates. This, in addition to numerous other losses among land-based Army and Navy squadrons. This destruction all but finished the job our carrier pilots had begun in the Coral Sea in May 1942. From then, through Midway in June, at Eastern Solomons in August, and especially at Santa Cruz in October 1942, our side had gutted the solid core of first-team professionals manning the Japanese carrier air groups. Along the way, over islands from Guadalcanal to New Georgia to Bougainville to Rabaul herself, our land-based fighters had destroyed the core of the Imperial Navy's land-based air groups. Beginning in early November 1943, we started to work on the Imperial Army's air force. We won no clear operational aerial victory during the Solomon Sea battle itself, but we certainly drove a long way toward capping the victory in our ongoing war of attrition, for we could replace our losses in men and airplanes while the Japanese could not.

We did not perceive it at the time—though we might have had we looked hard enough—but the Solomons air campaign had been decided. After November 11, 1943, the Japanese were unable—or unwilling—to wage more than a rearguard holding action, a meager attempt to put off the inevitable for . . . what? A miracle?

18

• • • • • • • • • • •

Fighting-17 had a lot going on besides flying and fighting. Our return from carrier duty after the Solomon Sea battle marked the end of our first two weeks in the forward area, a good time to assess the squadron's gains and losses.

On the loss side, so far, was one missing pilot, Lt(jg) Johnny Keith. He was never found. We had also lost several airplanes, all to enemy fire. That was all.

On the plus side of the ledger, we had received credit for destroying 28.5 Japanese airplanes and damaging 18 others. None of us had achieved ace status—5 confirmed kills—but several of us were closing on the mark. Ike Kepford and I were tied for leader with 4 kills each. Jim Streig and Teeth Burriss each had 2.5, and a handful had 2 apiece. Counting his 2 kills early in the war with Fighting-5, Johnny Kleinman had 3. Given the tempo of the action in late 1943—moderate —we were doing as well as or better than most other land-based fighter squadrons in the area.

In addition to the problem I had had with the reluctant ensign, it was becoming clear that the stresses and strains of our heavy schedule were wearing down several other pilots. One contributing factor, I believe, was that our mail did not catch up to us until around the time we got back from carrier duty. I was sure that that had an all-around negative effect, particularly on worried young men far from home for the first time in their lives. (We oldsters suffered, too. My wife had always been a lukewarm letter writer, at best, and getting just a few brief missives from her rankled. By way of comparison, I found many letters in that first batch from a young widow whose husband had been killed during our training period. I had never been a completely faithful husband, and the comparison under stress inclined to make me less so—as soon as I got the opportunity.)

One of our pilots who had done fairly well to that point somehow shot himself in the hand. This posed a rugged dilemma. Self-inflicted wounds occurred all too often in the armed forces, and they elicited draconian consequences—up to and including prison sentences—if intent was proved. In this case, I did much soul-searching and discussed the matter at length with Duke Henning and our flight surgeon— and ad hoc psychiatrist—Lyle Herrmann. Our consensus was that the wound indeed had been accidental, so we kept the matter in the family. This pilot did okay in our second combat tour.

One of the men who was not doing at all well by the two-week point was Sunny Jim Halford, who was hardly sunny anymore. He and Johnny Kleinman had never been particularly hot on the idea of another combat tour, but they had performed well, no doubt helped by the promise that they could go home immediately upon the squadron's relief for our first R&R leave. (Typically, land-based squadrons flew for six-week intervals separated by a lengthy break in the rear area.) It must be said that neither of them broached the matter; they hung in there. But Halford became increasingly and noticeably grimmer with each passing day. Finally, he aborted a routine CAP hop with the complaint of extreme nausea. Dr. Herrmann could find nothing physically wrong with Jim, but I felt that a psychosomatic illness was no less real than an authentic bug. I decided to send Jim home as soon as possible. And, since I had made the same commitment to Johnny Kleinman, I felt that it would be only fair to send him, too. Johnny was never happy about being in the forward area again, but even after he returned with his horribly bloodied face on November 11, he insisted upon carrying his share of the burden; he led his division on the thirteenth, albeit on a milk run. Much as I admired Johnny, and wanted him to stay, I could not muster the gall to try to con him into staying while Jim went home. I sent both of them south to Espiritu Santo on November 17, and they were both home by mid-December. I never heard from or of Jim Halford again, but I enjoyed lively and frequent correspondence with Johnny until his death in a senseless Training Command crash the following spring.

Duke Henning's fertile brain, plus our mutual disdain for some of the sillier aspects of "security," produced a useful if somewhat illegal means for getting our personnel aboard transport planes with high priority. Duke would draft and our yeoman would type orders for my signature, each beginning with the magic clause, "In accordance with highly classified instructions which cannot be quoted herein, the bearer will proceed . . ." Of course, the "highly classified" was our cover for sending someone somewhere to get some booze or, nearly as often, a spare part we could not acquire through normal channels. No one ever questioned it. We used it to get Halford and Kleinman back to Espiritu Santo without their having to wait for "space available." I was afraid to pull this dodge to get them all the way back to the States without inordinate delays because their pay status depended on honest-to-goodness transfer orders.

One of my early edicts resulted in my publicly walking back the cat. In early November, via ACIO channels, we got word that the other squadrons in the area had heard of my order, "Claim only confirmed kills; to hell with 'probable' and 'damaged' garbage." It turned out that the word was going around that Fighting-17 would claim a kill for *every* enemy airplane we believed we had hit. Thereafter, we conformed to the accepted reporting system.

* * *

I was frequently summoned to Munda to work with the Fighter Command staff, so I soon developed rapport with the people who made things go in our bailiwick. The boss, Col Oscar Brice, was an honest-to-God Southern gentleman whose wrinkled leathery face and hawk nose had been dyed by liberal ingestion of corn squeezings over the years. Oscar's characteristic smile was incandescent, and his wrath was equally spectacular. The good colonel knew his business and was extremely tolerant of new approaches voiced by subordinates within his blue-ribbon command. On the other hand, he had the shortest fuse I ever witnessed when it came to alibis and pusillanimity.

Colonel Brice's right-hand man was his ACIO, Lt Joe Bryan, a Richmond native and scion of one of the First Families of Virginia. Joe's forebears had served with distinction in every American war since Braddock's March. Joe had a keen, incisive mind, a lightning sense of humor, and a handsome, aristocratic visage that was the antithesis of Oscar's. This pair always had a flagpole with the Stars and Bars in the wind to mark their headquarters as the CP of ConForSols—Confederate Forces, Solomons.

Nearly always on hand for our informal conferences was LCdr Gus Widhelm, an authentic, 24-karat dive-bomber hero now commanding VF(N)-75, the Navy's pioneer night Corsair squadron. In fact, Gus's Corsairs, which arrived at Munda in September, had been the first Navy land-based Corsair squadron to reach the forward area. No dissembler, Gus cultivated the image of a diamond in the rough. A stranger to social graces, rough as a dry corncob, he was in every way a fighting man's fighting man. He had distinguished himself early in the war at Midway and Santa Cruz, where he drove and led SBD dive-bombers. His exploits had earned him a well-deserved pair of Navy Crosses in the days before many medals lost prestige from overgenerous distribution. With a toddy or two under his belt, Gus would open a conversation with, "Did I ever tell you how I won my first Navy Cross?" From anyone else, this would have been obnoxious, but not from Gus. For him, it was like showing snapshots of the kids. VF(N)-75 spent a lot of time in "alert" status, sitting on the end of the Munda runway, so Gus and his guys frequently came over to Ondongo to fly with us and keep sharp. They were always welcomed for their skill and experience, albeit with the standing proviso that they flew the tail-end-Charlie slot—except for Gus, who flew wing on me.

To us veterans of two weeks combat, it seemed that nothing much happened in the days immediately following our exciting November 11 combat. On the twelfth, sixteen of our Corsairs were tabbed to fly close escort on a PBY carrying the South Pacific Area commander, VAdm Bill Halsey, on his first eyeball inspection of the Torokina beachhead. Also that day, thirteen of sixteen Corsairs scheduled for an escort hop rendezvoused with forty-two SBDs and twenty-four TBFs over Baga Island and escorted them on a bombing raid against Kara airfield. The mission encountered no enemy fighters, and there was not even any antiaircraft fire over the target. A milk run.

November 13, Johnny Kleinman's last day in the air with us, was used up on three negative eight-plane patrols over Empress Augusta Bay and three two-hour patrols over a damaged cruiser. We saw no enemy aircraft.

For most of us, November 14 was just as dull, with three eight-plane missions covering a small naval task unit and two eight-plane CAP missions over Munda. We also mounted a four-plane escort for a Dumbo rescue mission in the Treasury Islands. The only excitement of the day was encountered by an eight-plane flight as part of an escort for fifty-four SBDs and eight TBFs that flew through extremely bad weather to bomb antiaircraft gun positions and supply areas around Ballale. The AA opposition was intense, but none of our fighters was hit and none of the bombers was shot down.

On November 15, at the conclusion of a negative two-hour patrol over Empress Augusta Bay, Lt Chuck Pillsbury, leading his and Butch Davenport's divisions, was directed to strafe ground installations around Chabai Plantation, off

Matchin Bay. Chuck led the fighters up Bougainville's coast and about 20 miles inland, flying very low. All eight Corsairs swept across the target area in line-abreast formation—always an impressive entrance—and sprayed .50-caliber rounds at numerous antiaircraft positions and buildings the pilots assumed were barracks and storehouses. At least two buildings were left burning and at least two AA positions were silenced. After leaving Chabai, Chuck turned his division north to take on the Buka and Bonis defenses. Chuck's was the first plane across Bonis. As he turned southeast across the runway, his Corsair was hit in the left wing by a 7.7mm machine-gun bullet and, worse, a 37mm shell. Chuck's wingman, Lt Wally Schub, also took a 37mm round through the fuselage of his Corsair, albeit without serious damage. The two Corsairs following Chuck and Wally were not hit and their pilots reported no observable results. Butch Davenport's division, which had turned back south after hitting Chabai, found a 60-foot tug off Kuriki Island. The craft was high and dry on a reef, so it was easy pickings for Butch's four Corsairs, which easily set it afire.

Also on November 15, our ongoing good terms with the staff at Fighter Command briefly came to a screeching stop.

I was stooging around over Torokina, leading my flight of eight Corsairs at 20,000 feet on a typical, boring CAP. About midway through the patrol period, we spotted a flight of a half-dozen twin-engine bombers to our northwest; they were heading more or less toward us.

The local fighter director had not yet alerted anyone, but it was prudent to check it out, so we eased out for a closer look. It seemed most unlikely to any of us that the Japanese would be sending out unescorted horizontal bombers at this stage of the campaign. While still some distance out, we all saw a Hellcat execute an overhead run on the bomber formation. I also saw a formation of six or seven other Hellcats holding altitude over the bombers. The whole show was too far away for me to see precisely what was going on, but it was by then clear that the bombers were B-25s. Nobody was getting hurt, there was no need for us to be there, so I swung back to resume our station. I could not help thinking about how dopey it was for that Hellcat pilot to play grab-ass with the bombers; someone might have gotten trigger happy and the result could have been fatal. Then I gave the matter no further thought.

At the conclusion of our mission, we were ordered to strafe Chabai, but the weather on the way up was lousy, so we cut across Bougainville to scour the northeast coast for targets of opportunity. Four of us strafed a known AA position at Arawa Bay from treetop height with no observable results, and the other division strafed a building at the end of the Kieta runway, also at treetop height and also without observable results. As the entire flight swung east over the water, we came upon a 40-foot barge which was just backing off Banaru Reef. We set it afire almost as an afterthought.

On our return home, I was diverted to Munda to "report immediately to Fighter Command." I found Colonel Brice in a lather. "Tommy," he began without his usual affable preamble, "your outfit had the escort job for the B-25s we sent to Buka this afternoon." This was true; while I was over Torokina with my eight, Dirty Eddie March had been undertaking his first truly responsible job of the deployment, escorting the Buka-bound B-25s as leader of another flight of eight. I nodded. "Well, Strike Command is raising hell. The flight commander of the B-25s reported by radio that the fighters peeled off much too soon after the bomb drop and that the bombers were left exposed to an attack over Bougainville by a flight of Hamps. Luckily, they escaped damage. Tommy, you know damn well I won't tolerate this kind of performance by our fighters. You go back to Ondongo and look into this. I want an immediate report on who was responsible and how come it happened."

"Aye, aye, sir. Will do!" I bade farewell to the colonel, Lt Joe Bryan, and the CO of an F6F squadron who was also present. I was by then quite literally sick to my stomach. VF-17 had never done anything even remotely resembling this fiasco. I was prepared to have Dirty Eddie publicly hanged, drawn, and quartered—for starters.

When I confronted Lieutenant March, he recoiled in amazement. "Not so, Skipper. We stayed with those guys till they were well into the Empress Augusta Bay area. I even saw you and our other CAP before we shoved off. There were no—repeat, *no*—Japs seen, no cries for help."

"March, I can't help that . . ." I was getting wound up, but my tirade was cut short by the jangling of the field phone.

"It's for you, Skipper."

I had the rime of extreme annoyance in my voice when I answered, "This is Blackburn. What is it?"

It was Joe Bryan. "Tommy, I just got word from one of the ACIOs. One of his F6F pilots reported at debriefing that despite their best effort to stop him, his squadron skipper made a firing run on a flight of our B-25s. You're off the hook. The colonel told me to apologize to you for him."

It was obvious that the B-25 flight commander had mistaken the square-winged F6Fs for the square-winged Zero variant we called Hamp. But that did not explain how the errant F6F CO had been able to stand by listening while Colonel Brice reamed me out.

"Why," I spluttered, "that crummy son of a bitch."

"Those were the colonel's exact words before he relieved him at once and ordered him home. Colonel Brice said, and I quote, 'If he dares show his face around here, I'll kill him.' Tommy, the Old Man wasn't kidding."

For once, it was a pleasure to walk back the cat as I made peace with Dirty Eddie.

November 16 was another busy, dull day. We flew four uneventful two-hour eight-plane CAP missions over a naval transport group, a division-strength CAP over Munda, and eight-plane Dumbo escort to Empress Augusta Bay, and a four-plane search around Elo Island looking for a downed P-40 pilot. The only near-action of the day fell to divisions led by Dirty Eddie March and Timmy Gile while they were escorting a flight of sixteen SBDs against ground targets near the Jaba River. This was our first authentic mission in direct support of the Marines on the Torokina beachhead.

Unfortunately, none of our guys saw a thing as the dive-bombers made a total of six bombing and strafing runs against targets in the trees.

We were bored, bored, bored, yet tense in the ever-present face of potential combat. We knew we could never afford to dope off. Between the big day on November 11 and November 16, no AirSols pilot shot down or even encountered a Japanese warplane in daylight. The only kill was a Betty claimed at 0420 on November 13 by the crew of a Marine twin-engine PV-1 night fighter. Of course, we had no way of knowing that the depleted Japanese air groups at Rabaul had been laying low, using the last few days to gear up for a new offensive effort. Fighting-17's honeymoon was about to end.

19

. . . .

The redoubtable Rog Hedrick led the way into VF-17's next action of consequence, on November 17. His flight was composed of his own division (Mills Schanuel on his wing, as usual, and Jack Chasnoff on Andy Anderson's wing) and Timmy Gile's (Danny Cunningham on his wing and Brad Baker on Paul Cordray's wing). Every one of the eight had at least one confirmed kill to his credit.

The flight was on station at 0800, 25,000 feet above Empress Augusta Bay. At 0830, Hedrick was electrified by: "Gem Three, this is Cocker Base. Many bogeys. Angels one-five. Distance thirty from Cherryblossom [Cape Torokina]. Vector two-five-oh. Buster. Acknowledge."

"This is Gem Three. Wilco. Out."

The flight had barely turned to the new course and was angling down at 325 knots when Gile spoke up: "This is Timmy. Tallyho! Bandits at two o'clock, thirty degrees down. Twelve Zekes right over eight Kates. Over." For a change, someone had spotted some targets before hawkeye Hedrick.

"This is Rog. See 'em. Timmy, swing left forty-five. Hit Kates from high side right as soon as we're clear. Over."

"This is Timmy. Gotcha, Rog! Will do. Out."

With that, Hedrick and Schanuel hurtled in at the unalerted fighters. Rog immediately flamed the flight leader while Schanuel nailed his wingman. Both Corsairs pulled out in steep chandelles to get into position at the enemy's two o'clock—up-sun from the Japanese formation.

While Hedrick and Schanuel were delivering their attack, Anderson and Chasnoff dropped back slightly to gain some freedom for maneuver. Andy selected the left-flank fighter and opened fire just as it went into a diving turn to the left. This left Anderson mousetrapped in a horizontal scissors executed by a pair of gutty Japanese fighter veterans. His "target's" wingman sheered right and then reversed course right onto Andy's tail. Andy heard the awesome sound of bullets striking his Corsair, so he abruptly pulled up, the least likely maneuver when under attack by faster-climbing Zekes. The Japanese pair did not follow and Chasnoff joined up to check Andy's fighter for visible damage, of which, apparently, there was nothing serious. The pair headed back into the melee, but as soon as Anderson got off a long burst at a moderately distant target, he saw that his left wing was burning. With the cockpit rapidly filling with smoke, Andy desperately attempted to slow to 300 knots so he could safely bail out. No joy there, so he flipped inverted, kicked free, bounced off the horizontal stabilizer, and fell to 1,000 feet before his chute blossomed.

Meantime, Chasnoff boresighted a Zeke coming down on Andy's tail. Trailing smoke all the way, the Japanese fighter commenced a vertical plunge all the way into the water. Without missing a beat, Jack went after Anderson's original target as soon as Anderson's burning F4U broke off. A quiet, studious, shy young man, Jack Chasnoff was transmuted into a berserker by the apparent loss of his friend. He coldly withheld his fire until he was so close to the Zeke that the cloud of slugs he transmitted simply shredded the fighter into an expanding puff of incandescent bits and pieces—nothing big enough to damage the Corsair as it barreled straight through the mess. Frigidly calm, Jack tilted his nose to see Andy splashing in, apparently uninjured.

As the lead Corsair team chandelled into the sun, Schanuel

lost sight of Hedrick thanks to a badly oil-smeared windscreen. After sensibly peeling out to prevent a rear-ender, Mills found himself all alone in the great blue sky. This was a weird but typical outcome of high-speed maneuvering in combat; one second, the sky is filled with dodging, twisting airplanes, and the next it is completely empty. Following long moments of anxious, thorough scanning, Mills prudently turned for home, for, all alone, he was easy meat.

Meantime, Rog had seen the Anderson-Chasnoff brannigan and he, too, searched high and low for Schanuel. Fearing the worst—he had seen Anderson bail out—he dived past Chasnoff and signaled "Join up." By then, for them too, the sky appeared to be completely at peace. Heartsick and despairing of two apparent losses, the pair touched down at 1045. They found that Schanuel had gotten in minutes earlier, unhurt but also fearing the worst.

Timmy Gile's attack in the torpedo bombers was equally aggressive. Though Timmy and Danny Cunningham apparently missed on their pass, Paul Cordray, the second-element leader, blew his Kate away with just a short burst. Both pairs lost sight of the evading Kates during their pullouts, so they climbed to 12,000 feet and headed north.

"Tallyho!" Cunningham had something! "Ten fighters headed this way at twelve o'clock, twenty degrees down."

Gile completed three overhead passes in quick succession and Danny, who somehow clung to his tail through strenuous maneuvering, counted three definite flamers. By the time Timmy came around for a fourth attack, the sky was empty and Cordray and Baker were out of sight. Timmy coolly led Cunningham back to their patrol station and circled over the bay for another hour. It's a wonder neither had a coronary due to the rapid deceleration from top-flight excitement to sheer boredom.

As Gile whistled into his first attack on the lead threesome of the six Zekes and four Tonys, Cordray and Baker went after a Tony on the west flank. Cordray missed and pulled up with a pair of Tonys on his tail. Brad Baker failed to materialize altogether. As Cordray climbed through 10,000 feet, the Tonys broke off and headed for Rabaul. They were apparently novices flying close formation without swiveling their heads. Cordray's F4U whipped down and Paul opened fire. The trailing Tony fell away burning and exploded on contact with the surface. Fully alert and eager to draw more blood, Paul spotted a pair of Marine Corsairs shagging several northwest-bound Zekes. He joined in what became a fruitless chase. The three eventually quit and headed back toward the beachhead. On the way, the trio spotted three Tonys, low on the water and heading toward Rabaul. Totally without communication, the Corsair pilots executed a coordinated attack from dead astern of the once-again unwary Imperial Army fighters. Paul's target took violent evasive action, but to no avail. Solidly hit, the Tony skidded right into the water and kicked up a huge splash. The Marines missed their targets and joined with Paul for the trip home, they to Barakoma and Paul to Ondongo.

Hedrick's flight had accounted for seven Zekes, a pair of Tonys, and a Kate. Timmy Gile's three kills had brought him even with the squadron leaders, Kepford and Blackburn, at four apiece.

On the other hand, Fighting-17 had suffered its first losses from the guns of enemy airplanes. We knew that Andy Anderson had gotten down, apparently in one piece, but we had no news on Brad Baker, who had simply vanished while Cordray was busy evading a pair of Tonys. Brad had been forced to ditch on November 11, on the way home from the fight over Task Group 50.3. We knew that if he was down in one piece and functional, he would know what to do, but that did not alleviate the worry.

Eight of us—my division and Butch Davenport's—got airborne at 0345 the next day, November 18. We were to be over Cherryblossom in time to intercept a possible dawn low-level attack of the sort that had slipped through and beaten up on our transports for several days running. Then, depending on the outcome of our trap, we were to launch an early-morning attack on any barges we could find around Buka. If all went well to that point, we were to fly a routine

CAP over Empress Augusta Bay while looking for signs of our two downed pilots and a Marine who also had been shot down on the seventeenth.

This mission marked the beginning of Butch Davenport's reputation and fame. Early on, it had been clear that Butch was a good pilot and a good leader. Moreover, in his capacity as squadron engineering officer, he had contributed mightily to the Hog's emergence as a viable carrier fighter. So far, on the scoring chart, Butch's only contribution had been a one-fourth piece of the Betty his division had downed after much effort on November 6. I expected great things of Butch, and he began to show his true colors.

My earphones came to life as we were nearing Empress Augusta Bay. "Big Hog, this is Butch. Believe I saw a light in the water. Request permission to break off and investigate. Over."

"This is Big Hog. Roger, Butch. Permission granted. Keep me posted. Big Hog out."

As Butch led his division down, my four proceeded to carry out the balance of the mission, which came to absolutely nothing.

The following is quoted from the Fighter Command intelligence report distributed to all the area's squadrons:

On the afternoon of 17 November 1943, Lt(jg) R. S. Anderson, USNR, VF-17, was shot down near Cape Torokina. His rescue the next morning is owed to the resourcefulness of Lt M. W. Davenport, USNR, of the same squadron. The pattern of Lt Davenport's procedure follows. It is one which all pilots can study to advantage.

Lt Davenport's division of four F4Us took off from Ondongo for a dawn strafing attack against Buka. At 0425, while proceeding up the west coast of Bougainville, he sighted a steady light in the water. The division investigated with their landing lights from a low altitude and found an object which might be Anderson afloat. They abandoned their mission, and, while the division circled above, Davenport turned on his emergency IFF [Identification Friend or Foe, a transmitter carried by each plane which displays a distinctive signal on friendly radar] and asked Dane Base [the nearest fighter director station] to take a bearing. It was reported to him as 295 [degrees], distance 32 [miles]. Soon afterward, the light went out, so the division went on patrol over Dane Base, their tertiary mission. As soon as dawn broke they resumed their search for Anderson and found him on their second run over the given course. Dane Base was notified, but no rescue boat [or Dumbo] was available. The division continued to circle above Anderson until fuel shortage forced one section back to Barakoma. Davenport and Lt(jg) Freeman were able to stay on station. Davenport was using [extraordinarily economical engine power and flight technique]. A PT boat finally picked up Anderson at 0900.

Davenport's alertness . . . and skill . . . cannot be too highly recommended. . . . Remember this. . . . It may be a direct means of saving someone's life.

As Butch and his wingman, Lt(jg) Chico Freeman, circled at only 200 feet over Andy in precarious, perilous balance against the laws of physics, Chico decided to help Andy's spirits with a poem and a girly picture. He scrawled the missive on the pad of notepaper strapped to his knee and zippered the sheet and the photo into the canvas pouch with the red streamer pilots used to drop messages to ships under conditions of radio silence. Chico was not much of a poet, but he had a good eye and nearly beaned Andy with the weighted pouch.

When Butch landed, he still had 23 gallons of fuel aboard after 6.75 hours aloft. Such fuel stretching was the result of a lot of experimentation we had undertaken during the boring patrol flights. The news jolted a lot of people into investigating and further developing the Corsair's unrealized operational capabilities.

Adding immeasurably to the legend was one of Andy's comments during a group visit to the sick bay, where he was healing a broken ankle, fractured rib, and a badly wrenched back. When one of the awed troops commented, "Lucky you had that flashlight," Andy recoiled in surprise.

"Lucky I had that flashlight? *What* flashlight? I didn't have any flashlight!" He had somehow neglected to clip his small standard issue waterproof flashlight to his Mae West life jacket.

Unlikely as it seemed, we could only surmise that Brad Baker or the downed Marine had held the light Butch had sighted. Of those two, Brad and the Marine, nothing more was ever heard. Possibly, Brad's luck had simply run out; maybe one unscathed rescue after a ditching was his limit. I fervently prayed that our mate had died at the controls of his Corsair, for, more than most, I knew well the feeling of drifting upon a sea that could suck life's heat from the body. It was terrible to think that the unknown man with the light had heard and seen Butch's division make those first low passes—had clung to life thinking that rescue was only a short time away. There is the story of a miracle in this, and of the cruel balance nature and the Fates impose.

We lost Andy to his injuries, for he had to be evacuated to the States to recuperate fully. But at least he was back. He was flying fighters again by the following summer.

20

. . . .

The ups and downs—days of boring routine missions punctuated by literally only minutes of sudden deadly action—were hard to take. It was difficult to remain in top form so we could fight when we needed to when all we had to do was bore holes in the sky.

On November 19 Fighting-17 undertook five negative two-hour patrols—forty sorties—over Empress Augusta Bay and one negative two-hour patrol—eight sorties—over Munda. November 20 was only marginally more rewarding: four negative two-hour patrols—thirty sorties—over a transport group, a negative two-hour one-division CAP over Munda, and an eight-plane escort mission with a light-bomber strike over Bougainville. The only action on November 20 came when Lt Lem Cooke and Ens Beads Popp smoked a Betty they found on the ground beside the Kara airstrip on their way home. Lem took the incident in stride, but Beads, who had arrived at Ondongo on November 18 following some detached duty on Espiritu Santo, thought he had really found the war.

On November 21 Fighter Command again assented to our proposal that we launch our first CAP mission an hour early to try to catch Japanese raiders bound for a dawn strike against the ships off Torokina. On their way north by 0400 were eight Corsairs led by Butch Davenport. On arrival at Cherryblossom, as agreed to in advance by Butch and his second-division leader, Dirty Eddie March, Davenport's division circled at 3,000 feet between Cape Torokina and volcanic Mt. Bagana while March's flew a northeast-southwest racetrack over the bay at 10,000 feet.

Just as dawn was breaking, Dane Base ordered Dirty Eddie to "Steer two-six-oh, angels twenty." (Butch was having radio problems and did not hear the vector order.)

The division was clawing for altitude when the sun appeared behind them. They had flown 25 miles from their original position when they heard the dreaded, "Base under attack!" (Three bombs dropped by an unseen intruder had detonated in the water off the beach.) The Corsair pilots did not need the follow-on orders that urged them to get back there as fast as they could. Within seconds, Dirty Eddie's four Corsairs were eastbound and angling down at top speed. Suddenly, as March was leading the way through 13,000 feet, a lone Tony flashed into view. It was on an opposite-course heading and going all out. Dirty Eddie tried a snap shot at a closing speed that had to be way over 500 knots. This tough shot was almost always a miss, and he did just that.

In the meantime, Butch, who was leading his foursome in his bushwhack position, spotted six Zeros coming in to the beachhead area, so he swung into action. He opened fire on the lead Zeke from four o'clock level. Butch clearly saw his bullets going in; the Zeke did not smoke, but the pilot bailed out. (The injured man, who was later picked up by our PT boats, claimed to have been sent down from Rabaul specifically to find out why so many of their planes were being lost on supposedly safe dawn strafing missions!)

Davenport chandelled out of his first firing pass and found a lone Zeke making a right-angle beam run on his Corsair from 1,000 yards out. Butch turned into the attack, but he passed below the Zeke and could not get his sights on. Butch completed a 360-degree turn preparatory to going after the missed target, which was climbing, but he saw that he could not catch him. He rolled over on his back and dived back into the main melee. At that moment, he saw a Zeke on the tail of his division's tail-end-Charlie, Ens Andy Gump Jagger. Butch instantly tried to get rounds into that Zeke—at least to scare him off. The Zeke pulled up and Butch lost him, but at least Jagger was off the hook. As Butch turned back into the fight yet again, he found a lagging single below at eight o'clock. Almost as soon as Butch opened fire, the Zeke began smoking and pitched violently downward to crash into the bay. Butch followed him virtually the whole way, just to make sure. By then, it was safe to do so; Butch's second kill was the last of the six Zekes.

Lt(jg) Chico Freeman, who was flying 200 yards off Butch's wing, set up his initial firing run on the number three Zeke, but he saw the number two Zeke open fire on Butch, so he shifted targets. A tough shot from three o'clock level produced hits through the Zeke's engine, and the Japanese fighter began an unambiguous final dive straight into the water. By the time the Zeke started its plunge, however, two other Zekes had opened fire from about 75 yards behind Chico's tail. Stomping full rudder, Chico skidded violently to the left. The closer Zeke slid past to port while the wingman broke to the right and climbed steeply away. Chico reversed course to follow the climber. At length, just west of volcanic Mt. Balbi, Chico opened fire from dead astern the Zeke, and his bullets started a fire in the cockpit. He saw a chute blossom from the open cockpit, but the shrouds caught on the tail before it deployed. The Japanese pilot rode the burning fighter all the way into the jungle below.

Lt Ray Beacham, Davenport's second-section leader, successively found his way into fights—several tail chases and one breathtaking head-on duel—but each of the Zekes evaded fatal damage through radical maneuvering. His bullets even sent a Zeke into a steep spiraling dive, but the Japanese fighter recovered. Finally, the Kittyhawk Kid found a Zeke low on the water, heading west. He gave his Hog full throttle and came up on the target's tail. Cutting his speed, Ray opened fire from 100 yards, and the Zeke flew straight into the water. On a hunch, Ray turned back over the floating wreckage of the downed fighter and, sure enough, he spotted a swimmer buoyed up by a black life jacket. He relayed a message through Butch Davenport to call out the local PT boats to grab the swimmer.

Ens Andy Gump Jagger was initially too far out on Beacham's wing when the action started, so he did not join right in. He quickly lost Beacham when the section leader chandelled out of his first firing pass, so he climbed and then dived into the Japanese formation by himself. He made several passes at four Zekes which had by then started to form a Lufbery circle, but all his bullets were wide of the mark. He tried to join another Corsair (Davenport's) that was making a left turn, but he was not yet in position when the other Corsair opened fire at a Zeke crossing his—Jagger's—path. Andy Gump's turn carried him right onto the tail of the Zeke, which had broken off to flee. Jagger instantly got his gunsight pipper on the departing Zeke and pummeled it into a tight, smoking downward spiral. Still 1,000 feet from the surface, the Zeke suddenly burst into brilliant flames and streamed a spectacular black plume until it arced in.

As the unflappable Chico Freeman joined on Davenport to begin the routine CAP that finished out the mission, he radioed Dane Base to put in a bid for the injured Japanese prisoner's gold teeth—in case the man died. Chico's laconic explanation: "I want to make a bracelet for my gal in L.A."

The November 21 action blasted Butch Davenport to deserved prominence. He had minutely planned the bounce and had executed it to perfection; his flight had bagged six out of the six Zekes encountered. Equally satisfying was the perfect reformation of the flight for the routine ho-hum patrol that followed. First the Anderson rescue, and now this. Butch was noticed by the front office and marked as a comer.

Tragedy struck the squadron later in what we thought would be a triumphal day.

Six Corsairs under Chuck Pillsbury routinely relieved the midmorning CAP over Empress Augusta Bay, and they flew yet another butt-grinding noon-hour CAP mission until relieved in turn by the early-afternoon flight. All six of Pillsbury's F4Us were directed to strafe targets of opportunity along the Monoitu–Kahili Trail, over which the Imperial Army had been resupplying their ground forces arrayed against the Torokina beachhead. Lt Wally Schub's division was unable to find the Monoitu Mission itself, but the four did expend most of their bullets on bridges and huts along the trail.

Meanwhile, Chuck and his wingman, Ens Bob Hogan, flew an independent course up the jungle-obscured trail and managed to flame five trucks. At about 1300, just before the pair reached Kahili, Hogan idly cut to starboard to pass around 400-foot Kangu Hill. He saw Chuck swing left around the same prominence. Though Bob neither encountered nor saw any signs of antiaircraft fire, that was the last he saw of Chuck. Bob circled offshore and called Chuck on his radio, but there was no response. Bob was by then running low on fuel, so he called the next CAP flight leader, who sent a division up to look for Chuck. No joy.

Fully a quarter century later, Chuck Pillsbury's virtually intact Corsair was located, purely by chance, in the dense jungle near Kangu Hill. Our comrade's remains were still strapped into the cockpit. One .25-caliber rifle bullet had gone through him from below and lodged in his skull. No doubt, Chuck died instantly, before the crash.

The demanding, mostly enervating routine continued unabated for yet another week. We remained busy and alert for the occasional bombing-mission escort, which carried us to potentially livelier locales than Munda or Empress Augusta Bay had become, but no Japanese fighters ever rose to meet us.

It was plain for all to see that the air and naval campaign in the Northern Solomons had reached a successful conclusion. For the rest of November 1943, there were virtually no hostile contacts in the air over the Solomons or Rabaul by Navy or Marine squadrons. Certainly, there were no contacts resulting in claims for Japanese aircraft destroyed or damaged in the air. The only time we got to fire our guns was in the course of strafing missions, and our fighters did encounter some Japanese antiaircraft fire, particularly over the northern airfields.

On November 28 my eleven-plane flight completed a routine two-hour CAP and vectored out to strafe an alleged radio tower at Motupena Point, Bougainville. The target was given top priority for destruction, and all hands were under orders to rake the area around the tower even if no targets were apparent. We were unable to locate the tower—if there was one—but we obediently made numerous firing passes over the indicated coordinates. In the end, after we had expended nearly 1,200 rounds apiece, Doug Gutenkunst reported falling oil pressure, apparently from a hit by an infantry weapon. Doug nursed the ailing Hog with its bullet-riddled oil cooler out over the water in Wilson Strait and then made a dead-stick landing. Doug was picked up within minutes—safely and without injury—by a crash boat.

Ground-strafing missions over wooded terrain had by then become fairly commonplace. The results, however, were always impossible to observe. We rarely found anything that would burn, such as trucks or fuel farms, and, as in the case of the phantom Motupena radio tower, we rarely even precisely located the object of the mission.

Some weeks after Chuck Pillsbury's disappearance and Doug Gutenkunst's dunking, a Japanese infantryman captured near Cape Torokina revealed the probable cause of both losses. Infantry units deployed along trails or other locales that were being routinely strafed by our fighters were under orders to form ranks under cover of the trees and, on command, simultaneously fire their rifles and light machine guns vertically into the air. This shotgun tactic was a neat method for getting the troops to overcome the feeling that they were helpless in the face of our offensive fighter tactics. In the case of Chuck Pillsbury, Doug Gutenkunst, and others, it proved to be a cheap, effective means for swatting the occasional Allied airplane from the skies. As soon as Fighter Command got the interrogation report, all routine strafing runs over wooded terrain were discontinued.

I received word during the last week of November that Fighting-17 was scheduled to go on a slightly premature R&R leave to Australia. I was not about to argue with the bosses in light of the zero action we felt we had been seeing. On December 2 thirty-four of us took off from Ondongo in our own fighters while the rest of the pilots and organic ground personnel followed aboard several gooney birds.

Our first stop was Henderson Field, Guadalcanal, where we could begin to unwind in the comparative luxury of the famous and infamous Hotel de Gink, a pilots' eating and sleeping establishment that dated from the darkest days of the Guadalcanal Campaign. There, we gorged on good *Navy* chow before repairing to the flourishing O Club for drinks, and then on to the nightly movie. Most of us were not yet up to carousing, so we hit the sack early.

Once again, I had the privilege and pleasure of dining with VAdm Jakey Fitch and his staff. This afforded me the opportunity to shoot myself in the foot.

After we had enjoyed our martinis and repaired to the dinner table, Admiral Fitch himself asked a question I was sure he had designed to get The Word to his soft-living staff from a real, hardened combat vet. "Tom, what do the guys up in New Georgia want that we can provide and that they aren't getting?"

Truly serious, I replied, "Admiral, they want beer. Few want to get drunk, but almost everyone had trouble relaxing. Beer would help." Out of the corner of my eye, I saw a scowl on the face of a senior staffer sitting across the table. Did he really expect me to request Parcheesi sets?

"Fair enough," the admiral replied. "We'll see if we can't improve that. The beer we have is not very good, but we have warehouses full of it down in Espiritu. Anything else?"

Feeling that I needed to inject a little levity into the proceeding, I told the admiral that our photoreconnaissance and intelligence boys had pinpointed the location of a cat-house for high-ranking officers on a hill overlooking Rabaul. I allowed as how I would like an opportunity to take the place out as soon as possible after Fighting-17 returned from leave. I gilded the lily a bit by relating the factual data on how Royal Air Force Mosquito light bombers found sport shooting up similar facilities servicing German brass based in France.

ComAirSoPac took this trifle in the spirit in which it had been offered, and he joined in the general laughter that began long before I concluded my half-serious pitch. Not so the owner of that earlier scowl, a senior captain who had been appropriately tagged with the sobriquet, Lord Plush-bottom. After dinner, this arrogant, verbose sycophant cornered me well out of earshot of the admiral. He looked at me with warmth akin to that generated by flatulence in a phone booth.

"Blackburn, your off-color remarks at the admiral's table were badly out of place. You and that hooligan squadron of yours are getting a lot of publicity Stateside." (This was news to me, but it turned out that the tireless aircraft publicity departments were pushing us along with their products, our beloved Hogs, their engines, and their propellers.) Plushy continued at full steam, "The headaches you gave Admiral Bellinger around Norfolk with your wild behavior are notorious. Now, what with bearded aces, nonreg attitudes, and despicable actions, you're hitting the headlines as Blackburn's Irregulars. This is painting a picture which reflects no credit on the U.S. Navy, and especially on this command. If you're really harboring ideas of a big publicity stunt like a strike on that alleged whorehouse—and I wouldn't put it past you—I'll see to it that you rue the day."

Plushy had given me more good news than grief, but I kept a straight face and answered, "I understand, Captain." I was neither terrified nor impressed by this prudish popinjay, but I knew that he could have me summarily relieved of my beloved command by making a case with the front office that Fighting-17's actions were the antithesis of those "in keeping with the highest traditions of the U.S. Naval Service." I knew that he would knife me if he could.

But could he? Most probably. We *were* nonreg and free-wheeling if not quite the hooligans Plushy made us out to be. Our very real discipline was not apparent to traditionalists of the prewar Navy. Beards we had, in profusion, but they were legitimate per Navy regulations even though few commands tolerated them. Our reputation from the Norfolk days was indeed somewhat gamy, and a few known peccadilloes had been just a hair short of court-martial. Activities that might not stand the light of day *had* been discreetly conducted. We had transported a significant supply of hard liquor from the States to Ondongo via *Bunker Hill* and *Prince William,* carefully packed in plywood cases labeled "Aircraft Instruments—Fragile." And there was a jeep in Espiritu Santo, complete with squadron insignia, that did not appear on the motor pool records. These were among the skeletons that could make us look unparagonical if they were ever uncloseted. On the other side of the coin, however, was our combat record: 2 small cargo ships destroyed, 11 barges destroyed, 2 Betty bombers destroyed on the ground, and 48.5 Japanese airplanes destroyed in the air. This substantial tally had cost us 3 pilots—still missing, but all in fact dead—2 aircraft downed by enemy aircraft, 3 aircraft downed by ground fire, and 2 aircraft lost in water landings brought on by excessive fuel consumption in combat. These numbers marked VF-17 as a winning team.

With these thoughts, I lost concern about Lord Plushbottom's stuffy reaction to our proper *joie de vivre* and headed for the shucks. In the morning we would take off for Espiritu and then ride out to immerse ourselves and our libidos in the fleshpots of beckoning Australia.

PART V

· ·

Fortress Rabaul

21

· · · · · · · · · · ·

With no ill will whatsoever toward the wonderful women of Australia, I must say that "Down Under" perfectly describes our two-week bout of unwinding. However, by the time we arrived back at Espiritu Santo on December 15 and 16, all hands were quite ready to take up the profession of arms again.

The first business at hand was wading through the mounds of savored mail that greeted our return to Espiritu. Among the treasured words of our loved ones were reams of newspaper clippings describing exploits of Blackburn's Irregulars in lurid detail, some of which was factual. So, Lord Plushbottom had not misspoken after all; the aircraft companies' publicity flacks had been more than earning their keep the whole time we had been in the forward area. The fact that we all innocently thought the publicity was deserved made us more obnoxious than ever.

For the moment, we faced an uncertain amount of another type of R&R—this one being best described as Regroup and Rearm. Among other chores was the need to inculcate several new arrivals into the mysterious ways of Fighting-17.

One "new" guy we did not have to work over hard was

Lt(jg) Bobby Mims, our former bad boy of Manteo and Norfolk. Bobby had sailed with us to Hawaii in October but had been felled by a burst appendix just as we got ashore at Pearl. None of us ever expected to see Bobby again—and many, not including me, were happy with the prospect. Bobby had other thoughts. As soon as he was released from the hospital, he began an all-fronts onslaught against all the regional powers, the object of which was to get himself reassigned to what he later described as "my beloved Fighting-Seventeen." Bobby was more than equipped to make himself a nuisance with which the various staff personnel people had to reckon or go nuts. They reckoned, and Bobby had marched into our temporary squadron office the day after the last of us had departed for Sydney. I was pleased to see Bobby, a superb pilot and a proven aggressive soul.

I was told shortly after my arrival that five new ensigns and jaygees, strangers all, had also reported in during our absence. However, all had been temporarily shanghaied to help ferry new F6Fs up to the forward area. The five reported in on December 27, and several more reported in over the next four or five days.

We set off with a bang to recoup the finer points of our flying and fighting skills the long layoff had no doubt dulled. On the other hand, our sojourn at Espiritu was far from all work and no play—given the rather limited play facilities. First and foremost for all hands seemed to be the rapid accumulation of restful sack time, "restful" being a trait of sack time I am sure nearly all of us had pointedly eschewed in Australia. We also had no trouble providing ourselves with ample quantities of beer—not the world's best, but good enough. The beach was superb, the surf was perfect, and the weather was uniformly temperate. The local O Club, complete with snack bar, was open every evening, and open-air movies were offered nightly. Feminine companionship was simply not available, but we managed to accept that one shortfall, all the time realizing that most male denizens of the base were years at a time between women.

Tons of fruitcake and shattered cookies—and no end of

affection described in a mountain of letters—did not suffice to make Christmas 1943 a happy one. Fortunately, it was a busy time for me. Endless reports had to be churned out and turned in to describe and analyze the combat and other operational actions of our first combat tour. And I had a big hand in bringing up to speed and evaluating all the new kids who continued to dribble in through the latter half of December. I got completely off booze during this period as it had in it the potential for too much self-pity. The hurt from the loss of Johnny Keith, Chuck Pillsbury, and Brad Baker still seared, and the possibly foolish thought, "Where did *I* fail them," kept surfacing.

We made many personnel and leadership changes during our layover in Espiritu. Among the changes was one set off by the unexpected visit of Lt Oc Chenoweth, a plowback instructor at Opa-Locka and, at the time of our reunion, the exec of a small, rather unexcelling Hellcat squadron that had operated out of Segi. I knew what I was in for almost as soon as Oc flashed a forced smile, not at all his own, in my direction one evening at the O Club.

I was fully wired into the scuttlebutt network by then, so I all but perfectly anticipated Oc's opener, once he got around to it: "Tommy, I want to talk with you about a problem we're having in the squadron."

I nodded, perhaps a touch wearily, for him to go on. "We have a good bunch of guys, but we can't take our son-of-a-bitch skipper any longer. He bugs us day and night. He lays our lack of combat success on the people flying with him, but we all know bloody well who screws up. God, I hear talk of shooting him down before he gets one of us killed. Will you talk to Fighter Command for us?"

I was in full accord with Oc, but Fighting-17 was not directly affected. I thus felt that I would be way off base if I got directly involved. "Oc, I know it isn't kosher, and you might get your butt fried for it, but I recommend that you go see Colonel Brice. Tell him privately what you just told me. The colonel is a square shooter and will respect your guts. I'm sure he won't put your head on the block for doing what you feel is best for the troops and the war effort. But I have to warn you; if Brice sees fit to can your skipper, he's going to can you, too—make a clean sweep before putting in a new man. I'm sure he won't fleet you to command the squadron. If he gets that far, you tell him that you've spoken with me and I will be more than pleased to have you in VF-17."

And that is exactly the way it happened, with one pretty major addition: Colonel Brice asked me to recommend a replacement CO for the F6F squadron. Rog and I concurred that Lem Cooke was a natural. Lem and I had never become close, but I had come all the way around in my respect and admiration for his flying and leadership skills. It was a good choice; the unhappy outfit was completely rehabilitated with Lem's warm but firm hand on the helm. And we benefited by enrolling another "castoff."

On the debit side of the ledger was the special case of Lt(jg) Jack Chasnoff. I was fond of this gentle man, a highly proficient, gutty pilot, but the loss of his dear friend and alter ego, Andy Anderson, during the November 17 air battle had left Jack a shaken, chastened man, and he had been going downhill physically since. I convened an informal board to discuss his future. Rog, Duke, and Dr. Herrmann unanimously agreed with my assessment that we would all benefit if he went home. I called Jack in for a heart-to-heart. As expected, he was understandably reluctant to leave, but I eventually brought him around to our view, and he agreed to take the Stateside Training Command assignment I proposed to him. Above all, I assured him that the transfer was no reflection on his courage or integrity, as heartfelt a bit of news as ever I uttered.

While disdainful of the Army Air Forces in general and their horizontal bombing in particular, we had noted with great admiration the development by 5th Air Force B-25s of the technique known as "skip bombing." This consists of a high-speed run, with all the forward machine guns blazing, at masthead height—or below—and the release of bombs just as the bomber pulls up to get over the target. Just as a flat stone skips off the surface of a lake, the bomb skips off the surface of the ocean to impact against the target vessel's side. As a further refinement, the bombs were equipped with delayed-action fuses so they would breach the hull of the target before detonating and after the attacker has flown clear. The accuracy rate was phenomenal; apparently, the bombs sometimes missed, but getting them to do so was not easy.

We had first heard of the skip-bombing technique around the middle of our first combat tour. Immediately, our heads filled with sugarplum dreams of nailing a fat Japanese tanker. Thus, during our last days at Ondongo, Butch Davenport, Timmy Gile, and I spent a good deal of time devising a way for our Hogs to lug bombs. At length, we settled on a modification of the catapult-hook structure.

All carrier aircraft have catapult hooks, which are attachment points for the loops of heavy wire that comprise the catapult "bridle." The bridle is the connector to the "shuttle," the business portion of the slingshot arrangement which accelerates the airplane from 0 to 80 knots in a few short feet. Manifestly, the cat hooks have to be attached to the main strength members of the airplane.

As with our tail hooks, we had no use for the cat hooks on land. So we unbolted the starboard hook of a spare old-model Hog and replaced it with a substantial steel plate. To this, our metal benders attached a standard bomb rack plus unstreamlined but adequate steel pipe for sway bracing. The ordnance gang worked up the arming and release rig to and in the cockpit.

Timmy and I both found the installation completely successful during several test hops, and we ordered up a total of eight bomb racks. However, the project went on a back burner for lack of potential targets within reasonable reach of Ondongo. While we were at Espiritu, however, we dusted off the jury-rigs and began further testing with the expectation of developing a surefire technique for scoring bomb hits from our Hogs.

While eight of our Hogs were being retrofitted with the new water-injection version of our standard Pratt & Whitney engines, Cdr Emerson Fawkes, the local Aircraft Overhaul and Repair Facility boss, heard of our homegrown bomb rack rigs. His first reaction was, "Tommy, it ain't safe," but I managed to talk him into taking a personal interest. He agreed to get eight good adapter rigs designed and built, then pushed the project with the Fleet Air operations section, and won an early approval. The eight juryrigs thus were replaced in short order by a like number of properly engineered versions. We flight-tested the new ones and, when they had proven out, we had them preserved and packed to take with us on our return to the forward area.

A lot of fighting was in progress up the line, and we were both ready and eager to get in on it. Since we had no word about our next deployment by the end of the first week of January, I grabbed Doug Gutenkunst to accompany me on a quick hop up to Henderson Field so I could learn more or begin my politicking, whichever applied. I was greeted at AirSoPac headquarters by Capt Al Morehouse, who heard me out before launching his own typically patient pitch: "Tom, we know you're rarin' to go and I wondered when you'd show up squalling. We're as anxious to get you back to work as you are to be back, but we're in a big state of transition. Flight ops are moving up to Bougainville. Right now, we only have the little emergency strip the Seabees put in at Torokina, but they're at work on a big bomber strip and an adjacent fighter strip. We expect to have both of the new strips running in a few weeks, and we will be moving squadrons in beginning January 24. We have FightingSeventeen slated to be among the first squadrons to operate off the new fighter strip. In fact, we're about ready to issue formal orders." Then, with a renewed, knowing smile, "I guess I don't have to ask if you'll be ready. Huh?"

We had about two weeks to get fully up to speed again. The time went by in a whirlwind of activities too varied and numerous to recall. We experienced a high and annoying level of personnel turbulence during the period, with all sorts of new blood joining and departing. I must admit to being the prime source of the departures. We had no way of selecting rookies other than trying them out and retaining or detaching them based on admittedly hurried assessments of their aggressive traits and flying skills. The result was that we did get rid of a few tyros we thought would not cut it, but we also wound up taking a few such back to the forward area because they arrived late and were not adequately evaluated. Fortunately, all the newcomers arrived with experience in cast-off old-model F4Us that had found their way to Training Command.

We lost two of our fighters which were totally destroyed in training accidents, but neither of the pilots was severely injured.

Fortunately, the comings and goings—except for the Cooke-Chenoweth trade—had zero impact on my flight- and division-leader assignments. Unlike many squadrons, the operational leadership jobs were not assigned in strict conformity with seniority; rank was, at best, secondary. Thus, the five other flight leaders were Rog Hedrick, Butch Davenport, Dirty Eddie March, Timmy Gile, and Thad Bell. The division leaders were Tom Killefer, Oc Chenoweth, Earl May, Paul Cordray, Ike Kepford, and Wally Schub. Several of these division leaders could easily fleet up to lead flights, and there were several section leaders who could certainly get their shots at being division leaders.

The last truly important piece of business before our January 24 departure was the headache we had given ourselves by amassing 148 cases of beer in the giant Quonset hut I shared with Rog Hedrick. How in the world were we going to get the cache from Espiritu to Bougainville?

We had had ample luck during our Ondongo tour at transporting the odd case of hard booze. Typically, camouflaged cases would be marked "Electronics Equipment— Fragile," and we got them delivered with no difficulty. But 148 cases of beer was too much to even think of masking within that scheme, and we *knew* that sending it aboard a ship would result in a total loss.

At virtually the last minute, our great Supply Corps outwitter, Lt(jg) Hal Jackson, arrived on my doorstep with a catbird grin—and a solution.

"Skipper! Rog! I got it! I got it!"

What is this jaygee doing here? "Got what?"

"How to get the beer to Bougainville!"

I was all attention. "Bless your bones, you crook. How?"

With rather studied indignation, Hal stared me down. "I am not a crook!" But the catbird grin came on again. "I'm just alert."

"So give!"

"Well, the most planes we've ever had in one flight in the forward area was twenty-four. And we did alright. Right?"

"Hal, press *on!*"

He did, with great fervency. "The flight going up to Bougainville will be the whole squadron. We'll never in God's world get jumped. But if we do, wouldn't four guns per plane and two hundred rounds per gun be plenty?"

"Jackson," I beamed as I saw his ploy, "I apologize for calling you a crook. You're a bloody *genius!* I'll have Duke write you up for a Legion of Merit."

That very day—within minutes, actually—we were out on the flight line figuring out the best and safest way to stow the beer cases in the huge ammunition cans. It was clear after a quick trial that we had room for all 148 cases.

On January 24 we flew the last hour to Bougainville at 25,000 feet. As we shut down on our hardstands at our base, each pilot solemnly handed a new church key to his Marine plane captain and bade him fetch and open two ice-cold cans of beer from one of the ammo cans in the wings. What an attention getter!

22

· · · · · · · · · · ·

The air war in the Solomons had taken a dramatic and decisive turn during Fighting-17's seven weeks in the rear area: The Japanese had gone over to an all but totally defensive mode. Moreover, their goals were extremely limited; they had given up the defense of their surviving bases on Bougainville in favor of conserving their declining resources for the defense of Rabaul against our inevitable direct onslaught.

By December 1943, the campaign in the Solomons had taken on a completely predictable pattern: As we seized or built new air bases, we launched progressively larger air assaults against those Japanese bases that came within our newly extended reach. They responded with aerial counterthrusts which we eventually and inevitably overcame. At length, we launched a new amphibious assault aimed at winning ground for yet new air bases. They attacked the new beachhead, and we proceeded to beat them at sea and in the air. This vital "stepping-stone" strategy had thus far carried us from Guadalcanal to the Russell Islands, to the New Georgia group, to Bougainville. Based on past performance, everyone—we and they—reasonably assumed that

Rabaul would be softened up for the inevitable direct amphibious assault.

In late 1943 or very early 1944, it was firmly decided to cordon off Rabaul and employ it as a focus upon which the Japanese could expend irreplaceable ships, planes, pilots, and, indeed, ground-combat forces. Rabaul was not to be assaulted by our ground forces because the cost would inevitably be enormous and the strategic gain minimal. Maintaining the mere *threat* of imminent assault would do the job. In fact, the same principle applied to the remaining Japanese bases on Bougainville; they would be assaulted only from the air. They and Rabaul would, in the words of the Commander in Chief of the U.S. Fleet, Adm Ernest King, be left to "wither on the vine." Unfortunately for many pilots and aircrewmen, a credible threat could be maintained only by means of an unremitting air offensive.

Our side used December 1943 and most of January 1944 to build up its air-assault force. Not coincidentally, perhaps, the lull in which we had found ourselves in late November had deepened until only the occasional Japanese snooper or night bomber was tracked by our radar and sent burning into the sea by target-hungry fighter jocks. The pickings were slim because the Japanese temporarily had no air assets to do more than harass our buildup on Bougainville. At the same time, until we could move adequate light bombers and fighters up to Bougainville, Rabaul—the only target the Japanese would surely defend in strength—was out of range to all but our medium and heavy land-based bombers. Our only other possible means for effectively hitting Rabaul—the carriers—were busy farther north, striking blows against shipping, airfields, and support facilities in the Marshall and Caroline island groups.

On December 10 our new Torokina fighter strip got its first permanently based air unit, the seventeen Corsairs of VMF-216, a fresh and unblooded unit. Within the week, as fuel and ordnance stocks were built up, hundreds of fighter missions were flying from or staging through the Torokina strip to undertake strikes and sweeps to the north. In addition, the Corsair night fighters of LCdr Gus Widhelm's VF(N)-75 were moved from Munda, as were the twin-engine three-man PV-1 night fighters of VMF(N)-531.

The establishment of the new Bougainville air bases gave rise to a new command echelon, Aircraft, Northern Solomons (AirNorSols), a direct subordinate of AirSols. While we were gone, the command of AirSols had passed from Army MGen Nathan Twining to Marine MGen Ralph Mitchell. ComAirNorSols was also a Marine, BGen Field Harris; he set up shop at Torokina as soon as our transports could land there. Working directly under General Harris were the old Fighter and Strike Command teams, including my boss, Col Oscar Brice. They also moved forward to Bougainville and set up shop at Torokina pending the completion of the new light-bomber and fighter strips—Piva Uncle and Piva Yoke, respectively.

While Rabaul itself was never to be directly assaulted, the Allies did have several amphibious assaults scheduled to go in elsewhere on New Britain. The first of these went off on December 15, when a reinforced U.S. Army regiment landed at Arawe, far to the east of Rabaul, on New Britain's southern coast. Interestingly, the Arawe landings were seen by our side as being an extension of Gen Douglas MacArthur's New Guinea offensive, and not as a continuation of the Solomons campaign. In any case, the landings at Arawe understandably drew some Japanese attention away from Rabaul's immediate plight.

The Arawe landings and the main show—a landing by 1st Marine Division at Cape Gloucester, New Britain's western cape, on December 26—were supported exclusively by the New Guinea–based 5th Air Force and associated Allied air units. AirSols had no part in the two New Britain landing operations, but we benefited from them in that the Rabaul-based 11th Air Fleet (Imperial Navy) and 4th Air Army (Imperial Army) were temporarily sucked out west to oppose them. Whatever losses the Japanese sustained over western New Britain naturally accrued to the advantage of the AirSols forces.

The first Bougainville-assisted strike against Rabaul took place on December 17, when a large fighter force took off from several New Georgia–area bases to stage through Torokina. The flight leader was Marine Maj Greg Boyington, the twenty-kill ace commanding VMF-214. His strike group comprised thirty Marine Corsairs, twenty-three New Zealand P-40s from Ondongo, and twenty-three Navy Hellcats. This was strictly a fighter sweep; no bombers were included. As similar missions had done over time at Kahili in mid-1943, this and future fighter sweeps over Rabaul were aimed at demoralizing the enemy by destroying his fighter force.

The Japanese had radar coverage of the approaches to Rabaul, plus radio-equipped spotters in the hills overlooking our Bougainville runways. Nevertheless, apparently they were caught completely unaware. The only opposition the raiders found airborne over the target was a lone Rufe, a single-float Zero variant. It and two of forty scrambling Zekes were blown out of the sky. In all, during the forty minutes Boyington's fighters remained over Rabaul, the Japanese got seventy of their fighters airborne, but the Japanese pilots largely evaded the smaller Allied fighter force. It was said that Boyington even taunted the Japanese on a radio channel he knew they used, but to no avail. In all, the New Zealanders got five Zekes, a VF-33 pilot got one, and a Marine got credit for the Rufe. On the other hand, three of the P-40s were downed with the loss of two pilots killed.

The tempo and strength of our new AirSols offensive against Rabaul picked up over the remainder of December and on into January. Our losses were heavy, but so were our gains. At length, the Japanese again stripped their carriers of aircraft, mainly fighters, and built up to a high of about three hundred operational aircraft deployed around Rabaul's five airfields. They were able to maintain that number more or less through the period by stripping replacements from operational squadrons throughout the Pacific and, indeed, from the home islands themselves.

On December 24 several of our cruisers and destroyers

directly bombarded the Buka-Bonis complex in northern Bougainville. As a result of this and a similar earlier bombardment, the Buka-Bonis complex was written off by the Japanese.

On Christmas day *Bunker Hill* and light carrier *Monterey* launched all available strike aircraft against Kavieng, the big air-base and shipping complex at the northeastern end of New Ireland which served as a stepping-stone for warplanes transiting between Rabaul and Truk. Succeeding carrier strikes against warships based at Kavieng—on January 1 and 4, 1944—met with heavier opposition and less positive results, but they did have the effect of drawing off at least 10 percent of the fighters that would have met our land-based strikes over Rabaul. After the January 4 strike, however, our carriers departed for the Central Pacific, and Kavieng was not further molested.

The first land-based light-bomber strike against Rabaul staged through Torokina on January 5, but it aborted in the face of a solid wall of heavy weather over the target. A repeat effort on January 7—the first to stage through Piva Uncle—met a similar fate and also aborted. There was some fighter action over Rabaul, and twelve enemy fighters were claimed against the loss of three Hellcats. Two of the SBDs crashed on the way back to their base.

The first successful light-bomber strike took place on January 9, when twenty-three Munda-based SBDs and sixteen Munda-based TBFs staged through Piva Uncle to hit Tobera airfield. The forty Japanese fighters launched to intercept the raid hung back until after the bombers had gone in, and they were engaged by the sixty-two-fighter escort. Our fighters claimed thirteen kills against the loss of one F6F and two P-40s. Only seven bombers were damaged, all by ground fire, and only one of those ditched.

The January 9 strike—rated a success by all interested parties on our side—set the pace for most of the rest of the air offensive against Rabaul. Coordinated dive-bombing and glide-bombing missions were undertaken just about every other day by one or two squadrons each of Marine SBDs and TBFs armed with 500-, 1,000-, or 2,000-pound bombs. On intervening days, Rabaul-area targets were hit by Munda-based B-25s and Munda- or New Guinea-based B-24s dropping 500-, 1,000-, or 2,000-pound bombs from high and medium altitudes.

All bombing raids were escorted by large forces of Allied fighters. In all cases, about a dozen New Zealand P-40s provided "very low" cover right over the bombers—mainly because they demonstrated execrable performance characteristics above around 14,000 feet. Most of the cover—stacked above the hapless P-40s—was provided by fifty or sixty Corsairs and Hellcats. Sometimes, P-38s accompanied B-24s from New Guinea bases. If so, they provided "very high" top cover. The only thing we saw of the P-38s was an early shower of their belly tanks. I don't know that any Japanese fighters were downed in any such debris storms, but they almost bagged me a few times.

The Corsairs and Hellcats were normally stacked in three flights of up to twenty each at 1,000- to 3,000-foot intervals above the bombers—low, medium, and high cover. On the approach to the target, as the entire mass of fighters and bombers neared an area that might be covered by enemy fighters, all the fighters accelerated from the cruising run-in speed of the bombers to 160–70 knots or more. This provided greater maneuverability and made it easier for the fighters to get to maximum speeds if need be.

The large increment of speed the fighters had over the bombers was compensated by a sinuous pattern of S-turns and weaves which allowed the fighters to keep proper position relative to the slower airplanes they were defending. The weave was a development of the familiar Thach Weave by which pairs of fighters and elements defended one another in combat—our analog of the defensive vertical scissors employed by Japanese fighters when they were under attack. Thus, in addition to slowing our relative speed as against that of the bombers, the weave also protected the vulnerable rear hemisphere of the fighter group. In addition to its other contributions, the continuous weaving vastly increased our visual scanning capabilities in our never-ending search for oncoming enemy fighters.

As the SBDs rolled into their dives and the TBFs angled down to begin their glides, the low and medium Corsair or Hellcat flights went down slightly ahead and so provided some measure of flak suppression by long-range strafing. At the same time, the high cover maintained its relative position about 4,000 feet above the strike bombers.

The best part about the entire strike technique was that it had been refined and proved effective earlier in the war, over Kahili and Buka. That knowledge increased everyone's faith in the outcome.

The early AirNorSols bombing raids against Rabaul, undertaken in the weeks before we returned to the fray, pointed up a stupefying weakness in the Japanese pattern of defense. From the outset—Boyington's December 17 fighter sweep—the fighters charged with defending Fortress Rabaul had been generally unwilling to accept the challenge of our fighters. So doing, they did not bother the relatively vulnerable light bombers during the run-in. After dropping their payloads, the bombers were usually strung out, scattered, and lacking tight fighter cover; they and the fighters were most vulnerable at this point, seemingly easy meat for the waiting fighters. Thus, most of the action occurred after the strike groups passed over the target and left the major portion of the AA fire astern. However, the Japanese proved to be base-bound—that is, they almost never followed our departing bomber formations much beyond the coastline—not even to bag easy kills against damaged, unescorted stragglers. Hundreds of our bomber pilots and crewmen owed their lives to this last oversight, for even a ditched crew had an excellent chance of getting home alive aboard an unmolested, closely escorted Dumbo.

We studied the emerging action from afar, using the closing weeks of our rest period to pore over reports and question veterans who happened to be passing through. We drew some early conclusions and concocted an innovation or two, but, for the most part, we wanted to get a strike or two under our belts before making up our minds.

On January 24, as promised, thirty-four of us took off from Espiritu and flew our Hogs to Guadalcanal to refuel. We all arrived safely at Piva Yoke by 1700 and, after sharing some of our beer, left the Hogs to our Marine ground crewmen while we went off to inspect our new home.

One of the first new experiences we had to get used to was the frequent *boom-swish* of outgoing artillery fire. The Torokina beachhead was enclosed in a 10-mile-diameter perimeter because the landings had never been intended to sweep the Japanese from all of Bougainville, but merely to provide room and protection for the Torokina and two Piva runways. Thus, as we soon learned with some trepidation, the active ground war still ebbed and raged only a few miles from our new home. Well, as long as the unsettling artillery eruptions were all outgoing . . .

The first contingent of our ground echelon was flown in the next day, January 25. On that day, also, we were told that thirty-two of us—nearly the entire squadron—were scheduled to accompany a mixed SBD-TBF strike against Lakunai airfield, overlooking Rabaul's Simpson Harbor, the next morning, January 26.

23

· · · · · · · · · · ·

We expected our January 26 debut over Rabaul to be rough.
The Japanese did nothing to disappoint us.

The SBDs made their run-in from the east at 14,000 feet,
across the southern tip of New Ireland and on to a position
just to the northeast of Lakunai airfield. The attack was
delivered from approximately north to south, and the SBDs
retired down the channel to a rally point five miles east of
Cape Gazelle. VF-17 provided medium and high cover, that
is we were positioned in two sixteen-plane flights at about
16,000 and 19,000 feet during the run-in. The Japanese
interceptors, mostly Zekes and numbering fifty to sixty,
initially were positioned from 15,000 to 21,000 feet.

As we crossed over St. George Channel to Crater Peninsula, we transitioned from the high tension of anticipation
to the frantic activity of a one-legged man in an ass-kicking
contest.

My division, which was part of the medium cover, was
not jumped before the dive-bombers turned their noses
down 60 degrees and hurtled groundward. As was standard
procedure, we dived with the SBDs but remained slightly
ahead of them so we could do our bit to help suppress the
murderous AA rising from around the airfield. We started

shooting as we passed through 8,000 feet, and we kept pouring out bursts until we leveled off at around 4,000 feet. The stream of SBDs dropped their bombs from 2,000 feet and recovered at about 1,000 feet as they headed for the rally point 10 miles to the south.

We encountered our first defender north of Rapopo airfield, a lone Zeke that made a head-on run at our level. My bullets hit him, first in the engine and then apparently in the wing root. He passed under me smoking and splashed in off Matupi Island.

I was an ace, Fighting-17's first.

After exchanging several unsuccessful snap shots with several other Zekes, Doug Gutenkunst finally nailed one of the Imperial Navy fighters from dead astern as it tried to get in among the SBDs. As Doug followed his flamer, another Zeke tried to set up on Doug with a low-side run. Doug was quick to discern the danger and honked his Hog around into a violent vertical bank. This put him in position to make a beautiful deflection shot at no more than 100 yards. The victim blew up. As Doug and I rejoined to assume position above the Dauntlesses, we saw that the opposition was keeping its distance from us.

Tom Killefer's four, which were flying as my second division, had a far rougher time. They dived down with us ahead of the SBDs, but almost immediately as soon as the AA on the ground opened fire, I saw a Corsair lose a wing to the intense fire. Several of our guys saw Bob Hogan's chute blossom, but no one was able to follow him down. Bob was never seen again. Hogan's wingman, Andy Gump Jagger, was caught by a pair of Zekes. He took a 20mm explosive round in his wing but survived by means of some very fancy maneuvering. He managed to rejoin the reforming group, and his tattered Corsair carried him home, albeit with some difficulty.

TK and Lt(jg) Jim Farley, one of the more promising new pilots, were jumped by six Zekes during the retirement over Blanche Bay. Tom missed a Zeke that was making a steep firing pass on the pair. The Japanese fighter followed through and hit Farley's Corsair, which crashed. The Zeke pilot erred when he pulled out into a vertical climb. TK had anticipated the maneuver, and he nailed him before joining on Doug and me.

Rog Hedrick was leading the top-cover flight at 19,000 feet when the SBDs and lower fighter flights began the attack. During the final approach phase, Rog's flight was jumped by eight Zekes screaming down from 22,000 feet. However, those Imperial Navy pilots did not press their attack. Even hawk-eyed Rog was unable to score discernible hits with a brief long-range burst.

Minutes later, as Rog's flight passed through 16,000 feet in concert with the dive-bombers, Windy Hill's Corsair took several 20mm hits which chewed up its left aileron and most of its tail surfaces. Windy spun down to 9,000 feet, recovered, and headed home alone. When he arrived, he had to make a high-speed, no-flaps landing. The wounded bird got away from him a moment after touchdown and flipped. The plane was totaled and Windy wound up in the hospital with a severe head gash. He was flying again the following week.

Minutes after Hill was shot out of the formation, Rog Hedrick suddenly found himself all alone. As he headed for the rally point, he encountered three single Zekes in quick succession. Each of them shot at Rog, and missed. Then, as Rog approached the SBDs, three more Zekes crossed ahead of his nose, setting up to hit the rendezvousing dive-bombers. Rog tailed in, but the Zeke pilots saw him and all three sharply pulled up. Rog coolly opened fire on the leader at the top of the latter's climb, then followed the burning debris most of the way to the deck. As soon as the Zeke crashed, he climbed back up, joined a Marine loner, and took up station above the retiring bomber gaggle. That was Rog's fourth *official* kill, but most of us believe it was his seventh *real* kill—at least.

Paul Cordray's division, which was the second in Rog's flight, was attacked by the same gaggle of Zekes that had initially feinted at Rog's division. Paul missed his first target, and a Zeke got solid hits into Cordray's wingman,

Lt(jg) Jamey Miller. Jamey, who was superficially wounded, spun out and fell to 6,000 feet before recovering while Cordray stayed right with him all the way down. The two found themselves in clear sky, so they headed for the rally point. On the way, just north of the rendezvous, the two were challenged by eight Zeros. Cordray flamed one of the Zekes with a clean tail shot and followed through with a head-on pass at a second, although with unobserved results. As Paul opened fire on the first Zeke, Jamey got another in his sights and sent him down in flames. Meantime, Paul chandelled out of his second firing run and worked into a nice setup from six o'clock high on another Zeke. His bullets drew smoke and flame, but the Zeke pulled clear by means of a violent evasive maneuver. When last seen, he was smoking but flying back toward the base. With that, Cordray and Miller rejoined the bombers.

Timmy Gile's flight of eight, part of my medium-cover group, came under fire from six Zekes as it started down with the SBDs. Timmy's troops successfully evaded the intrusion with no ill effects and leveled out at 7,000 feet. As Timmy led his entire flight straight into the widening melee over Rapopo, he missed each of three successive targets, but he set the fourth afire. Next, a dozen Japanese fighters bored right in after Timmy, and one of them got ample rounds into his wingman, Ens John Malcolm Smith. Gile turned in to Smitty's attacker, who broke off his pass and headed home with his mates in train. Smitty's hydraulic system was destroyed, but he managed a safe, extremely exciting landing at Piva Yoke.

By all standards, January 26 was Fighting-17's grimmest day so far, an understandable but nonetheless sad outcome of our first tangle over Fortress Rabaul. We had two pilots missing, but neither ever turned up. One pilot, Miller, had been slightly wounded and another, Hill, was in the hospital with head injuries. We lost three airplanes, and five others had sustained repairable damage.

On the plus side, our mission had been a success in that none of the SBDs charged to our care had sustained any damage. In addition, we got credit for eight confirmed Zero kills, one probable kill, and one Zeke damaged.

The loss of two comrades on our first day back shook Fighting-17 to its core. Our rather gloomy happy-hour conversation revolved around variations on the same theme: We faced six weeks in the forward area, and most of our flight time would be spent on missions to Rabaul; if we continued to lose two a day, we would all be dead in only nineteen more days; if we averaged "only" one loss per day, one of us would survive to tell the tale.

I kept thinking that it couldn't possibly be as bad as all that. In the first place, Farley had been a new guy on his first combat hop; at least in part, his inexperience had surely contributed to his death. Hogan, an old hand, a steady if not spectacular pilot, had been downed by a freakish hit that sheared his right wing. That sort of thing was always a possibility in the face of intense ground fire, but it had to be realistically classed as a random event. Or was I kidding myself? Were we locked in a game of attrition we could not possibly overcome?

The good news was that everyone appeared to have made all the right moves. Sections and divisions maintained cohesion as well as they could, or regained it. Everyone knew where the rally point was, and everyone but Hill, in his critically damaged Hog, rendezvoused there. All the training and experience were clearly paying off.

It remained to be seen if our adversaries would get their defensive act together. After enduring fighter and bomber strikes for nearly six weeks, the opposition was still clearly reticent to challenge us in any meaningful way. They certainly could outnumber us over the target on any given day, but they chose to launch interceptors in numbers roughly equal to our cover flights, and to deliver piecemeal or incomplete attacks. Everything I had heard on the subject before the January 26 mission was seen to be true by one or another of us that day. One new and potentially dangerous twist I thought I perceived on January 26 was a hitherto unreported willingness on the part of some Japanese formations to risk being hit by their own AA as they delivered unswerving attacks on our diving bombers and fighters. This could be accounted for by the well-recognized ongoing piecemeal commitment of new units to the defense of Rabaul; clearly some of the new units were better trained, more aggressively led, or less demoralized than the norm. If we found many more such over the next few weeks, then we really did face a serious prospect of heavy losses.

I had some solutions, some innovations, some thoughts I wanted to try out, but one mission hardly embraced a trend. As I had before leaving Espiritu, I decided to hold off on anything new until we had more experience.

After this mission, we did the usual debrief while wetting our whistles with some of the beer we had flown in from Espiritu. Just what we needed to simmer down from the extreme tension of a tough combat flight. We were still hot and sweaty from the hop as we tooled out to the jeep for the mile-plus ride from our ready room Quonset hut to the fighter pilots' camp.

I took the wheel as nine more piled on—four inside and five manning the rear bumper, running boards, and hood. We were still pretty wound up and eager to strip down for a long, cold shower, change into fresh khakis, get some chow, and hopefully catch a nap.

The road crossed the south end of the fighter strip, so someone carefully checked for aircraft before I proceeded at the overloaded jeep's best speed. As I slowed to eyeball the runway-approach airspace, we were confronted by a very young Army MP in crisp, starched khakis, MP brassard, nightstick, police whistle on a lanyard, and *white* gloves. We were all gaping at this specimen when it held up a gloved hand in an imperious "Stop" signal. I braked and leaned out. "Hi! What can I do for you?"

"Sir, you can't proceed with more than four people in a jeep. This is the limit allowed by regulations. Carrying more than four is not safe. All these extra officers will have to dismount and walk."

All the guys aboard the jeep were big. Many had fearsome beards. We were all lean and mean. A lot of us habitually carried .45-caliber pistols at all times. Four of the bearded ruffians wordlessly dismounted and advanced on the 5'6", 125-pound representative of law and order. The soldier paled visibly, but stood his ground. Though annoyed, I was concerned that the pilots would dismember him, so I quickly and loudly hollered, "Hey! Knock it off! Get back aboard. Now!"

As the pilots backed off, I turned to the shaken doggie. "Son, this jeep is the only transport we have. I know that you have your orders, but, as your superior officer, I'm countermanding them for now. We're going to proceed as before. I'll take it up with the provost marshal."

"Okay, Commander, but I'll have to report you for the violation."

"Certainly, son, you do that."

I never heard a peep from on high, and we were never bothered again.

Early on January 27, twenty-four of us, forty-five Marine Corsairs, and twelve New Zealand P-40s took off to escort twenty-four B-25s to Lakunai. The medium bombers were to hit in two equal squadron waves from 12,000 feet.

Japanese fighter interception of the lead bomber squadron was desultory. Wally Schub was leading his four just above the P-40s, which were in close-cover position with the bombers. About twenty of the Marine F4Us were stacked in divisions to 19,000 feet. Only one Zeke pilot had the temerity to press home an attack against the bombers. He flew right into Schub's sights and acquired crippling hits that blew off large parts of his fuselage. However, the Zeke did not burn or smoke and, since it appeared to fly from the sight under its pilot's control, Wally properly claimed a probable.

The second B-25 squadron and its escorts bore the full brunt of the Japanese reaction. Immediately after "Bombs away," sixty to eighty Zekes and Hamps attacked with a hitherto unknown ferocity.

Thad Bell's division—Lt(jg) Hal Bitzegaio on Bell's wing and Ens Beads Popp on Lt(jg) Earl May's wing—were at 19,000 feet, the top of the heap. The Zekes hit them first.

Bitz, who was on his maiden combat hop, countered well. He flamed a Hamp and shot up two Zekes in quick succession. By then, Bell was leading all hands through a climbing turn to get at a dozen Zekes he had spotted as they positioned themselves overhead. One of the Zekes caught Bitz's Corsair in the right wing with a 20mm explosive round that blew up the contents of one ammo can. Bitz spun out through a half turn, but recovered. As he did, a Zeke came straight up his tail. Bitz yelled, "This is Bitz. Help! Somebody get this Zero off my butt."

Most of our guys heard the "cavalry" respond. "Bitz from Ike. See you. I'll get him."

Miraculously, Ike Kepford arrived in time and indeed did "get" the Zeke. Bitz managed to join on some friends and nurse his shredded bird home to a safe landing.

As Bitz was being saved by Ike, Beads Popp, the division tail-end Charlie, saw Thad Bell's lead Corsair go straight up in a convulsive vertical climb and then fall away. Though Beads did not see a Zeke jump Thad, nor any rounds going into the division leader's cockpit, he was sure that Thad had been struck and possibly killed instantly by Japanese bullets. Whatever happened, when the dust settled, Thad had disappeared. No one ever saw him again.

Shortly after Bitz was culled from the division, May and Popp went into a vertical dive to deliver an attack on three Zekes that were dogging the tail of a lone P-40. May led Popp into a beam run from four o'clock on the nearest Zeke and opened fire. His target half rolled and dived straight in. The pair recovered at about 5,000 feet and rushed the bombers.

Kepford's division went into the fight just below Bell's and was jumped at the same time as Bell's. A skillful riposte against six Zekes 5,000 feet below them brought one Zeke into Ike's sights at seven o'clock level; it was destroyed. Ike's wingman, Ens Don McQueen, a new guy on his maiden combat hop, also bagged a Zeke, this one at ten o'clock high. Danny Cunningham, who was in the number three slot behind Ike, got in a well-planned shot from astern and above his target, which was destroyed. Kepford's foursome, which was still hanging together, was just pulling back up to 19,000 feet when the elements split up to deliver spoiling attacks on a gaggle of about twenty Zeroes. Nothing much was accomplished until Ike heard Bitz's plaint. After Ike saved Bitz, he and McQueen again climbed. Kepford spotted a Zeke chasing another F4U and executed a beam run from three o'clock. He opened fire early from middle range, more to rattle the Zeke pilot than to kill him. Still, he was credited with a probable. A great deal of chasing and shooting ensued down to 8,000 feet, at which point Ike and McQueen rejoined the bombers. The tireless duo then went on to repel two consecutive and uncharacteristically determined fighter attacks on the retiring B-25s. There were, however, no discernible results beyond chasing the Zeros off.

In the meantime, Danny Boy Cunningham, trailed by his wingman, was attacked by a Zeke from above. They split-essed away and, going to full power, got back above the bombers at the rally point. On the retirement, Danny saw a Zero formation to the south, over Cape St. George, and he headed straight for it. He was still far from the objective when he chanced to see a lone Zeke well below him. He executed a textbook high-side run, and the Zeke rolled away smoking, his propeller windmilling. Danny saw the Zeke strike the water, his second kill of the day and his third overall. With that, he led his wingman back to rejoin the bombers. (Had there really been a time when I felt that I had to transfer Danny because he literally did not measure up to a seat in a Hog?)

Though I have absolutely no direct recollection of this action, the records show that my flight of twelve got involved in a wild, swirling dogfight in which I suppose neither I nor Doug Gutenkunst found a target. On the other hand, my second section—Jim Streig leading Bobby Mims—initially dived away and lost the Zekes but found them again when they rebounded to 14,000 feet. The two pulled right up onto the tail of a Zeke which was in a chandelle away from the growing action. The two shared the kill with simultaneous bursts right into the Zeke's belly. They next spotted four Zekes overhead and two or more above and astern. Before our pair could respond, the two Japanese groups joined and came down to gang up on Streig's tail. Bobby turned in on one Zeke, came in from dead astern, and flamed him with a solid burst. Streig used Mims's attention-getter to escape by breaking left and diving away. In the process, however, he lost track of Mims, but he did find a lone Zeke at 3,000 feet. The Zeke was dispatched with a solid burst delivered from Jim's high-side run; it burned and crashed. Streig pulled out to 5,000 feet, but dived away when he saw a burst of tracer pass close aboard his fighter. He recovered at 1,500 feet without damage and again climbed back to 5,000 on a heading for Cape Gazelle. There, he saw seven or eight Zeros climbing away from the Rapopo runway. They were at 1,500 feet when Jim went for the nearest one. He delivered a firing run from abeam and watched the Zeke fall away to the right, all the way to the ground just outside the runway perimeter. Jim put on full power and headed out to overtake the retiring bombers. When he found them, he was making 310 knots at 1,000 feet.

After shooting the Zeke off Jim Streig's tail, Bobby Mims found eight or ten gray-painted fighters he was unable to identify but which he attacked nonetheless. He swung onto the tail of one of the gray fighters and put in a burst that sent it straight into the water. With that—2.5 kills in a matter of minutes on his second combat hop—Bobby chased after our retiring bombers. Eventually, Jim Streig joined on his wing for the trip home.

At the back of my formation, Dirty Eddie March's wingman, Lt(jg) Carl Gilbert, caught an arrow that blew a big hole in his wing. He nevertheless recovered and flamed a Hamp. When Gilbert began looking for Dirty Eddie, he saw nothing but a sky filled with Zekes, so he dived down to the water and turned for home. He was just getting abreast

Cape Gazelle when four Zekes set up on him. However, the four disengaged when Carl turned in to meet their challenge. Seconds later, his Hog was hit again by rounds from a Zeke that crept up on his tail. In Carl's words, he was "scared skinny" by the time he joined a pair of P-40s over the bombers. And he was "still twitching" when he finally got home.

Teeth Burriss and Andy Gump Jagger, March's second section, were nearly swept away by six Japanese fighters, one of which put rounds through the accessory section of Teeth's Hog, just aft of the engine and just ahead of the cockpit. Teeth dived away and came out on the tail of a Zeke, which jinked forward and down. Teeth stayed on him, ripped off short bursts down to only 50 yards, and watched the target smoke and dive into the water. Meantime, Jagger latched onto the tail of the Zeke that had shot Teeth up. The Zeke rolled away, but Jagger stayed with him and fired one burst after another until the Zeke began smoking. It looked as if the Zeke was a goner, but Andy Gump could not wait around to see him go in as he was anxious to rejoin Teeth. However, as Teeth was recovering from his kill, he saw Jagger's target go all the way in. Jagger was unable to rejoin on Teeth before Teeth's oil pressure went to zero and his Hog's propeller stopped as the engine seized up 120 miles from home. Teeth angled down for the surface and neatly skimmed in across an 8-foot swell. He got out of the sinking fighter without difficulty and waved to several friends who had already arrived.

During the early retirement, Lt Oc Chenoweth's section, which was the second part of Tom Killefer's high-cover division, was weaving 2,000 feet above the bombers when Oc spotted six late-arriving Zekes. The enemy fighters, which were coming in from the direction of Rapopo, were already well into their dives from overhead. Before Oc could act, the Zero leader made a run on his wingman, Ens Jim Dixon, but the Japanese pilot did not open fire. When tracer from another Zeke went by his own wings, Oc splitessed to the left and picked up the Zeke from out of the turn. Both fighters were on their backs when Oc opened fire from dead astern. Oc saw his rounds go in, and the Zeke began to smoke. At that moment, however, Oc had to kick up to the right to avoid several P-40s. When next he looked, the Zeke was cutting through the wave tops on its way in. By then, Dixon was long gone so Oc called him on the radio and arranged to rejoin over the bombers. They subsequently joined on a pair of Marine F4Us for the ride to Piva Yoke.

I circled over Teeth with three other Corsairs until a Dumbo Tom Killefer called out from Torokina arrived to pick him up. The wait seemed interminable. As I stooged around at 200 feet and 150 knots, I kept thinking, "Surely the Japs know we do this. Surely they'll send six or eight fighters out as a cleanup detail. We're easy meat, and the Dumbo will be easy meat when it gets here. I can't believe they're letting us get away with this!" However, Teeth was safely on his way home within an hour of ditching.

Our tally for the January 27 morning strike was impressive: sixteen Japanese fighters definitely downed and five probably downed. None of the B-25s was touched by enemy fighters. Our losses were Thad Bell missing and presumed killed and Teeth Burriss downed but rescued. Four of our fighters were slightly damaged and two were lost. The apparent death of Thad Bell was a severe blow to me—not that it was ever easy. I was closer to him as a friend than to most of the guys, and he had been one of the stalwarts from the first days—a good, solid leader who had *earned* command of a flight of eight.

Eight of us took part on an afternoon strike by fourteen B-24s, also against Lakunai. The Japanese put up a bunch of fighters, but none got close enough to be engaged. Even the AA opposition was meager. On the other hand, after sauntering through absolutely clear skies, the bombers put every one of their bombs into the water off the airfield. "Disgusted" does not begin to describe our feelings.

While not unaware of the high kill ratio we amassed in our first two days—twenty-four of them to three of us killed and five Hogs destroyed—we were still deeply concerned. As far as I could tell, the pattern had been established, so I alerted the wiser heads to get to work on solutions that would prevent us from being nearly decimated every time we went out. Out of the ensuing skull session came "Roving High Cover," perhaps our single best tactical contribution to the war effort.

24

• • • • • • • • • • •

When the day's ops drew to a close on January 27, I called my brain trust—Hedrick, Henning, Davenport, Gile, and March—to the Pilots' Mess for a skull session. Over some beers and potions of Black Death whiskey, we six started off with an attempt to assess the causes of our combat losses: What could we do to continue to accomplish our mission of getting strikes safely in and out without getting so badly chopped up ourselves?

The Japanese had shown well before our return that they would not try to counter fighter sweeps. By opposing only bomber raids, they could operate solely as hunters against the AirSols fighters tied to the bombers. This was a familiar ploy; AirSols fighters had done more or less the same over Empress Augusta Bay during our entire first tour. Alerted by their ground observers on Bougainville, they had a full report as to what was coming, and when. To obtain maximum results, their fighters could be guided on station by their radar, ready to take us on as we flew into the target area. As we had done throughout November, they usually pounced from higher up and out of the sun. I was certain that this tactic had culled Thad Bell from our ranks, just as several of us had culled Japanese flight leaders in November. Aggressively pursued with coordinated effort, these tactics could provide the Rabaul defenders with ample opportunities to attrit us with diminished risk to themselves at a rate that would make the losses of our first two days seem like a picnic.

Not unexpectedly, Rog Hedrick provided the basis for our thinking: "If we can hit them before we start our attacks, we could disrupt their plans and formations."

"Yeah," I rebutted, "that's great. But hit 'em with what? Fighter Command is going to schedule us to capacity in cover assignments. They're not going to hold still for any increase of exposure of the bombers."

Butch Davenport, in his capacity of maintenance officer, got the drift of Rog's premise and chimed in: "With our own mechs, plus the topnotch work of the Marine crews, we're averaging almost twenty-five percent better availability than other Corsair squadrons here. In effect, if we're committed to the cover assignments at the same rate as other outfits, we can still field as many as six fighters above and beyond our proportionate share, maybe more."

More mental lights started clicking on; I could feel the intellectual tension rise. What we began putting together was a tactic as old as war itself. It is not uncommon in ground warfare to detach a small unit to lurk well away from the main body so that it will be free to strike the enemy while his attention is focused upon the main action. Awareness of the Japanese tactics virtually led us to the obvious conclusion arising out of Butch's claim that he could provide extra airplanes.

As always, there was a down side. A small unit with no support was clearly vulnerable to being wiped out if the larger enemy force refocused even part of its ample power.

We were not treading new ground. I had been especially fearful of such a tactic going into our very first action over Bougainville on November 1. On that day, we had first— and only—seen twelve Zekes supporting eighteen Vals. I had immediately jumped to the conclusion that this was a bait run, that more Zekes were lurking in the up-sun position, ready to pounce as soon as we had committed ourselves to the obvious targets. The Japanese had not set up the trap as I had feared, but I never quite got over the sense that we could have been in a bad place if they had done the right thing.

Here was our opportunity to do the right thing.

While those of us who considered ourselves tactical geniuses blathered on at great length, Duke Henning quietly jotted down the notes that would soon form the basis of our formal proposal. When he thought enough had been said, Duke cut in. "Skipper, you know that Colonel Brice thinks we're tops. He'll listen to you and probably buy any reasonable proposal you make."

After reviewing Duke's notes, I jeeped over to the colonel's tent.

"Good evening, sir."

His usual "Hi, Tommy" was immediately followed by a shrewdly assessing pause. "Oh boy! I can see by the gleam in your eye that you've got a bright idea you want me to find favor with. Well, at least this is better than the goddamn phone calls from Ondongo you used to raise the dead with at night. Have a beer, and hold your latest brainchild until I get some protection for my flanks."

While I absorbed some of the colonel's beer, he called out his ACIO, Joe Bryan. As soon as the colonel replaced my empty beer bottle and he and Joe had opened theirs, he nodded, "Okay, Tommy, let's have it."

I explained our problem as we saw it, and what we thought the inevitable outcome would be. I pointed out that even our best and most aggressive pilots were not immune to the inexorable statistics, that the outstanding Maj Greg Boyington—then tied for the U.S. record of twenty-six kills—and his wingman had both disappeared without a trace on January 3. I cut it short when I saw signals from the colonel that he was only too well aware of our combat losses.

"Colonel Brice, we'll continue to meet all our flight assignments as laid on for us by your people. And we'll have ready fighters to cover aborts. Then, if we still have several planes and pilots ready to go, I'd like to use them at my own discretion. We'll keep you informed, of course."

The good colonel snorted. "What you mean, Tommy, is that you'll let me know what you did after you've done it!"

"Well, er, yes, sir. Uh, sort of."

The colonel leveled a knowing glare in my direction. "Maybe. Why don't you tell me exactly what you've cooked up now?"

I plunged on with the philosophical pitch Duke had cooked up—every squadron should have a Yale prof aboard—and concluded, "We'll send in four or six experienced guys, led by our best, at high altitude—say thirty or thirty-two thousand—about ten minutes ahead of the strike. They'll jump the Japs as they're forming up at altitude, before they're ready to begin attacking our incoming main formation."

At that point, Joe Bryan alertly chimed in, "What keeps the Zeros from figuring out what you're up to and ganging up on your unsupported dribble? They could shoot your asses off."

"Joe, damn little. This has occurred to us, too. My guys are willing to accept that possibility. Until we come up with a better answer to that question, I guess it's up to us to vary the timing and positioning patterns so we can keep 'em guessing."

After a brief, heavy silence, the colonel gave a brief, sharp nod. "Okay. *But* it's your responsibility to make damn sure you're not throwing away your best pilots and good aircraft. When do you want to try it out?"

"How about tomorrow morning?"

Bryan gave me a stare and a shake of his head, "Tom, you're out of your mind. Good hunting!"

Thus was the birth of Roving High Cover, or RHC. The official name came in as soon as Duke wrote up the first action report, the very next day. However, our guys quickly got to calling it the Gravy Train. Even the top Zero ace of the time, Lt Tetsuzo Iwamoto, wrote of us as "wolves . . . who pounce on the unsuspecting Zeros."

I led off twenty Corsairs at 0640 on January 28, 1944, and joined with eleven from VMF-211 and eight from VMF-215. The mission was to cover seventeen TBFs making a glide-bombing attack with 2,000-pound bombs on Tobera airfield. Well before we reached the target area, Rog Hedrick climbed to 32,000 feet and stormed ahead of the pack with five other Corsairs in tow; fittingly, he was to lead our first RHC bounce.

Based on their radar readings of the main body's approach, the Japanese launched fifty to seventy Zekes.

The RHC contingent approached the target area at 30,000 feet. As the bombers began their attack (there was another, separate formation of SBDs and their cover in on this, too), Rog spotted twelve Zekes in loose formation approaching at 24,000 feet from seaward. Typically, this bunch began breaking off to deliver loosely coordinated attacks in singles and pairs. As soon as the Zekes were committed to their attacks, Rog's six pounced from out of their own loose column of pairs.

Rog made three quick initial firing passes, but only one of his six machine guns responded each time, so the results were negligible. Worse, following the third pass, a Zeke got on Rog's tail as Rog zoomed up to regain altitude. Just as the Zeke appeared on the verge of stalling out, Paul Cordray, who was leading the second section, came up behind him and poured in a long burst with all six of his guns. The Zeke caught fire and fell away.

Hedrick made one more one-gun firing pass, also with no results, and finally got his whole battery working. At that point, he was 10 miles astern the by then retiring bomber formation, which was at 4,000 feet. He decided to close on the bombers but was arrested when he spotted a lone Zeke two miles off and slowly closing on the bombers. Suddenly, the Zeke pointed its nose down at an F4U flying close to the water. Rog fired at long range and missed, but the startled Zeke pilot pulled up in an Immelmann, and Rog followed. Rog cold-bloodedly closed to within 100 yards and fired all his guns into the Zeke's wing root and engine. The Zeke's canopy slid back and the pilot hurtled into the slipstream just before the plane caught fire. Rog strafed the chute, but his shots probably only bracketed it.

After blowing the Zeke off Rog's tail, Cordray and his

wingman, Lt(jg) Jamey Miller, recovered and made several passes at several Zeros, all without observable results. Miller clung to Cordray through his first kill and several subsequent firing passes. When a Zeke Paul never saw set up a high-side run on Cordray's Corsair, Jamey turned into him to commence a head-on firing pass. He saw many pieces of the Zeke's engine fly off under the impact of his guns, and the Zeke eventually nosed down. As Miller rejoined on Cordray and the pair nosed down to follow the plunging Zeke, they spotted five more Zekes. Paul selected one of the Zekes, which was 300 feet below him, and set up a beam firing run which sent that fighter into a flaming dive all the way in. That was Paul's second kill of the day, his sixth overall. Score Fighting-17 another new ace! Miller's Zeke rolled away, but Jamey got in a deflection shot from astern. He saw his tracer going into the Zeke's belly, and then the Zeke blew up. With that, the pair joined up on the bombers for the ride home. Miller's first kill, which no one saw go in, was scored a probable.

Hedrick's wingman, Ens Fatso Ellsworth, lost Rog at the very start of the action. He shot at a Zeke, but missed, so climbed back to 20,000 feet, where he found another Zeke climbing. Fatso turned up into the enemy fighter and got a long burst into its engine. The Zeke staggered and fell away smoking and tumbling, but could only be scored a probable. That was more than enough for the lone fatman, so he headed for the rally point, where he joined on a Marine Corsair's wing for the retirement.

The third RHC pair, Lt(jg) Hal Jackson and Ens Don Malone, went down with Hedrick on the first firing pass. One of four passing Zekes pulled up right in front of Hal, too good a target to pass up. Hal put a long burst right into the cockpit, and the Zeke erupted in flames. Hal rolled away from the blast and was on the verge of joining on Cordray and Miller when he spotted a Zeke making a firing pass on Malone's tail. As Hal came down, the Zeke broke off and dived away. Malone rejoined on Hal's wing and the pair flew to the rally point to begin a protective weave over the retiring bombers. However, Malone's plane had been badly damaged in the fracas and Hal's was very low on fuel. The pair broke away from the formation and headed straight for the barn. They landed early without further incident.

Maybe it was the RHC plan, and maybe it was superb flying skills, aggressiveness, or a hundred other variables, but the six RHC Corsairs bagged a total of four unambiguous Zeke kills, plus two probables.

Perhaps it was our RHC attack, perhaps it was other factors, perhaps it was in the eye of the beholders—whatever lay behind it, the Japanese main effort was disorganized, nearly inchoate. Only thirty or forty of the fifty to seventy airborne Zeros closed on our bomber formations, and not one of them got any rounds into any of the bombers. The fourteen Fighting-17 Corsairs providing medium and high cover had one of our best days so far: Dirty Eddie March, Tom Killefer, Doug Gutenkunst, and newcomer Ens Percy Divenny each creamed two Zekes; Bobby Mims scored 1 full kill, shared another with a Marine, and scored a probable; Ens Bill Meek, another rookie, scored a definite kill; and Lt(jg) Carl Gilbert got a probable. Together with the RHC total, that comes to 14.5 definite kills and 4 probables, virtually as good as our November 11 turkey shoot over the carriers. Moreover, though we had three planes badly shot up and two more holed, we lost no pilots and, in the end, none of our fighters. Our Marine coworkers got 15.5 confirmed kills and 4 probables.

Though extremely successful, our RHC mission of January 29 took a turn I had feared it might.

Led by Rog Hedrick, sixteen of our guys launched to escort twenty-four SBDs to Tobera along with a like number of Marine Corsairs and a dozen low-cover New Zealand P-40s. On the way, our formation had two aborts, both of them Corsairs that were to have been in on the RHC bounce. Despite the 50 percent operational attrition, the two remaining RHC pilots—Kepford and Burriss—elected to complete the bounce. By this time, Ike had 6 kills and Teeth had 3.5. They were big boys, but, like all boys, they were bound to step a little beyond the bounds when no one was looking. I later had cause to question their judgment, but I could not openly reproach them in light of the results.

While the bombers ground along into the approach at 14,000 feet—we had seven Corsairs at 15,000 and seven at 16,000—Ike and Teeth climbed to 30,000. The approach was made over Cape St. George and south of Duke of York Island. As the final approach was being completed, Ike and Teeth spotted a dozen Zekes below them, at about 24,000 feet over Cape Gazelle. They both climbed slightly and then dived right away at the Zekes.

The RHC pair did everything right. Trading the lead after each firing run, the two maintained perfect cohesion in one textbook attack after another. In ten minutes of continuous high-side and overhead firing passes, with sharp chandelles in between, they accounted for four Zekes apiece. Moreover, not only was the personal score of each pilot superbly enhanced, there is no question that they broke the spirit of the Japanese. Only fifteen Zekes challenged the retiring bomber formation from above in a series of uncoordinated, half-hearted attacks. The two Zekes that got through to the bombers were shot down by their gunners, and our guys got a total of two kills (Timmy Gile and Earl May) and three probables (Oc Chenoweth, Ens Jim Dixon, and Ens John Malcolm Smith). Lower down, the Marines had quite a battle on their hands with Zekes, Hamps, and Tonys climbing into the strike formation. Their Corsairs got eleven kills and five probables.

At the debriefing, a proud and pleased Rog Hedrick let down his reserve long enough to bellow, "This one was really a piece of cake! It was great—and then some—to see the burning Zekes raining down as we came in on Tobera."

Overall, the squadron's morale soared after these two sensational days, and Fighter Command was elated. But I found myself possessed of a concerned fatherly rage over the reckless temerity evidenced by Kepford's and Burriss's ill-advised though manifestly successful showboating.

Ike and Teeth came away from the January 29 mission as

our high scorers, Ike as a double ace and Teeth with 7.5. There was no jealousy evidenced by any of my other tigers; they just wanted to be sure their turns came up for the Gravy Train. It was all just as I had hoped—and just as I had feared.

At the pilots' meeting that evening, before the preflight briefing for the January 30 mission, I decided to lay down the law. "We've turned things around, and you men are showing all hands in Fighter Command the kind of stuff you've got." I paused for a moment to allow silent cheers and mental backslapping. *"But, . . ."* all eyes were back on me, "don't you *dare* get overconfident. There is no surer way of getting your ass in a sling. We will have *no stars* in this outfit! As I told you before we came up here, if I see anybody—*any*body—who shows signs of getting Zero Happy, I'll ground him, maybe for a while, maybe forever. That includes Rog. And he'll lay it on me if he thinks I've been bitten by that bug. There will be no contests for record individual kills in Fighting-Seventeen. That sort of thing only gets people killed."

I let that sink in and turned to another problem we were just beginning to experience; I was sure it was a direct outgrowth of the nascent Zero-Happy problem. "Hereafter, if you're late getting off because of a mechanical problem, you're more than welcome to try to catch up to the flight and finish out the assignment." It had always been thus, with good results. "However, if you're not joined up by the time you get within twenty-five miles of Cape St. George, you will turn around and return to base. It doesn't matter if you get it into your head that there are no Japs around. Always keep in mind Blackburn's First Rule of Survival: 'It's the guy you don't see who's most likely to cream you.' As we all know, they're superaggressive when it comes to bouncing singles. Separate pairs will not go in either below thirty thousand feet. No exceptions."

25

. . . .

The morning liftoff on January 30 comprised twenty VF-17
F4Us as part of the cover for a small flight of B-25s bound
for Tobera. The operation was routine in all its parts, and
the results were well within the norms we had established
in just a week: Hedrick scored another kill while his wingman, Ens Fatso Ellsworth, scored his first definite air-to-air
victory. Probables were scored by Lt(jg) Hap Bowers, Ens
Jamey Miller, Ens John Malcolm Smith, and Ens George
Keller. One Corsair brought back a wing chewed up by a
Zero, but none of the bombers was molested directly.

After lunch and a nap, Doug Gutenkunst and I went
down to the beach by the mouth of the Torokina River.
Though a godsend for us, Bougainville's beaches will never
put Waikiki out of business; the sand is coarse and coal
black—the detritus from lava from the volcanic Franz Josef
mountain range, which forms the big island's spine. Except
on very stormy days, the surf runs at all of 6 inches.

Doug and I got along perfectly despite the difference in
our ages and backgrounds. We were more brothers than
colleagues, more trusted friends than commander and subordinate. My only real bitch about my wingman's superb

fighting skills was his marked tendency in combat to sky out and take on the Imperial fighters on his own.

As we lolled and relaxed in the surf, the normal noise levels of engines being turned up for testing and the occasional bursts of fire from the nearby front lines suddenly altered drastically. Soon, all other noise was subordinated to the unmistakable throaty roar of numerous high-power engines.

"What's up, Skipper? I didn't know there was a launch scheduled for this afternoon."

"Me neither, Doug. May be a scramble."

We soon saw Corsairs lifting off from Torokina and Piva Yoke, while Turkeys—as we now called the TBFs—were climbing out of Piva Uncle to form up overhead. Doug and I did not exchange so much as a word as we hustled into our clothes and ran for the jeep. Minutes later, we screeched up to our line-shack, ready-room tent at the strip. By then, I learned later, seventeen of our hastily assembled pilots had climbed aboard any old Hog and gotten airborne on the run, in a catch-as-catch-can organization.

Doug and I whipped into the Marine cotton coveralls we preferred for our tropical flying and donned boondockers— the heavy Marine combat shoes that were the best footgear available in the event we had to bail out over land. As we grabbed our Mae West life jackets, cotton flying helmets, sheath knives, and pistols, Duke Henning briefed us on the run: "Some recon plane just radioed in that a Jap carrier is approaching Rabaul along with a small escort force."

The contact report had come in around 1500. While no time was wasted getting planes away to snoop the enemy task force, MGen Ralph Mitchell, ComAirSols, had by no means hit the panic button. He had gotten on the horn to Fighter Command, then to Strike Command, and had ordered them to "Scramble whatever fighters you can with a maximum of the ready Turkeys with fish. Get the flattop."

By 1640, the time Doug and I taxied out, more than twenty TBFs—half loaded with torpedoes and half loaded with 1,000-pound bombs—and forty Navy and Marine Corsairs were a half-hour out, barreling north-northwest at the best speed the laden bombers could make. Odd flights of bomb-laden SBDs were also on the way. Our seventeen VF-17 fighters were under Oc Chenoweth.

There was no carrier, so the strike went after the small game it could find at Simpson Harbor. The Japanese reacted to the unexpected incursion with a meager thirty Zekes and several flights of Imperial Army fighters, mostly Tonys. However, the AA barrage was fierce, as if the gunners deeply resented the breakup of their late afternoon sake hour.

As Doug and I came boiling in at full throttle in high blower, the scene over Rabaul was spectacular. The heavy AA was laying a thick carpet around the Turkeys, which were approaching at 14,000 feet. Just slightly lower down was an equally lethal array of tracer from the lighter AA. AirSols fighters were all over the sky, sending down burning Japanese fighters. Here and there, one or another of our fighters plummeted earthward trailing long plumes of thick black smoke.

Doug and I turned out to be a delayed version of the RHC as we came in out of the westering sun to surprise some of the enemy fighters preoccupied with the brouhaha below. I spotted six Zeros in loose formation of three pairs as they flew through a gentle turn at 20,000 feet. All of them seemed to be enjoying the show farther down; certainly none of them imagined our approach. I hit the number two man in the lead pair from a steep dive, a beam run that ended astern as he blew up under the impact of my rounds.

As we chandelled out of the attack, I spotted another pair setting up on a high-cover F4U. Doug and I got there in time and I set up a low-side run on the wingman. He dived away in a spiral, but I managed to get on his tail and stay there. Repeated hits set the Zero afire, and that forced the pilot to bail out. At least I did not have to follow the wreck to earth to claim a definite kill. However, I did have to recover from my attack. The tight turn pulled more gees than I expected, and I was on the ragged edge of blacking out. As the gray fog evaporated, I spotted the recently blossomed parachute. I swung back to finish off the Japanese pilot; if I didn't, I reasoned, he probably would be up to meet us the next day—smarter, and looking for me. Unbelievably the harness was empty. A closer look at the dangling straps revealed that they had burned through. At that moment, it was not at all pleasant to think about the Japanese pilot's 18,000-foot unarrested dive to the surface.

Doug had stayed with me all through the gyrations topping off the two successful attacks. As a reward, I turned the lead over to him. As we eased on down to about 10,000 feet to find a slot in the high-cover formation above our bombers, Doug made a high-side attack from four o'clock against a single Zero. When the target spun out it was smoking and apparently out of control. Next, about a dozen Zekes and Hamps jumped us, but we took violent evasive action and shook them off. As we recovered and rejoined over the bombers, Doug set up on a pair over the bombers and cut loose at the wingman, who split-essed to safety. Instantly, Doug shifted his attention to the element leader. I clearly saw Doug's round going in, but the Hamp disappeared into a cloud.

Having had an opportunity to lead two attacks, Doug graciously turned the lead back to me. As we again took station over the outbound bombers, I saw a Zero about 2 miles astern and boring straight in. I swung away, and Doug followed. I managed to set up a full-deflection shot that staggered the Japanese fighter and started a fire in the cockpit. Just as I stopped firing, however, the flames died out. I shot again, and the Zeke glided away. When last seen as I led Doug back to the bombers again, the Zero was in a 30-degree dive and heading down through 1,000 feet.

The rest of the Fighting-17 team did very well. Ike Kepford bagged a Zeke and a Tony, and Butch Davenport got a pair of Zekes. Oc Chenoweth got two Zekes and shared a third with his wingman, Ens Jim Dixon, a new guy. Mills Schanuel got a single, his third definite kill.

The victory—ten confirmed kills—was not without cost. Lt(jg) Tom Kropf disappeared without a trace, and Lt Ray Beacham's Corsair was badly shot up. Ray got the damaged Hog home, but by then his hydraulic pressure gauge read zero. He thus had no flaps, and the CO_2 emergency gear-extension system got only one wheel down. Making matters hairier, Ray reported that he had about 5 inches of avgas sloshing around in his Hog's belly right below the cockpit, the result of a busted fuel line. It was getting dark, and Ray prudently elected to make a water landing. The splashdown was rough; the one wheel violently slewed the F4U upon contact with the water. The crash boat pulled Ray from the water in seconds. He was briefly hospitalized with a broken nose, but he and we all knew he had fared well.

A Tony had nearly creamed Kepford; an ammo can in his right wing exploded from a 20mm hit. There was a big fire raging in the wing for a while, but Ike doggedly kept on course for home. The fire soon burned itself out, but at the cost of vital controls. The result was that Ike came in for a high-speed, one-wheel touchdown. The Hog violently ground looped and piled up, a total loss. Blessedly, it did not burn. When the crash crew yanked Ike from the wreckage, our high scorer was physically okay but a mite shaken in the emotion department.

Ens Beads Popp also washed his plane out on landing. Unbeknownst to him, he came in on a flat tire. The Hog pulled a spectacular ground loop that turned into a magnificent cartwheel. The pilot was unhurt, but he was naturally exuding giant beads of sweat on his nose, the unique personal reaction to high stress that had led to his nom de guerre.

Doug and I were among the last fighters in. By the time we got over the field, it was nearly dark and the crash and salvage crews were overwhelmed by the busted birds piling up on Piva Yoke. We were therefore diverted to Piva Uncle, the bomber strip. Its traffic pattern was saturated with a mix of F4Us, TBFs, and SBDs. Further, by then, the radio discipline no longer existed; the tower's control frequency was hopelessly jammed with competing high-tension chatter. Efforts by the tower personnel to handle the traffic by means of red and green signal searchlights were ignored.

It was all too evident that getting on deck in one piece was going to take some doing.

At length, I spotted a good-sized hole in the circle of planes on the downwind leg of the landing pattern and I decided to go for it. I gratefully slid in, and Doug followed at a thirty-second interval as I made our standard turning carrier-type approach. I laid on a perfect three-point landing as far down the strip as possible so I would spend the least amount of time getting off the runway. As I completed my rollout, I checked my rearview mirror to see if it was safe to turn. To my horror, all I saw was a huge ball of orange flame at the downwind end of the runway. I *knew* that Doug was in it.

Also in the inferno rising intensely against the black night sky was what had been a badly shot-up Corsair that had been driven by a seriously wounded Marine major. With neither lights nor radio, nor an operable hydraulics system, the Marine had been guided back to the field by his squadron mates, who had lined him up to the runway for a necessary straight-in approach. The Marine Hog was barely controllable. With no landing flaps available, it came in extremely fast. Moreover, blood from his head wound had left the major virtually blind. He and Doug collided at low altitude, right over the end of the strip. Neither pilot had a chance. It was nobody's fault; some malign fate had brought these two brave men into a space big enough for just one of them.

All hands in both squadrons were devastated. Combat losses were hard enough to take, but we could accept them, of necessity. This freak grisly accident was too much. Compounding the unacceptable was that the wounded major was seconds away from what would otherwise have been an epochally miraculous safe return.

I was wiped out. My beloved friend and loyal protector was a charred corpse. The final flight had been joyous, a successful scrap in which our team of two had come very much into its own.

On January 31 sixteen of us were assigned low and medium cover above the TBF component of a Piva-launched light-bomber strike against shipping in Karavia Harbor. The total loss of five of our aircraft the previous afternoon prevented us from mounting the usual RHC mission.

There was nothing worth taking on in Karavia Harbor, so the bomber leader diverted all his birds to Tobera. They made their approach over Cape St. George, up St. George Channel, over Duke of York Island, and then south over Londip Plantation. As the bombers made a right turn toward the target, we were approached by approximately forty Zekes and what looked to Chico Freeman like three Imperial Army Ki-44 "Tojo" fighters. There were not supposed to be any Tojos deployed around Rabaul—so the official records say—but the type's barrel-shaped P-47-like silhouette was absolutely unmistakable. In fact, Marine great 1st Lt Butcher Bob Hansen had been credited with two Tojo kills during the previous day's afternoon strike.

As so often happened, the interceptors stooged around until after the bombers had completed their drops and were retiring over Kabanga Bay. Even the typically aggressive AA defense was meager this day, and the heavier guns ceased firing altogether as the dive-bombers pushed over on the Tobera runway. The Japanese fighters began their runs from around 24,000 feet, but they were singularly unaggressive. Elements of three Marine Corsair squadrons flying top cover intercepted and got five kills and four probables, and one TBF gunner got a kill. However, during the run-in and early retirement, not one of the enemy fighters got as low as 14,000 or 15,000 feet, where we were tied down.

Well into the retirement, I saw a steeply diving Zeke slanting down on Teeth Burriss's fighter, which was number three behind my second-flight leader, Dirty Eddie March. I keyed my mike and yelled, "Teeth! Break hard right! Now!" But Teeth apparently did not hear my warning, for he continued in the gentle turn of his weaving pattern. The Zeke nailed him and followed through before any of our guys could get a shot off.

Teeth left the formation trailing smoke. His wingman, Andy Gump Jagger, followed him down until another single Zeke jumped them. Andy turned hard into this attacker, but the Zeke took violent evasive action and got away. When Andy turned back to his previous retirement course, Teeth was nowhere to be found.

We were able to send off a search mission on February 1 across the Solomon Sea to St. George Channel, straight up the track we thought Teeth might have followed as he limped home. We saw a submarine that dived before we got close enough to identify it, but nothing else was out there—no debris, and no raft.

We never learned Teeth's fate. Andy Jagger, who was miserable, had not been able to get close enough to Teeth's wounded Hog to check the extent or nature of the damage, or to see if Teeth was hurt. We all hoped Teeth had lived to make a water landing—he was one of our most skilled pilots and could have managed it if anyone could—but he could as easily have crashed. Though we marked him as missing, we well knew that Teeth Burriss was dead.

January's totals were 60.5 enemy fighters destroyed in the air—in only six days! However, we had also lost 5 pilots shot down and killed and 1 pilot killed in a midair collision. Altogether, 13 of our Hogs had been destroyed, 5 directly by enemy aircraft, 4 in crackups after being shot up by enemy aircraft, 3 in operational landing crashes, and 1 in the midair collision.

26

· · · · · · · · · ·

Though we got a search mission off after Teeth Burriss, the February 1 game was called on account of rain—a huge frontal system that totally shut down everything from Rabaul to Empress Augusta Bay. The rain was so bad that no one gave much thought to Hal Jackson's report that he had seen a drainage ditch filled with drowned frogs. Any flat place was calf-deep in mud, and the 10-foot-deep ditches the Seabees maintained on either side of all roadways were dangerous swift-moving streams. The entrance to my tent, a 5-foot-square area paved with empty beer cans, was maddeningly musical. By the second, even the gulls were walking.

The two-day respite was most welcome. In a mere week since we had taxied onto Piva Yoke's hardstands beneath the towering mahogany trees, we had had six consecutive days of furious, mind-numbing action. Six of our number were dead—one a day.

The living conditions at Piva Yoke were good—screened tents on wooden decks and plenty of showers with cool, sparkling water from jungle streams—but the down side had us all on edge. We often heard and sometimes saw tanks clanking down the main road running past the field, and we were treated constantly to the *boom-swish* of (thankfully) outgoing artillery fire. So far, each and every night, and most days, had been filled with the odd withering bursts of gunfire from the all-too-near front lines. We were constantly assured that there was zero chance of our being overrun, that two entire veteran Army divisions were dug in along or engaged in expanding the perimeter around us. The assurances would have been more credible without the sounds of gunfire. We all made sure our pistols were in easy reach and that we had plenty of ammo on hand. We begged, borrowed, or stole carbines until each of us had his own.

The bug population had been all but wiped out. There appeared to be no mosquitoes, but we all choked down our daily dose of vile, yellow-skin-producing antimalarial Atrabine. The only insect life that seemed impervious to the Seabees' DDT showers were the *giant* centipedes. We all learned to stow our shoes upside down and high off the ground at night, and to shake them out before donning them in the morning. One day shortly after our arrival, I unfolded my washcloth at the shower and found myself being stared down by a huge unfriendly-looking specimen.

Thankfully, the Navy supplied and prepared our food. The fighter pilots' mess was adequate in every way. We even had plenty of refrigerated fresh food. I cannot give the facility four stars, but it was light-years better than the Army-run Hotel Mud Plaza at Ondongo.

Recreation was primarily based on our own resources. Card games never ended, though the cast changed from time to time, and everyone spent hours listening to Armed Forces Radio and Tokyo Rose. The former was considered okay, but all hands preferred the latter's better selection of good jazz records larded with the highly comedic Japanese propaganda. Beer was the favored beverage, but we maintained a decent supply of Black Death whiskey and Lejon brandy, which was tolerable if mixed with grapefruit juice.

When flight operations resumed on February 3, Butch Davenport led off twelve of our remaining twenty-four Corsairs. His job was to help escort a flight of B-24s bound for

Lakunai. Only twenty-eight Japanese fighters were counted in the air over the target. As far as Butch's flight could see from their low-cover position, only seven Zekes actually engaged. Of these, Kepford got one and Chenoweth got a probable. Marines from two squadrons assigned to medium cover did a little better with five kills and four probables. There were sixteen P-38s along flying top cover, but I have no idea how they fared.

It was becoming obvious that the Japanese defense over Rabaul was crumbling. Individually, their few truly aggressive fighter pilots had been getting better at air-to-air tactics, but the overall effort had been in a deepening slump since we arrived. The pressure had dropped off to almost nothing on January 31, and it showed no signs of reemerging on February 3.

I led off twenty of our Corsairs on February 4. Once again, our charges were B-24s, this time bound for Tobera. I had a newly arrived lieutenant on my wing, a solid-seeming senior pilot I wanted to check out before moving him up to lead a section, or even a division.

Only twenty Zeros and ten Tonys appeared to challenge us. On the approach, however, Ens Perce Divenny, who had joined us in Espiritu but who already had two kills under his belt, made a really dumb mistake. Instead of opening the valve that released CO_2 into the Corsair's wing-purging system, he opened the adjacent valve, which actuated his emergency landing-gear system. Once down by this means, there was no way to get the wheels back up while in flight. We were by then too close to the target to allow Perce to abort, so, as soon as I saw the reason why he was dropping back, I radioed to tell him to tuck in beneath the heavy bombers. If Perce understood and did exactly what he was told—and stayed put—he would have it made; the Zekes would never be able to get at him.

We were retiring from the bomb-drop point when, to my utter horror, I saw Divenny's Corsair slowly dropping behind the B-24s. We could never figure out what happened; Perce was a cool hand, so the only theory that held was that his Hog suffered some sort of engine-power loss. In any case, by this time, the Zeros were nipping at our flanks, looking for an opening so they could get at the Liberators or bounce exposed fighters. Our job was to protect the B-24s, and we all had our hands full doing that, so I made the brutal decision to withhold cover for Divenny. Naturally, the Zeros—at least eight of them—pounced on Perce. As they started in, Earl May broke from his position in the bomber cover and led his wingman, Beads Popp, to the rescue. The two got to Divenny's lagging fighter, and they did get their talons into one of the Zekes. Earl got credit for an assist and Beads got full credit for the kill. However, the rest of the Zeros bore down on them and May and Popp had to dive to safety. A Zeke came down on Perce's tail and hammered him into a fatal dive.

As the retiring bombers were clearing the coast, six Zekes hit the formation from 500 feet above the low-cover flight. Attacking from the rear, these Zekes put in a series of aggressive high-side runs. The rear division, under Lt(jg) Paul Cordray, turned back to take on the Zekes, and the Zekes broke contact. However, when Paul turned again to rejoin the bombers, two Zekes slipped in and set up a firing pass at the rear element, Lt(jg) Hal Jackson followed by Lt(jg) Don Malone. Jackson was well behind Cordray and his wingman, and Malone was lagging even farther behind Jackson.

Cordray gave a frantic "Close up" zooming signal, and Jackson promptly moved in. Malone, who had a long history of lagging in formation, did not respond to the unmistakable series of short dives and zooms, nor even to "Don! Don! Close up! Close up," which Paul frantically broadcast by radio. When the Zekes pulled up at the conclusion of their single firing run, Malone's Corsair was burning and falling away. Attracted by Cordray's vain warning, several of us saw Don's chute blossom. We hoped he would get down safely, but we had to leave. No one ever saw Don again.

As soon as we landed, I confronted Earl May at the ready room and let him have it with my fury. I had been literally sick to my stomach when I saw Divenny going down, but I had made the painful decision to carry out our responsibility to defend the bombers. I had determined that we could not do that and cover Divenny, too. It was, in my mind, a tough fact of life that Perce had been lost because he had been unable to stay under the heavy bombers. The only thing that kept me from grounding Earl was the lucky fact that no enemy fighters had attacked through the hole his departure had left in our formation.

"Get this straight, Earl. Nobody has ever questioned your courage. You don't have to prove yourself like some show-off schoolboy. You had no goddamn business breaking out of your cover position with Beads to take on all those Japs. For what? Sure, you and Beads flamed one, but you damn sure didn't help Divenny. You were lucky as hell you and Beads didn't get it, too. You *know* that if the enemy hadn't muffed their chance they'd have had three easy kills instead of just one. Worse than that, you exposed the rest of us and the bombers. Our job is to get those klunkers in and out in one piece. I'm *proud* that we haven't lost one yet. They *depend* on us. This is a team operation. There's no place for some wild-ass who shoves off to be the heroic White Knight riding to the rescue. I will not tolerate this kind of shit. Is that clear?"

Earl was angry with me—his body language said as much—but he was wrong and I was right, and he knew it. I got a sheepish, "I understand, Skipper."

"If you weren't such a good man who's always done a top job before, I'd throw your ass out. As it is, you're no longer a division leader. You'll fly wing, where I can keep my eye on you."

I was so obviously angry for the rest of the day that no one got within 10 feet of me if he could help it.

My overall reaction and anger over the two losses might seem unreasonable, but both were firmly grounded in my lifelong perception of how duty must come before my personal feelings for my subordinates, strong as they were. All hands—even late arrivals like Perce Divenny—knew that our responsibility was to guard the bombers *at all costs*.

In part, however, the display of anger was a mask for my profound grief. The two unnecessary losses were almost more than I could bear. I privately judged myself at least a little culpable in both cases.

With respect to Perce's fatal lapse, I allowed the wing-purging and emergency landing-gear CO_2 bottles to remain side by side even though I easily could have gotten Vought or even our own mechanics to relocate one safely away from the other. The potential for error was *so* obvious! Amazingly, Divenny's gaffe had been the first of its sort in hundreds of combat sorties.

Malone's loss was a little different, and I bore more direct responsibility. All hands knew that Don had a marked propensity to lag. Maybe I should have ridden him harder, or moved him forward from the definitely vulnerable tail-end slot. We knew that the Imperial pilots, like us, were quick to spot and nail a laggard.

Worst of all was my conviction that I had seen both situations developing. I had certainly seen Divenny fall behind, and I am sure I had seen Malone do so earlier in the mission. In Divenny's case, I *could* have taken the chance and gone back or sent help, but I deliberately chose not to. In Malone's, Cordray could have gone to help, but Paul knew—and accepted—my thinking, so he did not danger-ously expose his division and put others at risk, as May had done.

These were two more painful examples of the loneliness of command. I found, after a long search through my soul, that I would not have acted differently in either case. But I had contributed to Malone's death by being too lenient; I should have grounded him because of his inability to cor-rect a long-apparent problem. It was a bomb that had ticked away—that I had heard ticking—until it blew up in Don's face.

27

. . . .

On February 5 twelve of our F4Us led by Dirty Eddie
March were assigned as part of the SBD cover on a joint
SBD-TBF strike against Lakunai. On the approach over
Duke of York Island and Crater Peninsula, the SBDs flew
at 12,000 feet and our fighters flew low cover at 13,000 feet.

Right between Duke of York Island and Crater Peninsula,
the formation was approached by a dozen brown-painted
Zekes coming in over a volcano called The Mother. Five of
the Zekes executed overhead runs against the SBDs just
before the dive-bombers pushed over on the Lakunai main
runway. As they did, and without ever losing his place in
the formation, Butch Davenport, who was leading the rear
division, depressed the nose of his Hog and caught one of
the Zekes with a 40-degree deflection shot. The Zeke burned
all the way in. It was Butch's fifth full kill; he was an ace.
None of the attacking Zekes laid a glove on the Dauntlesses.

On the retirement—straight out directly over St. George
Channel—six to eight Zekes were spotted over Tobera at
about 6,000 feet. Probably, they had just taken off and were
only just forming up. A pair of the new arrivals attempted
to put in a low-side run against Lt Wally Schub's middle
F4U division. However, Lt(jg) Country Landreth, the leader

259

of Schub's second element, dived at one of the attackers and got a good, solid burst into the target's engine. This Zeke went down in flames. At the same time Country was swatting his Zeke, Schub spotted yet another Zeke diving into his formation. The Japanese pilot turned away prematurely as Schub angled up to meet him. Wally got in a great belly shot from eight o'clock. The Zeke caught fire and fell all the way into the water. With that, the rest of the Zekes backed off and our formation was not molested during the remainder of the retirement.

Our only other mission of the day was a Dumbo-escort hop east of Buka. I turned the lead of my division over to the new lieutenant who was my temporary wingman. I happened to be the one to spot the life raft first, but I was pleased with the new officer's leadership, and I mentally noted that he was nearly ready for some unsupervised section-lead flying.

I led off sixteen of our guys early on February 6, but we had two early aborts. We were assigned to fly high cover over a formation of twenty-seven B-25s out of the Treasuries. Also along for the ride were twenty-four New Zealand P-40s, twenty-four Marine Corsairs from two squadrons, and eight F6Fs from Lem Cooke's squadron, out of Vella Lavella. The target was Lakunai again. As we got close, I turned the lead over to Wally Schub and peeled off for RHC along with my wingman and a section composed of Bobby Mims leading Hal Bitzegaio.

In absolutely clear skies, the B-25s approached Lakunai at 12,000 feet in reverse of the usual pattern, from south of Duke of York Island and north of Gredner Island before turning right to get in over the runway. Retirement was to be over the tip of New Ireland's East Cape.

At least forty Japanese fighters were spotted; sixteen were forming up over Tobera and the rest were over Rapopo. I decided to pile in against the Tobera bunch and timed my arrival from 25,000 feet for just before Bombs Away.

The first firing run was made from out of the sun at four

or six Zekes which were still over Tobera but heading in the direction of the bombers from 22,000 feet. I lined up on the first Zeke I saw and dived in at a 25-degree down angle from the five o'clock position. A very short burst instantly caused the Zeke to explode—a clean kill. As I was getting my Zeke, Bobby Mims flamed one of his own.

I recovered in a right chandelle and flew up through the expanding ball of debris of my kill at 23,000 feet. The entire division came out of the pass as a complete unit. As I leveled off, I saw another group of Zeros heading away to the northwest to intercept the bombers.

We caught up with the Zeros and dived to catch them at 20,000 feet, right over Lakunai. I led my division in and made an immediate high-side run from the left. My target started burning after I had fired only a short burst. Bitz also got a Zeke on the pass. Mims bored right up to the tail of what he later swore was a Tojo and, after nearly rear-ending the oddity, fired a short burst that sent the bottle-shaped Imperial Army fighter down in a shower of flames and debris. That was Bobby's fifth kill (including two half kills), so he, too, was an ace. Moments later, he got his sixth, another Zeke. He also scored two probables in this wild and woolly melee.

Meantime, before I completed my recovery from the first firing pass, another Zeke flew straight into my sights. I instinctively opened fire as I followed him into a tight diving turn. I kept putting out bursts until, at about 4,000 feet, I was on the verge of blacking out. I began to ease out of the spiral at just the instant my wingman saw my target flare up into a huge ball of fire. I continued to recover to my left and led my wingman up in a climbing spiral.

On the way up, I spotted a mixed bag of four Zekes and Hamps above me, but I declined to get into a fight without a sure altitude advantage. I poured on all my power and fought for altitude, but they never even approached. When I got to 22,000 feet, the four Zeros were still circling obliviously where I had left them, so I turned back down to get at them. As I was approaching, two of the Zeros vanished and the other pair dived away in opposite directions. I followed one Zeke into a radical dive, but it looked like he was going to get away, so I pulled out in a right chandelle. As soon as I gave up the chase, the Zeke turned sharply to the right and zoomed back up in a vertical climb.

This was an *old* trick. As the two planes are reaching the top of the climb, but well before the U.S. fighter is close enough to get in a killing shot, both begin running out of flying speed. Since a Zero was more maneuverable at low speeds than any of our fighter types, it could usually pull through the loop onto the tail of the attacker. We lost scores of airplanes and pilots to this maneuver earlier in the war, and I suppose we were still losing tyros to it over Rabaul. I was no tyro, so I put in a disquieting burst at long range and broke off as soon as I saw what the play was going to be. I saw my tracer fall right on the Zeke, but I was unable to observe any obvious damage before I had to go.

I was amazed and gratified to see how quickly the division again reformed on my lead. We had been running like a single piece of machinery all morning. I expected good things of Mims, who was one of the old Norfolk and Manteo hands, but I also got great performances out of the newcomers on our wings. I was particularly happy with my wingman, who, though he scored no kills, was proving out as an excellent pilot. As we headed out to join on the retiring bombers, Bobby flew up alongside to tell me via hand signals that he was getting low on oxygen. I signaled back, directing him and Bitzegaio to return to base immediately.

As my wingman and I were nearing Cape St. George, still following the retiring bomber group, we picked up a lone Hamp tooling along in straight and level flight at moderate speed. Talk about a death wish; this guy had clearly secured from General Quarters a mite too soon. We closed up his tail to within about 50 yards and never got a glimmer of reaction. The Hamp blew into a million pieces as soon as I began squirting rounds at him. My wingman's windshield was doused with oil and fuel, and he heard chunks of debris hitting his Hog as I led him through a fireball for the second time that morning.

The Roving High Cover ploy did *exactly* what it was meant to do; it broke the spirit of the welcoming committee before most of the airborne Japanese fighters could go after the bombers. Nevertheless, there were attacks on the main group.

Those Japanese who managed to stay out of the clutches of my RHC division attacked the standard high-cover fighters as the bombers were turning over Lakunai for the drop. This was the ideal spot for the interception because many of our fighters had to swing wide to stay with the bombers. The object was to pick off the outside fighters while they were most vulnerable.

As the B-25s turned, Wally Schub's second section—Lt(jg) Country Landreth leading Ens Clyde Dunn—went too wide to the outside. Then, as the bombers straightened out, Landreth and Dunn were sucked in behind their assigned position. Two or three Zekes at 17,000 feet—2,000 above our errant pair—pounced from dead astern just as the two Corsairs came right to cut back inside the bombers. At almost the same instant, Schub and his wingman, Ens Whit Wharton, were attacked by two or three other Zekes. This was the best example of a coordinated bounce we had experienced at Japanese hands in many a day.

Schub's section turned obliquely to the right—Wally said it was 135 degrees—and arrived in time to meet the second Zeke coming down on Landreth's section. Wally got a good burst in from two o'clock and below, and the Zeke fell away burning. He then led Wharton straight down to evade the trio of Zekes that had been closing on him all the while. Wally's intervention temporarily scared off the survivors of the team that had bounced Landreth and Dunn, but at least two pairs of these superb Japanese pilots managed to get in several high-side and overhead attacks in very rapid succession. Schub's and Wharton's Hogs were hit by 20mm rounds, but neither was disabled. At length, the Japanese withdrew and our two sections were able to rejoin. They scissored over the bombers the whole rest of the way home.

I was extremely proud of the manner in which my make-shift division had flown during the flight. All attacks were made in pairs that never came unglued, and the pairs smoothly reformed immediately at the conclusion of each individual fracas. Every attack was made from an altitude advantage, and all of us had the opportunity to decline to join with Japanese fighters that started out over our heads—just as it should be done. In fact, the entire action and all its parts had been executed exactly as prescribed in Blackburn's Unwritten Rules for Fighter Pilots. I do not believe any VF-17 foursome had ever attained that level of air discipline before. The results were gratifying: Mims emerged with three fresh kills and two more probables on his tally; Bitz had another Zero kill, his second; and I had bagged three Zekes and a Hamp, plus two more Zekes damaged.

I was elated with my temporary wingman, and I was all set to tell him that he had earned a trial slot as a section leader. When he approached me following the debrief back at Piva Yoke, he had a "look" on his face, and I thought he was going to ask for the lead assignment I had decided he had coming.

"Skipper, you're nuts! I want out of this. Now!"

I was more than just miffed; I felt betrayed. My startled immediate response was an inadequate "So?" Then I recovered and told him to go pack, that he could fly out to the rear before sunset. However, the last thing I said to him was from the heart: "I *am* sorry to lose you."

28

· · · · · · · · · · · ·

We tried something altogether new and exciting on February 7. Our choice, the sum of numerous evening skull sessions, was dubbed the Statue of Liberty Play, after its resemblance to the well-known football tactic.

In the playing field version, the quarterback stands with his arms cocked to throw a pass down the left side. The left end swings back and runs behind the quarterback, grabs the ball, and runs ahead to the right. Theoretically, the defense is focusing on the possible pass receivers, so the ball carrier is in the clear.

The basis for our flying version of the play was the base-bound strategy of the Japanese defenders around Rabaul. I could well imagine where that stupidity came from. No doubt, some staff cookie pusher had come to the brilliant conclusion that if their pilots did not fly past Point X their losses beyond Point X would be sharply reduced. He no doubt sold the idea to his boss in the plush, secure surroundings of a headquarters office, complete with maps and statistical tables keyed to validate the conclusion. If there were any Japanese pilots like us—folks who realized they were expendable to the whims of their leaders—they probably commented in terms to the effect, "Holy Fujiyama! Look at the latest order from headquarters: 'No pursuit, under any circumstances, beyond Point X!' Those staff jerks must be out of their minds.''

To which another veteran would certainly add, ''Never mind that, Ichi, look who *signed* the order.'' And there they were: base bound and losing their butts.

Our caper was to stay with the bombers until they had dropped their loads and were well out to sea, safely on their way home. Eight of our F4Us whose pilots had ample combat experience *and* plenty of fuel aboard would dive to the deck at moderate power and head away north, well out to sea. On reaching a point well to the northeast of the target, the Hogs would turn due west. On approaching New Ireland's east coast, the flight leader was to open his throttle to 95 percent of full power (in order to leave the other planes some reserve power to prevent lagging). Then it would be up and over New Ireland, right at treetop level, and then back down on the waves—so low that each Hog trailed a white wake. A final 90-degree port turn would set the Hogs up for a final run-in. At the last moment, the second division would split out abeam the lead division and the eight Hogs would rattle windows as they roared in just over the rooftops of Rabaul.

The theory was that we would achieve total surprise over the Japanese birds as they leisurely flew into the Lakunai traffic pattern. There would be *one* firing pass, all forty-eight .50-caliber machine guns blazing a path of destruction. Recovery would be straight ahead, and, still on the deck, we would retire over Cape St. George.

There were several caveats. If the Japanese anticipated the play—or were forewarned by observers or their radar—we stood a good chance of getting creamed by their fighters with an altitude advantage. There is no place to dive out when you are already hugging the deck. If that happened and there were enough of them, we would be lucky to get anyone out alive.

I had made my initial presentation to Colonel Brice on rainy February 2. I had lots of credibility in view of our on-going RHC successes, so I had turned on the charm and let the new idea rip. When the colonel and Joe Bryan had heard me out, the colonel had shaken his head in amazement. "You nut! Down on the runway at twenty-five feet? You'll probably get shot to ribbons by their light AA even if the Zekes don't nail you." He paused and eyed me with the shrewdest stare. "I suppose you're going to lead this." It was not a question.

"Of course, sir." There had been some give and take—to be sure!—but I left with the desired permission.

The February 7 strike was the usual midmorning call for twenty-four of our Corsairs taking part in covering the SBD component of a mixed SBD-TBF strike against Vunakanau. The remainder of the top-cover force was the customary mixed bag of Marine Corsairs. Eight of Lem Cooke's F6Fs plus eight Torokina-based New Zealand P-40s were low cover. For some reason, only sixteen of the scheduled twenty-four Hogs got to Rabaul. I thus had to call the four-plane RHC contingent down to beef up the high-cover group.

The formation closed on Vunakanau without incident, but we found the target closed in by a localized weather front. The bomber leader thus turned to his secondary target, Tobera, which was attacked from west to east.

The Japanese launched about forty Zekes, Hamps, and Tonys, which put in pathetically desultory attacks—less aggressive than usual. About all most of that gaggle did was try to impress us with an aerobatics display far out of range. However, several braver souls did try to throw in determined attacks, and several actually succeeded in pushing through the high-side and overhead runs on our formation.

Lt(jg) Earle Peterson, a member of Paul Cordray's division, was scissoring around in the number four slot, on Hal Jackson's wing, when he nailed one of about six Zekes making a concerted overhead run on the bombers. Peterson's firing run, which was from five o'clock below, produced solid hits in the target's cockpit and right wing root, and the Zeke flared up. Just as the burning Zeke rolled away, however, Peterson's Hog was drilled from dead astern by numerous 7.7mm machine-gun rounds and one 20mm shell, which exploded in the cockpit. Wounded and barely able to see through a shattered windscreen, Peterson rolled out, recovered, and started looking around for the rest of his division. Unable to find *any* friends, he flew directly to the rally point over Kabanga Bay, but there was no one there except a bunch of Zekes. He managed to skirt the area and set a course for home, but a lone Zeke found him and made a swift, surprising overhead run before pulling up directly in front of the wounded Hog's nose. Peterson opened fire, but he was unable to see the results. As he was passing New Ireland, he was joined by several Marine Corsairs, which escorted him back to Piva Yoke. We kept Peterson on the books for several weeks, hoping for a complete recovery from his wounds, but he never made it back to us.

Wally Schub's division, which was flying at 16,000 feet as part of Cordray's flight, was also attacked by the Zekes just as the bombers were turning into Tobera. Schub saw the Zekes, but he continued his weave over the bombers. This decision led Wally and his wingman, Whit Wharton, away from the Zekes, but Wally expected his second section to cover him. Unbeknownst to Wally, his second pair—Landreth and Dunn again—had been sucked back during the turn—an exact repeat of the previous day's error—and was not in position to cover Wally's pair. Wally's F4U began acquiring hits from one and maybe two of the attackers. A little later than Wally would have hoped, Dunn, the tail-end-Charlie, came around, saw what was going on, and thumped a snap shot at one of the Zekes. Miraculously, his rounds hit the Zeke and pried loose a stream of debris. The Zeke ran. Country Landreth also came around and joined in, executing a slightly belated high-side run on the Zeke that was putting rounds into Schub's Hog. Country's bullets hit the target; the Zeke's cockpit exploded and the Imperial Navy fighter went down burning.

Chico Freeman, who was taking a turn leading the second section of Rog Hedrick's medium-cover division, also came under attack during the turn into the target. The Hog was not hit and the attacker pulled away. Seconds later,

Chico managed to get in a beam run on another Zeke. He closed to within 40 yards and saw the Japanese fighter fly right through his stream of tracer. A piece of the Japanese fighter was blown off, but the plane successfully evaded.

As aggressive as this little bunch of Zeke pilots had been against our fighters, it did not escape our attention that they made no effort whatsoever to get in among the bombers. If anything, we were seeing the result of some inspired thinking on the part of a very few aggressive Japanese who had figured out where the medium-cover fighters were most vulnerable.

The entire formation retired down St. George Channel. Much to my disgust, the majority of rather unaggressive Zekes, Hamps, and Tonys followed us much farther than was their custom, nipping and feinting along a 20-mile track. The Marine Corsairs and Lem Cooke's Hellcats took these guys on, and they bagged a few. I was despairing of running the planned Statue of Liberty, but the Japanese eventually turned back, so the bombers no longer needed maximum cover.

The composition of the Statue of Liberty group was to have been two full divisions, eight Hogs in all. However, the two ironclad requirements—experienced pilots with plenty of fuel aboard—netted us only six participants in all: Earl May on my wing, Clyde Dunn on Country Landreth's wing, and Windy Hill on Chico Freeman's wing. We stayed with the bombers for about ten minutes after the Japanese fighters left, then dived away to the deck and proceeded up the east coast of New Ireland.

The adrenaline was flowing freely; we would know how well we had planned within the next half hour. I signaled all hands to fire a test burst from each gun followed by a salvo from all six guns. We would need all the firepower we could get, so it was prudent to check. Further exchanges of hand signals established that each Hog had at least 150 gallons of fuel aboard, more than enough for the minimum twenty minutes of full-power flight, plus cruise requirements and a prudent reserve.

We saw neither shipping nor any other planes until we recrossed the shoreline just north of Rabaul, blowing sand all the way. I was mindful that we had no idea if we were being observed by ground-based lookouts or radar; I tried to keep such thoughts from my mind.

My pulse was racing, my throat was parched, my nerves were taut as we pulled up to skim over the ridge and then dropped away to the rooftops. We were doing about 320 knots in roughly line-abreast formation—my pair in the center, Chico's on the right, and Country's on the left.

We saw no traps or ambushers, but we did see four or six Zekes and Hamps in the traffic pattern over Lakunai—their number one field. Was that all?!? But I had long since realized that our late start away from the bombers would mean fewer juicy targets. Obviously, most of the Japanese interceptors had already landed there or at any one of the other three operational fields.

There was nothing in the air dead ahead of my gunsights. Much as I would have liked to turn into the Zekes in the traffic pattern, we all had to fly pretty much straight ahead to avoid mutual interference, so I fired at several fighters on the taxiway, straight ahead. As soon as I started shooting, Earl May followed suit. We both saw chunks of debris and lots of dust kicked up by our streams of bullets, but we started no fires.

Country was in a better position to score. He got his talons into a Hamp that was climbing out of a missed approach with its wheels still down. Dunn squarely hit two Zekes in the parking area and smoked a third that was still airborne at the south end of the field. Country got credit for a kill because his hits had produced flames, but Dunn only got two probables and one damaged because none of his targets burned.

On the right, Chico and Windy roared down the west side of the strip, blazing away as they came. Chico's two airborne targets, a Zeke and a Hamp, were seen trailing black smoke and losing altitude, but no one saw them crash. Score two probables. Against orders, Windy pulled up to 1,000 feet to take on a Zeke in the approach pattern. However, the Zeke pilot was alert enough to take radical evasive action.

We were all clear of the field, still going flat out on the deck, before any of their guns got a round off in our direction. We throttled back to cruise power as we exited St. George Channel and then climbed to a cooler, more relaxing 3,000 feet for the run home. I cracked my canopy for a relaxing smoke and saw that some of the others had done the same. There were smiling faces everywhere I looked.

The ploy had clearly been successful, but far short of what we had hoped for. We all had expected to leave Lakunai littered with burning enemy fighters. Be that as it may, our intrusion could not have helped Japanese morale.

29
. . . .

We were rained out again on February 8, which worked out okay. The troops needed a day off and I had to steel myself to the dreaded duty of writing letters to the next of kin of our departed comrades. The only one I knew was dead for sure was Doug Gutenkunst; all the others were properly classified as missing in action. So all the letters except for those to Doug's mother and fiancée could be leavened with words of hope and encouragement. By hideous coincidence, my letter to Doug's mother never got to her, nor did the Navy Department's telegram. In the heart-wrenching sequence that ensued, Mrs. Gutenkunst's first inkling that her son was dead arrived in the form of a phone call from a sobbing woman, Doug's fiancée, who had just received my letter to her. Part of the fallout eventually reached me in the form of a reprimand. What a sad and unfortunate close on a very deep friendship!

Our February 9 cover mission was more of the same against diminishing odds. Oc Chenoweth and Earl May scored a solid Zeke kill apiece, and Mills Schanuel damaged a Hamp from his RHC leadership position.

On February 10 sixteen of our F4Us under Oc Chenoweth

accompanied a B-25 strike to Vunakanau while I and six others escorted a simultaneous B-24 strike against Tobera. The opposition was meager, but we scored three kills: one Zeke apiece by Davenport and Ellsworth over the B-24s and a shared Zeke kill over the B-25s by Bitzegaio and Jagger.

As the bombers were departing, I detached my entire flight from the B-24s and picked up two extra airplanes from Oc's B-25 group. The objective was a low-altitude sweep up along the coast well to the north and west of Rabaul in search of multiengine airplanes we thought might be hiding out there. It had only just dawned on one of my geniuses that we had seen absolutely no transports or bombers of any sort since the start of our second tour. Reason dictated that the Japanese, who we knew were forewarned of incoming strikes by ample radar and observer coverage, were sending their bombers and whatever transports they had out early. We were certain they still had bombers based around Rabaul, for there were plenty of large, well-maintained revetments in evidence at several of the larger fields. It stood to reason that a careful search would eventually reveal the location at which they were orbiting while our bombers were hitting the fields.

The search produced none of the expected results, none of the easy kills we eight had been contemplating all morning. My report, which made its way through channels, drew an eventual response from our side's intelligence wizards. It turned out that we had seen no bombers or transports because everything except fighters had been pulled out of Rabaul in early January. It was nice of our guys to tell us.

On the way up the coast that day, we did stumble upon a very small ship—a 100-ton, 125-foot wooden schooner—tied up to a dock in an out-of-the-way harbor. We worked out all our frustrations on that meager target, and I wrote it up in my report almost as an afterthought. Strangely, this routine dustup was treated as a very big deal by the higher-ups, and it was even cited in the text of one of my two combat awards. It is galling that the things I felt were my really major contributions—the RHC ploy and, above all, the fact that my squadron never lost a bomber it was charged with protecting—were to be officially ignored.

Nothing at all happened on February 11. We undertook escort duties for two bombing missions to Tobera and one for a Dumbo that plucked an entire B-25 crew from the water southwest of Buka. One of the Tobera raids drew out some Japanese fighters, but they never got close to the bombers and were handled by our Marine compatriots, who failed to score.

February 12 was another dull day. We sent twenty-two F4Us with the day's B-25 mission to Tobera, but no enemy aircraft were sighted.

Danny Cunningham finished off a Zeke on February 13, and one of our F4Us was damaged when gunfire from another Zeke blew up the ammunition cans in its right wing.

Again, for us, nothing of note occurred on February 14. The B-25s we escorted made it in and out over Vunakanau through meager and inaccurate heavy-caliber AA and no fighter opposition.

We saw no action on February 15, but it was a red-letter day nonetheless. Elements of the 3rd New Zealand Division went ashore in the Green Islands, four tiny, flat islands 117 miles east of Rabaul. We flew a total of seven two-hour patrols over the islands and the transport force, but we never saw an enemy airplane. More of the same ensued on February 16. The thing that made the duty so nice was that one of the islands was slated for conversion to an emergency airstrip for our wounded birds. It would be half the distance from Rabaul than our closest existing bases, on Bougainville.

We experienced several amusing incidents during the week-long dry spell. Or, perhaps we only remember them because we had the time and leisure to file them away in our memories.

On one return hop from the Green Islands, Tom Killefer led a low-level reconnaissance over Tuli Island, 60 miles northeast of the Greens. When TK and the others got home they *officially* reported seeing many beautiful, big-breasted, cocoa-colored women infesting the place. Sure.

The premier performance was made by Ens George Keller, an eager young new guy who had already been through some heavy action with us. Georgie was tabbed to go back to Guadalcanal to ferry a brand new TBF up to Piva Uncle. The way it worked was that the squadron was asked to make a pilot available—a routine headache—and Georgie was sent because he had originally trained as a Turkey pilot. In fact, we looked forward to these ferry missions because it provided us with the means for major booze purchases. The fact that the airplane in question was a TBF—with huge storage spaces—made this mission all the more worthwhile. Ensign Keller was entrusted with a rather large bankroll and very explicit instructions, the breaking of which, we assured him, would certainly mean his life. The central admonition was that he was not to leave the plane under any circumstances from the moment the booze was loaded until it was safely turned over to a senior squadron officer. (We were not above stealing another squadron's hooch if given the opportunity, and we would not blame another squadron for bagging ours. However, we *would* blame the youngster into whose care the booze was consigned.)

Duly briefed, Georgie bravely set forth. Unfortunately, he left with incomplete advice, for it had dawned on none of the old hands that Georgie was new to the area and that this was to be his first trip alone over the bypassed little fortresses in the Shortlands.

Our man accomplished his mission in stellar fashion at Guadalcanal. Affecting the air of a complete rube, Georgie used his engaging charm to drive extremely hard bargains. He wheeled into the wind at Henderson Field with the Turkey's bomb bay loaded down with a dozen cases of rotgut whiskey, six cartons of brandy, and thirty cases of canned beer. We who awaited him would have been proud of how well he had eked out the booze fund had not fate and inexperience intervened in the proceeding.

Georgie was motoring along at 5,000 feet, plump, inattentive, and content as he approached the venue of the Ballale Postgraduate School for Frustrated Antiaircraft Gunners. Before Georgie knew quite what was happening, he was shaken from his reverie by the flash-*crack*-and-black-puff signature of heavy-caliber AA. Before he could react, he heard a giant *kebang* and felt the new Turkey's airframe shiver violently.

As Georgie later told us, "I thought it was the end of the world." For him, as far as we were concerned, it might as well have been.

Now fully alert, our dashing hero of the air reflexed admirably with a violent push-over into a steep diving start of some extremely radical evasive action. Sensing that a great deal was amiss, Georgie cool-headedly leveled off at the first opportunity and dropped his main gear before all the hydraulic fluid bled out of numerous holes in the system. As soon as he was clear of Ballale, he called in for clearance for a deferred emergency landing.

Safely tucked away in a Piva Uncle revetment thirty-five minutes after the shooting incident, Georgie shakily shut down the Turkey's engine and went to examine the damage. It was almost total. The new torpedo bomber smelled like a saloon on New Year's morning and the beat-up bomb bay doors were dripping beer suds. Georgie felt they might as well have been dripping his life's blood. He called for help as soon as he found a lucid moment.

When the welcoming committee got into the bomb bay, we found scarcely an intact bottle; only a welter of sodden cardboard and broken glass. Beer was still trickling from three hundred ruptured cans.

As if the loss of our booze were not adequate punishment, Strike Command informed me that they did not appreciate receiving this mint TBF in its diminished condition. It needed a major rework—following cleanup and deodorizing. They added that they thought I would like to know that fragments from a bursting 37mm AA shell had started a fire as they severed gasoline and hydraulic lines and shorted out wiring. I heard them out to that point and then tartly rejoined that I had heard that the flames, fed by the flammable fluids and alcohol fumes, had not destroyed the bomber only because they had been quenched by the foam and carbon dioxide from the gushing beer—that maybe this was an idea worth pursuing for installation in all their light bombers.

We did not, as threatened, take Ensign Keller's life, but we did apply a new nickname that would immortalize the incident. In the air, his radio call remained Georgie, but on the deck he was known only as Dumbo.

30

....

For reasons beyond our ken, the air war over Rabaul picked up again on February 17, when I led twenty VF-17 fighters to help protect a mixed SBD-TBF strike against shipping in Simpson Harbor. For the first time in about two weeks, the Japanese challenge force was composed of up to fifty fighters—Imperial Navy Zekes and Hamps and Imperial Army Tonys and Oscars. Some of the desperation of the defenders could be seen in the commitment of the latter type, the inferior and easily downed Nakajima Ki-43.

The approach was made over St. George Channel and Credver Island, where the bombers started letting down through the overcast. The Japanese fighters intercepted our formation just as it turned left over Keravia Bay. We were stacked between 14,000 and 16,000 feet, but the leading wave of Japanese made their approaches from about 12,000, through broken clouds that made it extremely difficult for us to engage.

Ens Clyde Dunn, who was making his first hop as a section leader, shot down a Zeke during the initial attack. Moments later, during the bombers' final run-in, four Tonys ganged up on Dunn's wingman, Dumbo Keller, who had radioed Clyde to begin scissoring with him. Dunn did not respond; even a burst fired beneath his wings by the under-standably concerned Ensign Keller brought no response. As Dunn flew on straight ahead, Dumbo was forced to dive away, the first step in his ultimately successful struggle to evade the Tonys. Keller later reported that he saw no enemy planes on Dunn's tail, but Dunn was never seen again.

Ens John Malcolm Smith, who was flying wing on Timmy Gile, spotted at least a dozen Zekes climbing into the fight from over Blanche Bay. He warned the others in his division, and all four turned back the way they had come to prevent the Zekes from getting onto the tails of the bombers. Moments after the opposing forces deployed to engage, Smitty lost track of Gile. As he recovered from a chandelle, he saw a Zeke approaching from port at his altitude; it looked to Smitty like the Zeke was trying to join up on his wing. Smitty turned into a quick beam attack, fired a long burst, and watched the Zeke spin down in flames. After recovering, Smitty looked around for some F4Us to join, but there was no one around. He did see the bombers nose over into their dives, so he dived to 8,000 feet. There, as he had hoped, a Zeke was setting up on the vulnerable SBDs. Smitty damaged the Zeke in a beam attack, but the Japanese fighter rolled over and dived away. Certain he had done a day's work, Smitty flew toward the rally point off Cape Gazelle. Before he got there, however, he spotted an Oscar slightly below and heading in the same direction. A stern run brought Smitty to within 1,000 feet of the Oscar, and a good if distant burst sent the Imperial Army fighter diving away with gas streaming from holes in its wing tanks. Smitty declined to follow the Oscar; rather, he climbed away with the intention of continuing on to the rally point. Still well short of the objective, he was bounced from dead astern by a Zeke. The Japanese pilot had Smitty's Hog perfectly boresighted; numerous 7.7mm rounds holed both wings and sent Smitty diving away in radical elusive twists and turns. He managed to shake the Zeke and rejoin the rest of us at the rally point. He was given credit for one

Zeke downed, one Zeke probably downed, and one Oscar damaged.

The AA barrage over the target was meager this day, but it was not inaccurate. Lt(jg) Jamey Miller's plane was hit 10,000 feet over the target, and about 5 feet of his right wing was blown off. The airplane spun down to 5,000 feet before Jamey got out. When last seen, he was in one piece, and he even waved to his wingman before the latter was forced off by more fire from the ground. As with all our parachuting pilots over Rabaul, Jamey Miller was never heard from again.

After the bombers were safely on their way home, I led off another six-plane Statue of Liberty sweep. Staying above the overcast, we zoomed back in over Kabanga Bay from the direction of New Ireland. The Japanese should have been returning to their roosts by then, but we saw absolutely nothing. I led the crew to Blanche Bay, but there was nothing there either. We saw several fighters climbing out over distant Tobera, but there was no time to go after them. We left in a hurry, fearful their fighters might be waiting to pounce from out of the clouds.

On February 18 while Dirty Eddie March led off sixteen Corsairs to escort the first of two B-24 squadrons bound for Vunakanau, Rog Hedrick moved eight of our fighters into position for an RHC bounce. As the bombers flew in at 20,000 feet, and heavy-caliber AA burst above and below them, only about twelve Japanese fighters made a direct challenge, and only two of those seriously attempted to make firing runs. Portions of our high-cover divisions turned to meet the attack, but the Japanese declined to engage. It looked to Dirty Eddie and his crew like it was going to be another humdrum milk run. For them, it was. But for Hedrick's eight, February 18 was a big day.

The bombers were scheduled to arrive at 1115, so Rog had timed his arrival for 1040. The RHC approached from the south over Wide Bay at 32,000 feet and made a wide circuit of the area. As they circled, the two divisions split apart, Rog's going to 29,000 feet and Timmy Gile's going to 26,000.

As Timmy got over Blanche Bay, he spotted eight Zekes deployed in two four-plane divisions; they were at about his altitude in a climbing turn. Certain that his division had been spotted, Timmy tried to climb to an altitude advantage, but the Zekes kept climbing, too. Nevertheless, the Hogs got to 30,000 feet before the Zekes, and from there Timmy led his birds in to undertake successive section runs on the opposition. The Zekes dived away and the action developed into a running fight. Finally, over Keravat and following repeated unrewarding firing passes, our guys cut off one Zeke at about 25,000 feet. The Zeke split-essed, but the entire Corsair division threw in a pass from five o'clock and set the Japanese plane afire. The Zeke, which spun all the way in, was fully credited to Timmy Gile.

Suddenly, two Zekes appeared on John Malcolm Smith's tail. Smitty coolly followed Timmy into a tight 180-degree turn and on into a flat dive. The Zekes turned back and Gile chandelled after them. Smitty mistook Gile's initial turn-back for the opening part of a scissors, so he crossed beneath Timmy and turned back on the opposite course, thus losing Timmy altogether. As Smitty started a climb over Cape Gazelle, he saw a fighter approaching in a slight left turn and on an opposite heading. Our young hotshot turned to join on the other fighter's wing and saw that the other fighter was turning to join on his. Eventually, Smitty woke up to the fact that he was getting overly friendly with a Zeke pilot as confused as himself. Our man recovered first, within 1,800 feet of the other fighter, and set up perfectly astern of the Zeke. He coldly held his fire until the range had closed to 800 feet. The Zeke never varied from its course and a long burst sent it spinning down. Smitty recovered from his reflexive chandelle and followed his target down, pouring in bullets until the Zeke started burning.

Meantime, after losing Smith, Gile was attacked by a Zeke that climbed straight up on his tail. Timmy put his fighter into a 30-degree dive and rocketed from 20,000 feet to 10,000. He finally shook the Zeke as he was crossing over Cape Gazelle, where, lo and behold, Smitty appeared and joined up. The two shaped a course for home and arrived without further incident.

As Gile and Smith maneuvered to evade the two Zekes on their tails, Gile's second section—Earl May flying wing on Paul Cordray—went down into a high-side beam run on two other Zekes. May missed both targets, but Cordray sent one of them spinning out of control and smoking. Our pair, which never broke formation, turned toward Vunakanau to join on the bombers, but they got into a running fight with eight Zekes on the way. Still hanging together, they threw in a section run at all eight Zekes, but three of the Japanese fighters ganged up on Cordray, who dived into a layer of clouds at 16,000 feet. May had it all figured out; he called Paul to tell him to zoom back up into the clear so he, May, could shoot the Zekes off his tail. Paul did not hear the call and continued to dive. He eventually evaded the three Zekes and joined our retiring high-cover divisions.

Meantime, Earl May decided he did not like being alone, so he turned east again to chase the bombers. On the way, he came up behind a Zeke, which slow-rolled just as Earl was about to open fire. The Corsair followed the Zeke into the roll and put out rounds that flared the fuel tanks in both wing roots. The Zeke stalled and fell in. Earl continued on over the coast of New Britain and crawled up the tail of another Zeke single he found. This Zeke also slow-rolled when Earl opened fire, and Earl again followed his quarry through the roll. Once again, the Zeke went down in flames. Suddenly an ace, Earl was also suddenly out of targets. He joined on the retiring bombers.

Rog Hedrick made his first contact in the fight Gile's division had picked with the first eight Zekes it had found. His division began picking up the pieces south of Vunakanau at about the time Timmy's formation was breaking up. Rog and his wingman dived in from 29,000 feet and Rog caught a Zeke in a stern run at 18,000 feet. The Zeke burned. As Rog recovered, he spotted another Zeke below him, so he set up another stern run. This Zeke pilot saw him coming and dived away, but Rog stayed on his tail and blew him up with a short burst at 12,000 feet. By then alone, Rog turned back to Cape Gazelle. He was circling there when he saw a loose column of eight Zekes climbing through 15,000 feet a few miles east of Tobera. True to form, Rog waded in and came down astern the lead Zeke. As usual with Rog, a brief burst produced flames. As the Zeke fell away, Rog prudently withdrew before the other seven Japanese fighters could engage him. He joined up on the B-25s, which were well into their retirement.

Our box score for the day was three Zekes downed by Hedrick, two Zekes downed by May, one Zeke downed by Gile, one Zeke downed by Smith, and one probably downed by Cordray. That's seven, and probably eight, for no losses.

Eight of our planes were involved in escorting an afternoon SBD strike against the radar station on Cape Gazelle. The mission was completely unopposed.

Many an evening, the opposition sent over a twin-engine heckler at very high altitude. On the evening of February 18, the invader outwitted our two Torokina-based night-fighter squadrons and flew inland toward the Piva complex. Silhouetted by searchlights, Washing Machine Charlie circled and loosed an occasional bomb. Typically, the bombs fell into the jungle. The routine had become such old hat that no air raid condition was set. All hands went about their business and no one even bothered to douse the lights. As on most such nights, the higher-ups gave our AA boys an opportunity to relieve the ennui of their duty.

The bursts of 90mm rounds, the sweeping searchlight beams, the red gobs of 40mm rounds—it all made a fine show. As on many previous nights, TK and I stood in the open, drinking beer from cans, admiring the fireworks display, and debating some weighty philosophical point. Suddenly, from the beach area—close and to the west—there came a giant *WHUMP,* unmistakably an exploding bomb. Seconds later, and much closer, we heard *and saw* the second *WHUMP*. There were no foxholes nearby, so TK and I leaped toward the nearest tent, where the only possible cover was the floorboard. Unfortunately, I got there first. Even TK's solid 190-pound frame and considerable momentum were unequal to the task of driving either of us through the 6-inch clearance between the boards and Mother Earth. Nearby, Big Jim Streig remained sane enough to remember that he recently had dug a foxhole outside the opposite wall of his tent. From a prone position on his cot, Jim levitated over the intervening table and bunk and went straight through the side of the tent, taking with him the two-by-four framing timber. In the process, he managed to graze and daze Lt(jg) Hap Bowers, who had somehow slept through the racket going on outside.

The stick of bombs ran out just as the unexpected and unopposed low intruder—a lone Judy torpedo bomber—reached the edge of the pilots' encampment. All we saw of him were the blue flames of his exhaust stacks as he hauled ass back out to sea. What was this, a new wrinkle in the Statue of Liberty play?

31

. . . .

We approached Rabaul on February 19 in the throes of great anticipation. We hoped that the Japanese, who had been showing a renewed enthusiasm for jousting, would send up even more fighters than they had on the two previous days.

Twenty-four of us were assigned high cover for the TBFs and high and medium cover for the SBDs, and we had four planes tabbed for RHC. On the way to the target, however, we had four aborts, so I pulled in two of the RHC Corsairs, leaving only Oc Chenoweth and Danny Boy Cunningham for the Gravy Train.

While the rest of us stayed close to the slow-movers bound for Lakunai, Oc and Danny roared ahead and arrived at 1005, almost twenty minutes ahead of the main strike force. They came in at 30,000 feet, circled, and let down to 24,000, at which point they located six to eight Zekes 18,000 feet above St. George's Channel. Oc instantly selected one of the Zekes for his target and led Danny into the run-in. The Zekes saw our pair coming on and broke in all directions. Oc's target dived away, and Oc followed him to 12,000 feet while Danny broke off to cover him from 18,000 feet. The two Corsairs were vastly outnumbered and thus extremely vulnerable. Oc dispatched his Zeke, which Danny saw as it crashed on Cape Gazelle. Oc then climbed back up to rejoin Danny, and the two made a team run on another lone Zeke. Oc overshot the target, but as the Japanese fighter pulled up to get in what he thought would be an easy belly shot at Oc, Danny burned him with a solid burst.

The Corsair element recovered and headed for fresh hunting grounds to the west, over Blanche Bay. On the way, both pilots saw several Zekes below and on the same course. Once again, Oc led Danny down. Once again, Oc overshot. Once again, the target pulled up to shoot at Oc. And once again, Danny Cunningham blew the Zeke away. This was Danny Boy's fifth kill.

Unfortunately, the F4Us became separated during the recovery from this run. Oc spotted a lone Zeke and made a stern run, but only one of his machine guns responded, so the Zeke got away. Oc turned out of the fight to get all his guns working, then headed for a group of Zekes he saw hovering at 10,000 feet between Duke of York Island and Rabaul, right over the arriving bombers. He made a stern run on the nearest Zeke and set it afire. As soon as the Zeke pilot bailed out at 4,000 feet, Oc turned back toward Cape Gazelle, where he saw a group of Tojos sneaking up on the bombers from low on the water. As Oc turned into a pair of the Tojos, the wingman snap-rolled to avoid him and flew into the water before Oc fired a shot. Oc was given credit for the kill, his third and last of the day, a total of 8.5 overall.

Danny was at 5,000 feet near Simpson Harbor when he lost Oc. He went full throttle and blasted off for Blanche Bay. On the way, he saw another F4U, assumed it was Oc, and turned to join up. However, the other F4U turned north in pursuit of a Zeke. As Danny roared on to catch up, he saw another Zeke coming down astern the other Corsair, so he turned hard into him. The Zeke saw Danny coming, pulled through his dive, and again attempted to close on the tail of the other F4U. Danny stayed on the Zeke and closed to within range. A single burst sent the persistent but stupid Zeke pilot to his death in a burning airplane.

After recovering at 3,000 feet, Danny climbed away in the direction of Cape Gazelle to join the bombers. As he approached, he saw a single Zeke loitering outside the bomber screen and a little above it. Almost routinely, he came up astern the unsuspecting Imperial Navy fighter and opened fire at 150 yards. The Zeke instantly burst into flames and went all the way down in an uncontrollable turning dive. Danny rejoined the bombers, a seven-kill ace, richer this day by four. Nothing in the world could have better justified my early decision to let the little scrapper stay with the squadron.

Though the Japanese were thought to have launched upward of fifty fighters, the strike group was not molested much on the run-in; only a few Zekes made feints in its direction. On the retirement, however, the Zekes became intensely aggressive. Six of our F4Us guarding the TBFs were directly challenged by a large contingent.

Lt(jg) Mills Schanuel and Ens H. B. Richardson were all that was left of their division, the division leader and his wingman having aborted. Mills spotted seven of the oncoming Zekes at 19,000 feet, 3,000 feet overhead and on the port quarter, so he led Richardson around and tried to pull up into the enemy fighters. The effort was cut off when all the Zekes pitched over and came on at our pair. One of the Zekes got right onto Richardson's tail and opened fire. This brand-new rookie levelheadedly dived away. When he got to 3,000 feet, the Zeke pulled out of the chase, but not before shooting off Richardson's tail wheel and somehow blowing the doors off his main-gear wheel wells. Schanuel had been able to follow the chase, albeit outside of firing range, so he was on hand as Richardson recovered. He led his wingman directly back to Piva Yoke for a safe landing.

Timmy Gile's leading high-cover division had to fight its

way through a group of Zekes and several Tojos which had interposed themselves in Timmy's path. Timmy's wingman, Ens John Malcolm Smith, caught a Tojo at 14,000 feet and set it afire with a neat stern-quarter shot. Immediately after recovering from this run, the section made a similar run on another Zeke. This time, Timmy was the first to fire. A long burst started the Zeke burning and spinning down. It was seen to crash, thus giving Timmy his eighth confirmed kill. By then, the rest of the Japanese fighters had withdrawn, so Timmy and Smitty climbed back to rejoin the retiring bombers.

In the meantime, Gile's second section—Earl May followed by Beads Popp—had initiated a run against the same cloud of Zekes and Tojos. Earl dived on a Zeke and engaged him in a head-on run in which the Zeke vaporized into a ball of flame and metal. The pair recovered at 3,000 feet and headed toward Cape Gazelle. The Japanese fighters, mainly Zekes, were all over the sky, and a bunch of them joined to attack May and Popp with successive stern firing runs. Our pair not only managed to repulse the attacks by going into the standard protective scissoring mode, they shot down a total of three—two for May and one for Popp. The action suddenly ended when all the Zekes simply vanished from the arena. Breathless and sweating, our wolves pulled up and gingerly rejoined the bombers.

The only other action of the day was one for the history books. For me, it started just as the Japanese fighters began working on us over St. George Channel, when I heard a cry for help from one of my little lambs: "Skipper! Skipper! This is Ike! Ike! Three have me boxed. I'm headed north."

"This is Big Hog. Roger Ike. Good luck." I had no idea where Ike was. We were totally committed to our escort assignment; there was nothing I could do except sweat and face the pain of the probable loss of yet another comrade.

Ike had started the mission as leader of the high-cover

division that had included Schanuel's and Smith's element. When Ike's wingman had developed engine trouble and turned back near Buka, Ike had stayed with the TBFs until the strike reached Cape St. George. The cover at that point appeared adequate, so Ike decided he should turn back in consideration of the fact that he had no wingman.

As Ike began an easy turn to the right, however, he saw "something" low on the water off Cape Siar. He went down to investigate and found a Rufe single-float Zero heading north at 1,000 feet. Unable to resist such an easy kill, our high-scoring ace settled down on the Rufe's stern and set it afire with a short burst.

Just as the seaplane fighter hit the waves, Ike saw big trouble coming: at least twenty Zekes were letting down through a huge cloud 16,000 feet over New Ireland. Four of the Zekes were coming right at Ike in a loose column. The Zeke leader caught up with the lone Corsair from dead astern and opened fire. Ike popped his flaps to dump speed and then pulled up as the Zeke unavoidably overran him. The timing was perfect and Ike got in a good belly burst that sent the Zeke leader crashing in flames.

When Ike recovered, he was at 1,000 feet and making a rather meager 200 knots. The other three Zekes were in line-abreast formation. Two were on his starboard quarter, preventing him from turning east toward the Green Islands, and the one to port stood between him and Bougainville. After screaming for help, Ike did what he had to do. He turned his nose north, put his Corsair into a shallow dive, and shoved the throttle forward to the firewall. Ike also had a new asset at his disposal, 250 horsepower not previously available. Ike was flying one of the squadron's eight Corsairs that had been retrofitted in Espiritu Santo with Pratt & Whitney's new water-injection system. As Ike roared north, he wound the engine up to 2,750 rpm and 62 inches of manifold pressure. There were few aircraft in the world that could match that performance. With a speed advantage Ike estimated as being about 10 knots, he slowly pulled ahead and nosed over to put some nearby New Ireland hills between himself and the enemy. His Corsair's nose no sooner crossed the beach than the water-injection system faltered and the engine missed. Ike pulled back the throttle control and frantically pushed it forward again. The water injection caught, then died, and the engine missed again. The chase was only four minutes old.

What to do? Ike's Hog was indicating 305 knots. His water injection fluid was used up, but his engine seemed to be running okay at the normal combat-power setting. He decided to stay on course to the west-northwest, and did so for fifteen or twenty minutes, until his fuel was down to about 160 gallons. The Zekes were hanging on, so Ike had to go for broke. He made an ultraviolent turn to the left, just off the wavetops, in hope of getting away to the south past the three trailing Zekes. The Japanese fighter on his left tried to turn inside Ike's radical turn, but, too eager, he dug his left wing into the water and cartwheeled to destruction. The two fighters on Ike's right were caught flat-footed and got sucked wide. They gave up the chase as Ike crossed New Britain at Open Bay. Ike kept up his run for home at full speed for ten minutes after the pursuit ended, then slowly throttled back.

Ike was late getting home—so late that we believed we would never be seeing him again. The last anyone had heard, he was being chased north by three Zekes. Despite our universal exhaustion, all hands remained out on the flight line, not far from Ike's hardstand. We conjectured aimlessly about what might have happened after that last plaintive radio call. We all feared the worst.

We literally could not believe our eyes when the single Hog marked "29" taxied in. We streamed out to the hardstand as the huge prop stopped and the grinning mechanics chocked the wheels. A pale and exhausted pilot wearing a sweat-soaked flight suit struggled out of the cockpit with the plane captain's help. When Ike held up three fingers, we went into a frenzy. He had been in the air for 4.2 hours and returned with less than 40 gallons of avgas aboard.

Ike's three kills—including the self-destructing Zeke—brought his total to sixteen. Other pilots had been awarded the Congressional Medal of Honor for less. Ike, however, got the Silver Star.

Fighting-17's February 19 total was thirteen Zekes, two Tojos, and one Rufe.

Three of our divisions escorted a B-25 strike to Lakunai the next day, February 20. We saw no Japanese fighters. Indeed, we never saw a Japanese fighter again—or any Japanese airplane. As we soon learned, the Japanese had withdrawn every flyable airplane they owned from Rabaul beginning at dawn, February 20. There was nothing flyable left by the time our morning strike arrived overhead. Coincidentally, then, the Air Battle of the Solomons and Bismarcks ended eighteen months to the day after the first Marine fighter squadron arrived to defend the skies over Guadalcanal's newly won Henderson Field.

When the full breadth of the Allied aerial victory at Rabaul was revealed in the form of ongoing nonopposition in the air, we felt that ComAirSols, especially Fighter Command, had won it. And well we might have. But the totality of the victory had as much to do with large events outside our ken as it had to do with the months of aerial combat culminating in the daily grind over Fortress Rabaul.

By early February, AirSols was able to mount daily attacks—weather alone interfered—aggregating as many as two hundred bombers and fighters. The Japanese were willing to take on our strikes, but they lost airplanes and pilots at a tremendous rate. The combination was crushing, for, though they were able to replace the airplanes with others of more-or-less similar quality, the only fresh pilots they had to spare were rank novices drawn from the flight contingents of three of their carriers.

The clincher came in February in the form of numerous strategic blows, some quite far afield. By then, the Allied Central Pacific Offensive was well under way, having begun in late November 1943 with the amphibious strike into the Gilbert Islands, at Tarawa and Makin. During the first week of February 1944, the successful leap into the Marshall Islands, at Kwajalein Atoll, effectively outflanked the Truk anchorage from the north and provided the commander in chief of the Imperial Navy's Combined Fleet with the first intimations that Truk itself might be the next target. In a way, he was right. For two days, February 17 and 18, VAdm Raymond Spruance's Fast Carrier Task Force—*nine* carrier air groups—subjected Truk to withering air strikes. Among other accomplishments, carrier pilots downed seventy Japanese fighters and bombers in the air and damaged or destroyed numerous others on the ground. Unfortunately, we had tipped our hand as early as February 4, when an extremely gutsy long-range Marine photoreconnaissance bomber overflew the anchorage. Thus, the main target, the bulk of the Combined Fleet—the main strength of Japanese surface naval power—had withdrawn permanently to the home islands on February 10. Nevertheless, the Japanese were extremely shaken by the power and fury of the great Truk Raid, and they immediately made the decision to abandon Rabaul to what appeared to be its imminent fate—a direct amphibious assault. On the night of February 17–18, Japanese paranoia was further influenced by twin bombardments undertaken by our destroyers at Rabaul and Kavieng. At the former, five of our destroyers sailed right up St. George Channel and delivered—the hard way—3,868 5-inch rounds against shore installations at Praed Point and throughout Rabaul town.

Virtually as soon as the last of our strike aircraft left the scene on February 19, all their airplanes were ordered to prepare to fly to bases out of our reach in the rear. Only about thirty damaged and grounded fighters and reconnaissance types were unable to make the mass morning exit. All that remained at Rabaul was a powerful infantry defense force, a formidable artillery array, and all the AA batteries we had been facing for months. These Japanese remained vigilant for a direct amphibious assault that never came and, as Admiral King predicted, they withered.

Postwar estimates revealed that only about 70 Japanese

fighters were withdrawn on February 20, though some Japanese claimed there were up to 120. Further, it appears from incomplete and contradictory Imperial Navy records that our virtually daily attacks over a two-month period had destroyed at least 250 Japanese fighters in the air. No Imperial Army records of the Rabaul defense were ever located. Our records, quite possibly inflated, reveal 789 kills. Between December 17, 1943, and February 19, 1944, AirSols lost 151 warplanes of all types. The Japanese claimed 1,045 kills. It is doubtful that accurate statistics—or anything nearly accurate—will ever be determined. Whatever the real numbers, we won and they lost. Our victory was complete, for we accomplished exactly what we had set out to do.

What "exactly" we had set out to accomplish turned out to be news to me well after the event. While it was going on, we all saw our Rabaul missions in the context of assisting the bomber forces in their ongoing efforts to wear down the Japanese, to make their continued use of the airfields as difficult and resource-consuming as possible. In our eyes, the daily destruction of Japanese fighters was secondary to getting the bombers safely in and out.

Our perception was exactly backward. As crass and cold-blooded as it seems now, the only reason we had bombers along was because the Japanese had demonstrated an unwillingness to commit their fighters to challenging our fighter-only sweeps. They had done so in December, at the outset of the Rabaul offensive, and had had their butts broken. Thereafter, they only launched responses against our bombers. So, unbeknownst to us worker ants, our bosses sent the bombers mainly as a means to provide us, the fighters, with ample targets. Any damage the bombers themselves inflicted was considered a bonus.

The beauty of this strategy was that it worked so well. Fewer than twenty-five Allied bombers were lost as a result of damage sustained over Rabaul. Fighting-17 lost *no* bombers entrusted to our care, and we accounted for 106 confirmed kills. Moreover, solely because of our direct aerial offensive against all of Rabaul's air bases, not one of our ships nor any of our shore installations came under meaningful enemy air attack after November 1943. The only exceptions were periodic night nuisance raids by Washing Machine Charlie.

For all that, Fighting-17 was not quite out of the war.

32

• • • • • • • • • • •

We continued to escort strikes into Rabaul. It remained twitch-producing work both because we did not yet know for a certainty that the Japanese air groups had permanently abandoned the place, and because of the usual worrisome but ineffective AA opposition over the targets. Combat air patrols over the newly occupied Green Islands were truly a bore—aimless circling that produced nothing but acute aereo asserosis.

After two days of facing clear skies over Rabaul, it seemed like a good idea to go see Colonel Brice about an idea that had been brewing since before we completed our first combat tour. I jeeped to the boss's tent after the February 21 mission, and, following the usual amenities, I got down to the cases: "Colonel, I'd like your permission to go see Peggy O'Neill"—Marine Col David O'Neill, the chief of AirSols Strike Command.

"Holy cow, Tommy, what are you cooking up now?"

I grinned. "Sir, you'll remember that we cobbled up some bomb rack adapters last November. Well, as you may remember, we flight-tested them with five-hundred-pound bombs, then put them on the shelf. Our thought has always been that they would be handy in case of no air opposition, which is what we seem to be seeing now."

The boss had a pained look. "Yes, I do remember," he answered, with more than a hint of resignation in his voice. "I'll admit it really slipped my mind, but a light is dawning. Go on."

"Well, sir, when we got back to Espiritu in December we demonstrated the bomb racks for the FairWing ordnance guys. They were appalled by the Rube Goldberg rig; the consensus was 'Great idea, but they ain't safe.' So, they designed and manufactured properly engineered adapters for the F4Us. We brought eight sets with us when we rejoined them in January. We want to put them in operation."

"Maybe. What's Strike Command got to do with this?"

From his expression, I knew that we were about to be in business. "Matter of protocol. I figure we're sliding into Strike Command's territory. I don't want Peggy pissed off at us enough to kill our baby. Secondly, we need material support from his outfit. We jury-rigged the racks last fall with moonlight requisitioning. We have eight bomb racks, but for starters we'll need fifty five-hundred-pound bombs and fuses. And we'll need some of his ordnancemen for a few days. Our troops are red-hot with fifty-caliber machine guns, but even the best of them is rusty in the bomb department."

"Commander Blackburn, you're a devious schemer!"

"You know, Colonel, a very attractive lady in Sydney used those exact words not long ago!"

We went together to Colonel O'Neill's digs beside neighboring Piva Uncle. Oscar Brice gave him a rundown, adding that he posed no objection.

Colonel O'Neill started off with, "Tommy, your guys are getting bored, and you want to stir up some excitement. Right?" I shrugged and nodded. "That doesn't surprise me, but no jousting with AA batteries! Okay?"

In my best Waikiki beach-boy pidgin I answered, "Nevah hoppen!"

Peggy smiled. "No shit? Well, in that case, I'll issue instructions to my people to give you whatever you need."

The installations were rapidly completed and exhaustively ground tested. Then Timmy Gile and I took off, each with a live bomb, and made individual low-level bombing runs. Each observed the other from a respectful distance as we made runs on a beached barge hulk from 25 feet. The releases worked perfectly. The five-second delay fuse in the tail of the bomb enabled us to get well clear before the great eruption of water, sand, and barge bits blossomed.

The bombs were the standard General Purpose (GP) type designed for use against conventional surface targets. They could withstand moderately severe impact without breaking up. The explosive was relatively stable; it would not blow up unless activated by a detonator or subjected to prolonged high heating. The detonator was touchier, but, theoretically, it would not explode until "armed," a process effected by release of a multibladed fan-type device that spun a fixed number of turns during flight subsequent to release. The fan was kept from spinning prior to release by a wire that went between two of its blades, and the wire was held in place by a pair of clips not unlike ladies' bobby pins. If the pilot wanted to jettison a bomb not meant to explode, the "arming wire" stayed in place on the fuse as the bomb was released. When a detonation was desired, the arming wire was held tightly by the pilot-controlled latch on the bomb rack. If so, as the bomb fell away the wire pulled free of the arming fan, shedding its clips. The fan then spun so that the fuse could function on impact. With the fuses we were using, the bomb did not detonate until five seconds after first impact. Taking off and flying with the arming control in the cockpit set on "safe" meant the pilot could reasonably expect no disaster in the event a bomb fell off as a result of an arrested or hard landing. However, the pilot did have to remember to change the control from "safe" to "arm" prior to release. Many "dud" bombs were merely the result of pilots forgetting to arm them. After landing, the ordnancemen routinely checked to see if the wire was still there; if so, the pilot had irrefutable evidence that he had at least done his part of the job properly.

As soon as I returned from my mission to Strike Command, I went to see Duke Henning, who had been supervising the nuts and bolts of flight scheduling since we had lost Chuck Pillsbury in November. This, in addition to his formal assignment as ACIO.

"Duke, dig us up some targets in the Rabaul area that are free of AA coverage. I'm looking for bridges, warehouses, and the like. While you're looking, I want the following pilots to have made two successful live drops before the twenty-fifth: me, Gile, Hedrick, Killefer, Freeman, Landreth, May, and March. Also Kurlander and Ellsworth are to make at least one drop each. I'll explain later."

"Aye aye, sir. Sounds like a roll call of the squadron's leading studs."

"Never mind." Duke was right on the mark, but I did not want him to know that yet. My problem was that the squadron did not lack for highly competent, gutty pilots. I picked this team because I knew its members were the squadron's leading girl chasers. It seemed appropriate to the mission I really had in mind.

The preliminaries proceeded with the expected growing pains—bombs that would not release without coaxing, duds, early drops, belated drops, you name it; they all cropped up. The bugs were squared away in due course and the mystified-but-eager bomb droppers grew confident that they had mastered their new craft. The ordnance experts agreed.

Several days after my first visit, I took Duke to a return engagement I had set up with Colonel Brice and his ACIO, Lt Joe Bryan. "Colonel, we're set to go on that project I first discussed with you and Joe at Munda. As you recall, Joe had some aerial photos of Rabaul town. You'll recall that we discussed the nature of the target in great detail." I was jerking the skipper's cord, but I really did want to see if he would remember on his own.

Joe caught on first. "Ah! You mean that you're finally ready to strike a blow for morality and clean living?"

"Precisely, Joe. We'll be known for our punishment of wickedness and vice. We'll earn a well-deserved accolade as the Galahads of the South Pacific. However, there's a—excuse the word—*hooker* from another quarter. A certain captain on Admiral Fitch's staff has vowed to see me hung from the yardarm if we pull this off and it gets publicized. He ain't kidding. I have to ask that this caper remain very closely held info: just General Mitchell,"— ComAirSols —"Peggy O'Neill, and yourselves. I won't tell my pilots anything they don't have to know until the mission has been successfully completed. Even then, if asked by the wrong people, I'll lie about its ever having happened. With the colonel's permission, I don't even think we should turn in an after-action report if no one gets hurt."

The colonel went for the whole scheme and invited me out for a drink while Bryan briefed the still-mystified Henning on the precise nature of the target and provided him with the necessary charts and photographs. When it was all over, we had permission to bomb what appeared to be the official cathouse for the Rabaul region's senior officer contingent.

The weather for the Rabaul area for the morning of February 26 was forecast to be free of rain squalls. Perfect, for I would not consider taking the added, unnecessary, risk of flying at night at low altitude into that area without excellent visibility. Many good pilots had been lost in the South Pacific when clouds had rock linings instead of silver ones. I ordered our ordnancemen, now fully up to speed, to hang a 500-pound GP bomb on each of eight F4Us. The eight primary pilots, plus the two in reserve, were routed out of their sacks *very* early and assembled in the ready room at 0400.

The scheduling blackboard that greeted the enormously curious pilots read:

CHATTE FLAMBÉE
TAKEOFF: 0500

17-F-1 Blackburn   17-F-7 Hedrick
   -8 May   -21 Landreth
   -25 March   -23 Gile
   -5 Killefer   -31 Freeman

Standbys: Kurlander, Ellsworth

After the necessary preliminaries by Duke regarding weather, radio calls, and survival data, I took over the briefing.

"In my fractured French, this caper is *Chatte Flambée*. I'll translate when we get back. For your protection, I won't explain the purpose of the mission until after we get back here. If it works as I think it will, the Japs are going to be very, very mad. If you get knocked down, and are taken prisoner, honest lack of foreknowledge might save your skin.

"I'll use seventeen hundred rpm at twenty-eight inches manifold pressure, in automatic lean [fuel mixture] for cruise. Our run up there will use up the fuel in the wingtip tanks [unprotected integral tanks, purged with carbon dioxide before combat]. Full fuselage tanks will provide us with more than enough gas for any foreseeable needs. With these eggs aboard, that power setting should give us one hundred ninety knots [indicated air speed] at three thousand feet. The run-in will be very similar to the Statue of Liberty to this point [indicated on the wall chart] ten miles north of the center of Rabaul. My division will make an easy one-eighty [degree turn] to come in on the target west to east. Rog, you'll do a three-sixty and then come in from the northwest. Cross over the target one minute behind us. The lead division will retire straight ahead on the deck 'til halfway across the channel. Then we'll make an easy one-eighty to the left, climbing to five thousand feet. The second division will make a hard ninety left immediately after bomb release, then join up on me. We'll swing back well clear of heavy AA range to see what we can before coming home.

"On the final leg to drop point, fly a regular loose vee of four. Intervals of about one hundred feet. Division leaders will give a 'Stand by' at about five seconds, then 'Drop.' In the event you don't hear 'Drop,' pull the chain when you see the division leader let his bomb go.

"We'll strafe on the last part of the bombing run.

"I know it sounds goofy, but the object is eight near—*very* near—misses on the center building. We'll put bullets into the structure, and I expect that our bullets will torch off any vehicles parked close aboard. If we blow up the main target, that's just the way the highway squirrel squashes.

"Obviously, the closer to line abreast and at your division leader's level the wing planes are at bomb release, the healthier it will be. Rog and I, as usual, will use power settings of twenty-five-fifty rpm at forty-four inches of manifold pressure. Wing planes have three-hundred-twenty-five horses in reserve at full bore. But if you're caught in a trailing position, for God's sake don't be a hero. Break clear to the left and abort your run. Even if an earlier bomb blast doesn't get you, the flying debris you can't see will!

"Certainly, there are lots of questions on your minds, but unless they are strictly on what I've told you, I won't answer them 'til later. I'm asking you to buy a pig in a poke. We've got two spare pilots standing by to replace anybody who has the good sense to think this is a nutty operation." Silence greeted this remark. "If there are no questions, let's go! Down with *sin!*" The guys looked at me, clearly thinking The old bastard has really lost his marbles. I did not elaborate.

Before climbing into our birds, each of us performed an operation in addition to the routine preflight inspections—such as kicking the tires; we tried to shake the bomb to be sure it was tightly held by its rack and sway braces, and inspected the arming wires for security and proper installation. The ground crewmen had decorated these ugly weapons with chalked graffiti such as "This one's for you, Tojo" and "Last Rising Sun, Watanabe-san."

*   *   *

We made the standard carrier-type join-up and doused all the lights except the blue ones on top of each wing. These lights, which were visible only at short range and from above, supplemented the exhaust flames for formating purposes. We headed southwest for 20 miles at 1,500 feet to deceive Japanese observers on Bougainville, then we swung northeast to keep well clear of all the islands.

Steady on course at 3,000 feet at cruise power, I lit a cigarette and relaxed. As always at night, I was flying on instruments. Closing one eye during the Zippo lighter's brief flare kept my night vision acute. The cockpits glowed faintly from the red instrument lighting; I could barely make out Earl May on one wing and Dirty Eddie March on the other. Turning the master gun switch from "safe" to "fire" activated the dim yellow light of the aiming crosshairs, circles, and pips of the gunsight reflected in the center of the windscreen. I actuated the gun-charging controls to "fire," thus putting a live round in each of the six gun breeches. Then I fired a short burst from each pair of guns: inboard, center, and outboard. Finally, I set all three gun switches to "on" and followed with a few rounds from all six guns at once. The tracers arcing ahead crossed the line from my eyes through the crosshairs and then the firefly cone expanded as it curved off and down into the blackness. Finally, I put the master gun switch back to "safe" —all ready to shoot as soon as that all-important control was reset to "fire." The other seven planes followed suit in accordance with our long-established doctrine.

As dawn broke, we dropped to 50 feet off the water and turned west to approach New Ireland. We climbed just enough to safely clear the treetops as we crossed the beach. On the other side of the island, we eased back down to minimal altitude and increased to combat power and speed as we approached our initial point due north of the town of Rabaul. The sea had gone from invisible to gray to deep blue flecked with whitecaps indicating a surface wind of 15 knots. As expected, the whitecaps and the wind streaks showed that the wind was southeasterly and steady. We would not have a problem with lateral drift from a strong crosswind on our bombing runs, and there would be minimum turbulence from the wind spilling over the ridge on which the target sat.

With the sun about to break over the jungles of New Ireland, we had ample light to see our objective clearly. Coming in from the darker semicircle of the west minimized the possibility of early visual acquisition by an alert Japanese coast watcher.

Amazingly, the attack went precisely as planned. Rog's division had to hit the easternmost of the three buildings; as he later reported, he could not see the center structure at the last minute because it was blanked out by smoke and dust.

No gunfire from the ground was seen until we were effecting rendezvous of—blessedly—all eight unscratched airplanes. The AA that we saw as we were leaving was wild and uncoordinated. There were no "hung" bombs; all the bombs had released at the target. Postflight inspection revealed an arming wire still dangling from the shackle on each bomb rack, clear evidence that every plane indeed had made a "live" drop.

As we tooled back to eyeball our handiwork, the main building was still standing but smoking. Flames and black smoke rose from several vehicles parked beside it. Rog's division had flattened the eastern building.

An hour later, we were all back on the deck at Piva Yoke, ready for debrief. All hands were very excited and pleased. There were smiles galore. I was immediately beset by pilots shouting "Hey Skipper! How about that?" and "Did you see?" and on and on. The ground crewmen were beaming too, though they didn't know exactly why.

"Please! Let me talk! Quit shouting questions at me!" When all had settled down, I went on, "My fractured French, pronounced '*shot flombay*,' very roughly translates as 'singed pussy.' See, that center building used to be the British Officers' Club. The Japs renamed it The House of Flowers. Until this morning it was a spo'tin' house for Jap officers, the centerpiece for the maintenance of their morale. You can reasonably say that those samurai bastards came for a little ass, but lost much face instead. Well done!''

I reported the results direct to Colonel Brice, received a hearty pat on the back, and then filed a completely bogus after-action report for the benefit of the prudes up the chain of command.

In addition to getting the target, Fighting-17 started up a whole new industry for fighters. Beginning within the month, Corsairs throughout the Pacific were routinely bombing Japanese targets. We were aware that this development would have occurred anyway; however, we took pride in the fact that the crude rigs we fabricated at Ondongo in November 1943 were the first. By war's end, the Navy and Marines were fielding whole squadrons—mainly Corsairs—designated as fighter-bombers.

Epilogue

· · · · · · · · · · ·

After two weeks of utterly boring no-results missions, Fighting-17 flew for the last time on March 6, 1944. Butch Davenport led fourteen Corsairs in a barge hunt along the west coast of New Ireland and the northeast coast of New Britain and left six small barges and a 125-footer smoking. Later, eight of our Corsairs escorted an SBD strike against Lakunai, and in the very last mission, eight Corsairs escorted three TBFs against shipping in Simpson Harbor.

We were officially relieved by VF-34 on the afternoon of March 7. Beginning at 0615, March 8, our thirty-five airworthy Corsairs began lifting off from Piva Yoke. The last man off, Lt(jg) Country Landreth, heard a thrilling new sound as he was taxiing out to the runway—the *swish-boom* of incoming artillery fire. As Country lifted his wheels from the runway, he saw two TBFs burning fiercely in their revetments at Piva Uncle. The next day, we heard, the Japanese mounted a major ground assault against the Torokina beachhead. They never penetrated to the airfields —as we had long feared—but they put up a stubborn fight that lasted several weeks. Our nonflying personnel and several extra pilots were safely lifted out of Torokina by transport on the tenth. By then, the Piva runways had been closed because of the incoming artillery. Two of our ground crewmen who came out on that flight had been slightly wounded by shrapnel only moments after Country Landreth had lifted off.

Our return to the rear area was marked by a deafening silence from the headquarters of ComSoPac, Admiral Halsey. No sayonara—much less "Well done"—when we departed. Then and later, recognition by most higher headquarters of our status as, by far, the top scoring squadron—Navy or Marine—to date was niggardly, to put the best face on it.

My fantastically successful tour as a pilot and as CO—including seven of my eleven confirmed kills—was memorialized by the award of a second Distinguished Flying Cross. Since by then the USAAF was awarding the DFC to most any pilot who became airborne twenty-five times west of Hawaii, I declined the honor. In 1947, following a servicewide review of wartime awards by the Navy's Board of Medals and Awards, I was summoned to the office of Secretary of the Navy James Forrestal, who pinned a Navy Cross on my number one blue uniform just below my golden wings.

The stellar Ike Kepford, who, with sixteen kills, was the Navy's leading ace of the day, initially received a Silver Star and a DFC. All the services, including the Navy, had been and were later awarded the Congressional Medal of Honor for a lot less. Depending on whom you use as authority, at war's end Ike ranked sixth or seventh in the list of Navy and Marine aces. Eventually, he received two Navy Crosses—one basically for his superb performance in the defense of the carriers on November 11, 1943, and the other covering his overall performance.

Not so fortunate were the distinguished Hedrick and Gile. Rog's nine kills and 250 combat hours, Timmy's eight and 200 hours "earned" each of them a pair of DFC's. These minimal awards were never upgraded.

It is my belief that the aircraft companies' balls-out campaign via the press earned VF-17—emphasizing "Irregulars," "castoffs," and other nicknames—the enmity of many seniors who, like Plushbottom, saw us as a bad destabilizing influence on "good order and discipline."

Our recognition, then and subsequently, has come from our contemporary peers, from the Navy and Marine pilots who came on later, and from objective authors. It is heart-warming forty-plus years later to be admired as having been a member of *the* Fighting-Seventeen—near or at the top of any listing of Navy or Marine Corps fighter squadrons.

We were flown back to Pearl shortly after parting with our Hogs at Espiritu. After the warmest of receptions—well publicized—by Commander Air Force Pacific, we were turned loose on Waikiki for super R&R. Not me, for long. I was summoned back to Washington for grueling skull sessions with the high brass and the aircraft companies. It afforded me the privilege and joy of early reunion with my wife and family. On the negative side were sessions with reporters, complete with unnerving flashbulbs destroying my shaky composure at random intervals. Prior to heading back to the West Coast, I was assured by the Detail Office of immediate assignment as Air Group Commander (CAG) aboard a big new Fleet carrier. This was not to be, but that's another story.

On April 10 all hands—who'd come back to CONUS aboard, of all ships, *Prince William*—mustered at quarters at NAS, Alameda. I tearfully read the official orders decommissioning Fighting Squadron Seventeen. Some months later, a new F6F squadron was commissioned under that designation. I am happy to report that our heirs performed with immense distinction and success until VJ Day. The skull-and-crossbones insignia is still flying: It, under various numerical designations, has served proudly in Korea, in Vietnam, and most recently off the coast of Libya in 1985.

The decommissioning ceremony was followed by an uninhibited party to end all parties, hosted by Chance Vought Aircraft at the Mark Hopkins Hotel "atop Nob Hill in San Francisco." Then the Jolly Rogers scattered to the winds to begin their well-deserved month's shore leave before reporting to new duty stations.

For many of us, the combat action, if not the war, was over. Not so for the redoubtable Hedrick, by far the best fighter pilot with whom I ever served. He returned to the headaches and heartaches of forming a new squadron—this time as CO of VF-84, one of the many by now with Corsairs. They got into combat in late 1944 flying from *Bunker Hill*. In February 1945, following the combat death of his air group commander, Rog was fleeted up to CAG. Among Rog's Fighting-84 pilots were several VF-17 alumni—Chico Freeman, Fatso Ellsworth, and John Malcolm Smith. Rog scored three more aerial victories, Chico ran his total from two to nine, and Smitty fulfilled his early promise by adding seven to his Rabaul total of three. Unfortunately, *Bunker Hill*'s deployment was cut short by two kamikaze hits on May 11, 1945. One of the suicide planes vaporized inside VF-84's ready room. Among the many fighter pilots burned to a crisp was that nifty guy Chico Freeman.

Rog retired in 1958 with the rank of Rear Admiral. He subsequently prospered as a residential building contractor in Southern California.

Timmy Gile, Country Landreth, and Danny Cunningham returned to combat in F4Us in early 1945 as members of VF-10, aboard *Intrepid*. Unfortunately, none of the three scored further kills. However, Paul Cordray scored his seventh while flying from the same ship with VBF-10, also in the bent-wing bird. Timmy wound up as a VP with the financial giant Morgan Stanley. Paul died young—in bed—in 1963.

Country knocked himself down in March 1945. He was strafing an ammo dump on Honshu that blew sky high as he was making his pullout. It fatally wounded the lube oil system, forcing him to ditch. He was picked up by the locals, grilled (fortunately they never discovered that Country knew a lot about the upcoming Okinawa operation), and thrown into a POW labor camp. He there saw Greg Boyington, who everybody thought was long since dead. Landreth was the only "missing" VF-17 pilot or alumnus to be repatriated at war's end. He went on to a long and distinguished Navy career.

Following their month at home, Dirty Eddie March and Tom Killefer were sent to Florida to instruct in the Advanced Training Command. Soon after reporting aboard, they were joined by Lem Cooke. Their boss during this tour was Jumpin' Joe Clifton. By astonishing coincidence—it must have been that!—these three *and* Duke Henning plus Bob Anderson were among the Plank Owners when Air Group 74 *(Midway)* was formed and commissioned in May 1945 with me as CAG and Lem as CO of the thirty-six-plane fighter-bomber Corsair squadron. Air Group 74 had finished training and was ready to go into combat when VJ Day changed our world.

In early 1946 Dirty Eddie, who'd been training for the NCAA decathlon and thus was in superb physical condition, was killed off in a week by a mysterious, violently virulent flu bug. TK was mustered out in late 1945, and after a year as a Rhodes scholar in England, earned his degree at Harvard Law School. He was a VP at Chrysler but amicably parted brass rags with them before that company's great bailout by Uncle Sugar. He went from there to be president of a prestigious New York bank. Cooke left VBF-74 to join one of the Navy's experimental test units. He was killed in 1949 when the jet fighter he was wringing out developed a control malfunction and took him in. Earl May got it also, flying at the Naval Air Test Center in 1951.

The Navy kept Kepford busy in nonflying activity until after VJ Day. He was underdecorated but overworked making appearances and speeches to sell War Bonds and urge plant personnel to produce. As a civilian, he started out as a soda jerk in a Rexall drugstore. In 1956 he became president of the company.

Butch Davenport resigned his commission in 1949 after a final tour at the NATC, flight testing our early jet fighters. He went to work for a small manufacturing company and helped build it into the now much larger and very prosperous firm of which he became president. Butch is the only VF-17 member still driving an airplane regularly. (Remember shy, studious Jack Chasnoff? This most successful corporation lawyer and his wife tour the country—still—on a big Harley-Davidson motorcycle.)

I served in a variety of challenging and rewarding assignments, including that of CO of the big carrier *Midway* on which I had made the first landing and served as CAG thirteen years before. By mid-1962, the Navy sensibly decided that it didn't need an Admiral who could not handle his booze. Thus, twenty-nine years after graduating from the Naval Academy, I retired as a Captain and began growing wine grapes and raising blue-ribbon golden retrievers in California's Napa Valley. Following harrowing years of battling alcoholism—endless recoveries followed by ignominious relapses—I was finally reprieved from that hideous squirrel cage at the outset of 1981.

Other squadrons later surpassed our record of 154.5 kills, but in our day, we were the Navy's top guns. A lot of that had to do with lucky timing and positioning—and because Vought and our Navy and Marine mechs kept us equipped with a full complement of well engineered and maintained hogs. But the lion's share of the credit is due the pilots—all of them, living and dead—not just me nor Rog, but *all*. We were a cohesive, superbly successful *team*. It is for them, then, that I grant Big Hog "permission to leave the ship" with a quote from Shakespeare's *King Henry V*. Herewith Henry's exhortation to his troops the night before their stunning victory in 1415 over the French at Agincourt:

He that outlives these days and comes safe home will stand a tip-toe when these days are named. . . . He that sees old age will strip his sleeve and show his scars. . . . This story shall the good man teach his son. . . . And gentlemen who were then abed shall think themselves accurst that they were not there, and hold their manhoods cheap whiles any speak that fought with us.

Appendix
· · · · · · · · · · ·

Roster of Fighting-17 Officers
October 1943–March 1944

NAME	NICKNAME(S)	NOTES
Anderson, Robert S.	*Bob, Andy*	Det. 11/24/43
Baker, Bradford W.	*Brad*	MIA 11/17/43
Beacham, Sheldon R.	*Ray*	
Beeler, Edward E.	*Ed*	Det. 2/4/44
Bell, Thaddeus R.	*Thad, Juggy*	MIA 1/27/44
Bitzegaio, Harold J.	*Bitz*	
Blackburn, J. Thomas	*Tommy, Tom*	Ace
Bowers, George F.	*Hap*	
Burriss, Howard M.	*Teeth*	Ace, KIA 1/31/44
Chasnoff, Jack W.	*Jack*	Det. 12/10/43
Chenoweth, Oscar I.	*Oc*	Ace
Cole, Marvin W.	*Ace*	
Cooke, Lemuel D.	*Lem*	Det. 1/10/44
Cordray, Paul	*Paul*	Ace
Cunningham, Daniel G.	*Danny*	Ace

Davenport, Merl W.	*Butch*	*Ace*
Diteman, James E.	*Dite*	
Divenny, Percy E.	*Perce*	MIA 2/4/44
Dixon, James C.	*Jimmy*	
Dunn, Clyde R.	*Clyde*	MIA 2/7/44
Einar, Robert W.	*Ine*	
Ellsworth, John O.	*Fatso*	
Farley, James	*Jim*	MIA 1/26/44
Fitzgerald, Louis A.	*Lou*	
Freeman, Doris C.	*Chico*	(*Ace* in VF-84, '45)
Gilbert, Carl W.	*Gibby*	
Gile, Clement D.	*Timmy*	*Ace*
Gutenkunst, Douglas H.	*Doug*	KIA 1/30/44
Halford, James A.	*Sunny Jim*	Det. 11/22/43
Hedrick, Roger R.	*Rog*	*Ace*
Hill, Robert H.	*Windy*	
Hogan, Robert R.	*Bob*	KIA 1/26/44
Innis, Donald A.	*Stinky*	
Jackson, Robert H.	*Hal*	
Jagger, Frederick A.	*Andy Gump*	
Keith, John H.	*John*	KIA 11/1/43
Kelley, Louis M.	*Lou*	Det. 11/22/43
Kepford, Ira C.	*Ike*	*Ace*
Killefer, Tom	*Tom, TK*	
Kleinman, John M.	*Johnny*	Det. 11/22/43
Kropf, Thomas F.	*Kropf*	KIA 1/30/44
Kurlander, Melvin M.	*Mel*	
Landreth, William L.	*Country*	
Malone, Donald T.	*Don*	KIA 2/4/44
March, Harry A.	*Dirty Eddie*	*Ace*
Matthews, Marvin	*Matty*	
May, Earl	*Earl*	*Ace*
McQueen, Donald R.	*Mac*	
McQuiston, Louis T.	*Cue*	Det. 2/6/44
Meek, William P.	*Willie*	
Miller, James	*Jamie*	KIA 2/6/44
Mims, Robert	*Bobby*	*Ace*
Peterson, Earle C., Jr.	*Pete*	Det. 2/19/44
Pillsbury, Charles A.	*Chuck*	KIA 11/21/43

Popp, Wilbert P.	*Beads, Peter*	
Richardson, Harold B.	*Rich*	
Schanuel, Mills	*Mills*	
Schub, Walter J.	*Walt*	
Smith, James M.	*Smitty*	(*Ace* in VF-84, '45)
Streig, F. James	*Jim*	*Ace*
Wharton, Whitney C., Jr.	*Whit*	

Bibliography

Boyington, Gregory. *Baa Baa Black Sheep*. New York: Bantam Books, 1977.

Hammel, Eric. *Guadalcanal: Starvation Island*. New York: Crown Publishers, Inc., 1987.

———. *Guadalcanal: The Carrier Battles*. New York: Crown Publishers, Inc., 1987.

Lord, Walter. *Incredible Victory*. New York: Harper & Row, 1967.

Miller, John, Jr. *Cartwheel: The Reduction of Rabaul, U.S. Army in World War II: The War in the Pacific*. Washington: Department of the Army, 1959.

Mondey, David. *Concise Guide to American Aircraft of World War II*. London: Temple Press, 1982.

———. *Concise Guide to Axis Aircraft of World War II*. London: Temple Press, 1984.

Morison, RAdm Samuel Eliot. *Breaking the Bismarcks Barrier*, Vol. VI, *History of United States Naval Operations in World War II*. Boston: Little, Brown & Co., 1950.

Okumiya, Masatake, et al. *Zero!* New York: E. P. Dutton & Co., Inc., 1956.

Olynyk, Frank J. *USMC Credits for the Destruction of Enemy Aircraft in Air-to-Air Combat in World War II.* Aurora, OH: Frank J. Olynyk, 1982.

————. *USN Credits for the Destruction of Enemy Aircraft in Air-to-Air Combat in World War II.* Aurora, OH: Frank J. Olynyk, 1982.

Shaw, Henry I., Jr., and Mjr Douglas T. Kane. *Isolation of Rabaul,* Vol. II, *History of U.S. Marine Corps Operations in World War II.* Washington: Marine Corps Historical Branch, 1963.

Tillman, Barrett. *Corsair: The F4U in World War II and Korea.* Annapolis: U.S. Naval Institute Press, 1979.

————. *Hellcat: The F6F in World War II.* Annapolis: U.S. Naval Institute Press, 1979.

Documents

"Fighting Squadron Seventeen Log," Basil Henning, *10/27/43–2/16/44, 2/17/44–3/7/44*

"VF-17 War Diary," *9/28/43–3/31/44*

"VF-17 Action Reports," *10/27/43–11/29/43, 1/26/44–3/5/44*

Acknowledgments

• • • • • • • • • • •

If I hadn't learned it in many hard ways before, this writing would have convinced me fully that "no man is an island."

The quintessential Virginia gentleman and Unreconstructed Rebel Joe Bryan of Richmond, Virginia, suh, has been patient, tolerant, encouraging, and infuriatingly right over the many gestatory months. Thanks, Colonel.

Other talented professionals in the wordsmith field who have given unstintingly include Barrett Tillman, Adm Chris Cagle, Sallie Coolidge, Carl Solberg, and the Stockdales— Sybil and Jim. I'm truly grateful.

For aid in the military and aeronautic aspects I've been shamelessly and successfully crying MAYDAY. Rescuers have been squadron mates Rog Hedrick, Butch Davenport, Country Landreth, Windy Hill, Tom Killefer, and, the pearl beyond price, Basil Duke Henning. Boone Guyton, Bob Dosé, and Marvin Harper have fleshed out and squared away recollections wasted by forty-odd years. I hope you approve of your foster child.

The light of my life, Jamie, continues to be my delightfully unobjective instructive critic.

Acknowledgments

Finally, last but most, my deepest appreciation goes to the brave men, living and dead, who *did it* so that there is a tale to tell.

Tom Blackburn
Jacksonville, Florida

Index